The Foreign Policy of
Rajiv Gandhi: An Analysis

SADANAND HADAGALI

INDIA • SINGAPORE • MALAYSIA

ISBN 979-8-89066-840-0

Table of Contents

Message

ALL INDIA CONGRESS COMMITTEE

24, AKBAR ROAD, NEW DELHI - 110 011

Phone : 23019080

Sonia Gandhi
President

July 09, 2008

Dear Dr Hadagali,

Thank you for your letter of 16th June 2008 and the enclosed copy of your doctoral study on "The Foreign Policy of Rajiv Gandhi". I appreciate the research and hard work you have put into this endeavour and am touched by your sentiments for Rajivji. I send my very best wishes for success in all your future endeavours.

With good wishes,

Yours sincerely,

Dr Sadananda Hadagali
No.34, Gyanaba Layout
2nd Main, 5th Cross, Narayanapur
Dharwad
Karnataka - 580 008

Foreword

It is a great privilege to write these few lines of appreciation for Dr.Sadanand Hadagali's research study titled **"The Foreign Policy of Rajiv Gandhi – An Analysis".** Dr. Hadagali's study focuses on the substantial influence that Rajiv Gandhi had on the formulation of India's foreign policy and his noteworthy contributions to dealing with issues of global consequences.

Bharata Ratna Shri Rajiv Gandhi has chartered a new path, beckoning the nation to the twenty-first century. While Pandit Jawaharlal Nehru and Indira Gandhi established the framework for restructuring the nation's socioeconomic systems, Rajiv Gandhi contributed significantly to the construction of a new India, which has begun to establish itself as a leading global force. Rajiv Gandhi deserves the recognition of India which is considered as a modern country around the globe. During his stint as Prime Minister of India, he played a vital role in giving the nation a contemporary outlook. Throughout his political career, Rajiv Gandhi left an indelible imprint on Indian politics and governance. As the youngest Prime Minister of the world's largest democracy, Rajiv Gandhi travelled to all most all the countries, both Communist and non-Communist. His historic accomplishments in pursuit of foreign policy objectives, which included fostering world peace and enhancing India's relations with the rest of the world, elevated him to the status of an icon.

The author has systematically analyzed Rajiv Gandhi's diverse positions, including Chairman of the SAAARC, Chairman of the NAM, leader of the Six-Nations Initiative on Peace and Disarmament,

Crusader against Apartheid, and more. In reality, Dr. Hadagali's work illuminates how Rajiv Gandhi emerged as a successful world leader who fearlessly addressed the complex issues that confronted the nation and world over. It is noteworthy how he succeeded in maintaining amicable relations with most countries across the globe, including India's immediate neighbours, despite the tense relations on one or more pretexts. The work also examines and analyses forcefully the influence of the leadership factor, which is primarily responsible for formulating a country's foreign policy, and regards it as one of the significant determinants of foreign policy.

The author has succeeded in making good by highlighting Rajiv Gandhi's leadership in the context of various issues of international ramifications with which he dealt decisively by bringing them to their logical conclusion. I hope this pioneering work will fill some gaps and provide readers with valuable information's about Rajiv Gandhi's leadership in foreign policy formulation.

This study examines various aspects of Rajiv Gandhi's foreign policy and demonstrates how, even in the most challenging circumstances, he managed to find peaceful solutions to the contemporary conflicts. The discussion revolves around India's approach to dealing with our immediate neighbours, the Middle East, the Superpowers, the African continent, and so on.

I take the pleasure of congratulating, Dr. Sadanand Hadagali, for granting me the privilege of penning this foreword.

Bangalore   **18th November, 2023**

Dr. M. Veerappa Moily.
Former, Chief Minister of Karnataka,
Former, Union Minister,
Former Chairman, 2nd Administrative Reforms Commission,
Former Chairman, Parliamentary Standing Committee on France.

Preface

The book relies on the research study entitled **"The Foreign Policy of Rajiv Gandhi: An Analysis."** It is truly a path-breaking study that can enable readers to learn about India's foreign policy under the multidimensional leadership of Rajiv Gandhi, the then Prime Minister of India. This volume is unique in that the author is not from an academic background but still has exhibited his resolve to demonstrate the value of the academic knowledge he has received to bring out academic rigor in his analysis. This book makes such a distinction because the author has contributed significantly by covering all aspects of Rajiv Gandhi's foreign policy. This book attempts to understand the leadership factor in making the country's foreign policy from the perspective of the questions that relate to the influence of leadership on the conduct of India's foreign policy and international relations. This work would not have been possible without the inspiration of my beloved teacher, Professor S.S.Patagundi, whose support is noteworthy.

This work, "The Foreign Policy of Rajiv Gandhi: An Analysis", analyses India's foreign policy under the dynamic leadership of Rajiv Gandhi and also attempts to capture the multifaceted roles played by Rajiv Gandhi as Chairman of the NAM, SAARC, AFRIC Fund, Crusader against Apartheid, and mediatory role in bringing the warring groups to the table.

I take this opportunity to express my gratitude to Madam Sonia Gandhi, former AICC president, for the best wishes and kind words conveyed through the letter. I also thank M. Mallikarjun Kharge,

President AICC, New Delhi, Mukul Wasnik, General Secretary, AICC, Dr. P.L.Punia, former Member of Parliament (Rajya Sabha) and Chairman, National Commission for SC, K. Raju, National Coordinator, AICC, Dr. G.Parmeshwar, Home Minister and former Dy.Chief Minister, Karnataka, Dr. H.C.Mahadevappa, Social Welfare Minister, Karnataka, A.H. Vishwanath, Member Legislative Council Karnataka and former Minister, B.K.Hariprasad, Member Legislative Council, Karnataka, P.M.Narendraswamy, Member Legislative Assembly, Karnataka and former Minister, F.H.Jakkappanavar, Vijay Kulkarni, KPCC Members, Sharanappa Kotagi and P.H.Neeralkeri for giving valuable feedback on the document. Equally significant was the encouragement of the former Chief Minister of Karnataka, Dr. M.Veerappa Moily, who was gracious enough to pen the foreword to the document.

I thank Dr. M.H.Chalawadi and Dr. Vinod Annigeri for their valuable suggestions and all possible assistance whenever needed. I am grateful to several friends, and well-wishers for their encouragement and support, namely Nehru Olekar, former MLA, H.R.Algur; former MLA, Shambhu Kallolikar, former IAS officer Tamil Nadu; Ravi Malik, A.Venkatesh, C.S.Sharma, Ashish Vajpayee, G. Srinath, Robert Daddapuri, Basavaraj Gurikar, Danappa Kabber, Dr. C. D. Sarikar, Dr. S. C. Natikar, Debashish, and others. I would also like to thank Notion Press, Publishers, Chennai, for the high-quality professionalism and punctuality in publishing this volume. Finally, I would like to express my gratitude for the support and love of my family, especially my wife, Veena, and daughters, Rajani, Renuka, and Rakshita.

Dr. Sadanand H. Hadagali, **Dharwad**

CHAPTER – I

Introduction

No country in the modern world is self-sufficient, and no country can live in isolation, whether it has a democratic, communist, socialist, dictatorial, or military form of government. It is because every country in the world has a variety of needs and desires that cannot be satisfied by any one country alone due to scarce or limited resources. Therefore, in order to fulfil their various requirements, the countries are interdependent. This reciprocating nature among the countries resulted in an utter need for cooperation and coexistence in a global society to satisfy their vital needs that constitute a part of their national interests. Further, the dependence of one country on another and vice versa, aimed at fulfilling their needs, gave rise to interdependence. This interdependence compelled the countries to get themselves involved in international relations. As a result, in modern times, no country can avoid involvement in international affairs, regardless of its political system. Each nation adopted a set of well-defined principles, a rational guide, i.e., foreign policy, to provide a definite purpose and direction and to regulate a country's behaviour while conducting relations in the international arena. A nation attempts to secure the objectives of its national interest through its foreign policy and interactions with other countries. Hence, in the present world, foreign policy has become one of the key instruments in international studies.

The leadership factor plays a significant role in formulating the country's foreign policy, irrespective of the political system. It is the leader's responsibility to design foreign policy and make appropriate policy decisions, keeping in mind the interests and objectives of the country. James N. Rosenau, in his "Linkage Theory," makes reference to the linkage between inputs and outputs, i.e., actors and policymakers. He states, "In order to facilitate the development of linkage theory, we now expand the foregoing into a larger framework in which twenty-four aspects of politics that might serve as or give rise to outputs and inputs have been identified, along with six aspects or (from a polity perspective) sub environments of the international system that might generate or receive outputs and inputs."[1] Rosenau considers the executive, who is a governmental actor (national leader) in his Linkage theory, as a significant factor in the making of foreign policy.

In fact, in the present world, the situation has come to such a point that the very survival of the human race is directly dependent upon the pursuit of the right kind of foreign policy by a leader. This kind of foreign policy, no doubt, helps to strengthen friendly relations between the countries and reduce conflicts and tensions. Therefore, while formulating foreign policy, a leader should always keep in mind that the national interest of a country is paramount. Jawaharlal Nehru declared in one of his major foreign policy speeches, "Whatever policy we may lay down, the art of conducting the foreign affairs of a country lies in finding out what is most advantageous to the country... We may talk about peace and freedom and earnestly mean what we say. But in the ultimate analysis, a government functions for the good of the country it governs, and no government dares do anything that, in the short or long run, is manifestly to the disadvantage of that country. Therefore, whether a country is imperialistic, socialist, or communist, its foreign minister thinks primarily of the interests of that country."[2]

---

1   James N. Rosenau, (ed.) Linkage Politics , Essays on the Convergence of National and International System, The Free Press, New York, 1969, p-49.

2   Quoted in J.Bandyopadhyaya, The Making of India's Foreign Policy, (Determinants, Institutions, Processes and Personalities), Allied Publishers, Bombay, New Delhi, 1980, p-232.

In a democratic country like India, ordinary citizens have little role to play in the country's foreign policy formulation. They are entangled with numerous domestic issues and lack sufficient knowledge of international affairs, unlike Westerners, who are opinion-makers in the foreign policy process. Foreign policy issues are frequently ignored in electoral politics because the general public is disinterested in them. However, since the mass public is predominantly uninterested in external affairs, the leader in the government who represents the people enjoys wide latitude while making decisions on foreign policy matters. In this regard, the leaders' perspectives are crucial in foreign policy formulation. Therefore, "the much-boosted and so-called grandiose foreign policy of India is a one-man show. It is formulated by only those who supported the ideas of one man, keeping away the large masses of this country and without making them understand."[3]

Nowadays, the study of personality factors as a determinant of foreign policy is receiving a greater degree of importance than any other branch of politics. As a result, the personality of a leader as the governing factor started playing a predominant role in the formulation and execution of a country's foreign policy. This kind of foreign policy naturally bears an imprint of a leader's values, talents, likes and dislikes, and personality. Thus, foreign policy is considered the projection of domestic policy, but in real terms, it is the projection of leadership. In recent times, several leading scholars have highlighted the importance of foreign policy in their ways. According to a scholar, a nation without a foreign policy is like "a ship without radar, which drifts aimlessly without any direction by every storm and sweep of events."[4] Therefore, framing foreign policy has become an essential

---

3   S.R. Patel, Foreign Policy of India: An Inquiry and Criticism, N.M. Tripathi Co Ltd., Bombay, 1960, p-1.

4   Norman J.Paddelford and George A. Lincoln, The Dynamics of International Politics, Macmillan, New York, 1954, p-195.

activity for every leader in the present-day world, irrespective of the political system to which they belong. Generally, the leader formulates foreign policy in such a manner that its main objective is always to strengthen friendly relations between the countries of the world and to substantially reduce conflicts and tensions, thereby promoting international peace and harmony.

The Statement of the Problem:

Several variables and forces influence the foreign policy formulation. According to James N. Rosenau, "foreign policy inputs are geography, culture and history, technological and economic development, social structure, moods of public opinion, political accountability, government structure, value, talents, experience, and personality of leaders, external and internal situations, etc."[5] To quote Padelford and Lincoln, "Fundamentally, foreign policy has its roots in the unique historical backgrounds, political institutions, traditions, economic needs, power factors, aspirations, peculiar geographical circumstances, and basic set of values held by a nation."[6] All these factors and forces interact and determine the country's foreign policy. However, the leadership's personal aspirations, ideas, and beliefs play a dominant role and would be the most essential factor in formulating foreign policy. Regardless of the political system, the leader of the ruling political party will be in charge of the foreign policy institutional mechanism and will have a dominant and more assertive role in determining the country's foreign policy.

---

5   Quoted in Prakash Chandra's. International Relations,(Foreign Policies of Major Powers and Regional Systems) 2nd edition, Vikas Publishing House, New Delhi, 1994, p-2.

6   Quoted in V.N.Khanna, Foreign Policy of India, Vikas Publishing House, New Delhi, 1997, p-7.

Since the final shaping of foreign policy is the handiwork of the leaders, the impact of their views and personality is quite obvious. Endorsing this view, Prof. Galbraith observes, "Foreign policy, to an extent, is a reflection of the fundamental instincts of those who make it."[7]

Foreign policy is thus, "a product of a complex interplay of history, geography, past experiences, present circumstances, the perception of the ruling elite of national interests, and ideological consciousness, besides domestic, regional, and international affairs."[8] Therefore, the foreign policy of every country is generally designed in such a manner that it primarily represents the preferences and priorities based on the perception of global matters of the leader involved in the task of foreign policy formulation.

Though several factors influence India's foreign policy, the views and principles advocated by the undisputed leaders of the Indian freedom movement have a considerable impact. The foreign policy of a free India was shaped primarily by incorporating the thoughts of Mahatma Gandhi, the father of a free India. The influence of Mahatma Gandhi was so assertive that he even recommended the application of ideals such as peaceful coexistence, brotherhood, and cooperation advocated by him as the governing principles of India's foreign policy.

Further, the influence of Jawaharlal Nehru, the first Prime Minister of a free India, was decisive in shaping India's foreign policy both before and after independence. He was considered the pioneer and architect of India's foreign policy. As a leader, Jawaharlal Nehru was more concerned with foreign policy matters than with the job of Prime

---

7   Prakash Chandra, in Supra No.5, p- 4.

8   V.P.Dutt India's Foreign Policy, Vikas Publishing House, New Delhi, 1984, p-1

Minister. He once stated, "Prime Minister Ship is not my profession, and I would have resigned, but for one thing, and that is my interest in the foreign affairs portfolio. In this field, I came to know much more than anybody else in the country. And it is because I feel that by running the External Affairs Ministry I may do something good and useful for the country, that I have not resigned my office."[9] This clearly shows that Jawaharlal Nehru used foreign policy as a strategy to project his interests, preferences, and priorities based on his perception of global issues.

The present study seeks to investigate and analyze the influence of the leadership factor, which is primarily responsible for India's foreign policy formulation. The leader always projects his personality while developing the country's foreign policy. However, whether a country has a democratic, socialist, dictatorial, or military form of government, its foreign policy should invariably reflect the aspirations, likes, beliefs, and views of the intellectuals, scholars, diplomats, and the vast majority of the country represented by political leaders. Such a foreign policy, no doubt, becomes the rational foreign policy. However, in today's world, the perception of the leader is always the determining factor in the formulation of foreign policy, let alone other aspects. In the Indian context, foreign policy is primarily influenced by the leaders' perceptions, leaving aside the other dominant factors, which are usually considered secondary. This is so because the Indian political system is primarily personality-oriented. Since the leader's personality traits influence the formulation of foreign policy, there are bound to be deviations and variations in the country's foreign policy.

The purpose of the study is to examine the role of Rajiv Gandhi's personality in the formulation of India's foreign policy. Hence, we

---

9　　Quoted in S.R.Patel Supra No.3, p-34.

assume that Rajiv Gandhi, as the prime minister of India, made a substantial contribution to dealing with the problems of foreign policy. It is pertinent to study Rajiv Gandhi's influence on foreign policy in light of some significant developments with international ramifications, like the Indo-Sri Lankan Accord, the shift in Sino-Indian relations, the transfer of technology from the US, etc. The study also examines the change and continuity of India's foreign policy during the period of Rajiv Gandhi.

This study covers the period from 1984 to 1990. 1984 is considered one of the most significant and eventful years in the domestic and international politics. In 1984, Rajiv Gandhi assumed the office of Prime Minister, ushering in a new era of promoting peace, friendship, cooperation, and goodwill with most countries around the globe, especially with India's immediate neighbours. As a part of this, Rajiv Gandhi took concrete steps to consolidate India's relations with her neighbours, especially Sri Lanka and China. Therefore, the year 1984 has been taken as the starting point for the study.

The Scope of the Study:

The scope of the study is to focus on India's foreign policy from October 31, 1984, i.e., the day Rajiv Gandhi assumed the office of Prime Minister to the day he relinquished his post. It was the most significant and formative period in assessing Rajiv Gandhi's crucial role in India's foreign policy formulation.

The foreign policy of Rajiv Gandhi can be examined in light of the historical background of India's foreign policy, the influence of some dominant political personalities, and the events that led to the formulation of India's foreign policy. As it is virtually impossible to discuss all the foreign policy issues, the study has been restricted only to dealing with neighbouring countries concerning Sri Lanka and

China, and the two Super Powers, which figured prominently in the formulation of foreign policy during the regime of Rajiv Gandhi.

When Rajiv Gandhi became Prime Minister, there had been significant developments in both internal and external relations. The study only discusses such events in detail, notably in external affairs, which emphasizes the decision-making methods of the Prime Minister as the head of government. Some significant events with lasting consequences have also been examined to shed light on Rajiv Gandhi's personality.

The Review of Literature:

The study of the personality characteristics of a leader concerning foreign policy is an intriguing and new subject in the modern world that has gained enormous importance in the international sphere. It is high on the agendas not only of political scientists and statesmen but also of foreign policy experts in general. Hence, the studies of personality factor have received the utmost attention and importance in international studies. As a result, the study of personality factors has been considered one of the most significant domestic determinants of foreign policy.

There have also been some studies on the personality and leadership factors that have proven beyond doubt that the involvement and influence in the formulation of foreign policy is significant. "Several hundred studies have shown significant preferences within mass publics, several elite case studies and exploratory comparative analyses have made plausible arguments for the presence of significant personality influence on policy decisions in a variety of important areas."[10] Because of the importance attached to foreign policy, many

---

10   The American Political Science Review, Issue No.-70, 1978, p-434

intellectuals, diplomats, scholars, and foreign policy experts have contributed considerably to this area of study from this perspective.

An overview of the literature is necessary to understand the contributions of scholars to foreign policy from the perspective of the role of leadership. By reviewing the major works done in the field, it may be easy to understand how this study is distinct from the previous studies.

Theoretical Study of Leadership With Reference to American Foreign Policy:

James N. Rosenau's work on National Leadership and Foreign Policy (A Case Study in the Mobilization of Public Support) deals with the role of various types of actors, both governmental and non-governmental, in shaping American foreign policy. The author discusses the crucial role played by national leaders in shaping the contents and effectiveness of American foreign policy. Further, the author considered the American President to be the national leader whose decisions are final and who influences all the actors while deciding on foreign policy alternatives.

India's Foreign Policy from a Historical Perspective:

The book of Bimla Prasad, "The Origin of Indian Foreign Policy," represents the ideas and reactions of the key personalities of the Congress Party to world affairs and their influence and contributions in formulating the country's foreign policy. It also discusses the individual dominance of some elites particularly that of Jawaharlal Nehru, who adopted and passed various resolutions on foreign policy (world affairs) during Congress party meetings. Though the author adopted a historical approach, it is a valuable contribution to understanding foreign policy studies.

Domestic Politics and India's Foreign Policy:

The work of J.Bandyopadhyaya's entitled "The Making of India's Foreign Policy," focuses on the involvement of some crucial determinants in the making of foreign policy, and considers personalities as one of the fundamental determinants of foreign policy. Further, the author contends that the study of fundamental determinants involved in foreign policy making has been largely ignored not only by politicians and statesmen but also the scholars specialized in Indian foreign policy even.

Shashi Tharoor's work entitled "Reasons of State, Political Development, and India's Foreign Policy under Indira Gandhi, 1966-1977", makes an effort to examine the influence of Indira Gandhi on the making of India's foreign policy. According to the author, Indira Gandhi's assertive personality greatly influenced India's foreign policy during her long tenure as Prime Minister of India. The cabinet which was the vital organ to take decisions on foreign policy matters "was reduced to a little more than a committee of ratification."[11]

The work entitled "India's Search for Power: Indira Gandhi's Foreign Policy 1966-1982", by Surjit Mansingh discusses the dynamic role played and the hegemony of Indira Gandhi as a leader in India's foreign policy decisions. The author argues that Indira Gandhi, both as leader and head of government, always carried the overall responsibility for foreign policy, but her direction was more than institutional. She concentrated decision-making primarily in her own hands rather than delegating it to the ministers or bureaucrats of the External Affairs Ministry.

---

11   Shashi Tharoor., "Reasons of State, Political Development and India's Foreign Policy Under Indira Gandhi: 1966-1977, Vikas Publishing House New Delhi,1982, p-116

S.S.Patagundi's work on "India's Foreign Policy: An Elitist Perception" discusses how the Indian elites perceive foreign policy matters despite a separate External Affairs Minister and a host of other Indian Foreign Service officials. Further, the author also attempts to discuss the role of political elite's perception in the formulation of foreign policy.

V.P.Dutt's book "India and the World" examines the leaders' perceptions and their influences on the formulation of India's foreign policy. Discussing the role of Jawaharlal Nehru, who gave concrete shape to the foreign policy of non-alignment as one of the basic principles of India's foreign policy, opposed the surrender of India's right of independent judgment to any outside country and becoming anybody's camp follower. Indira Gandhi and Rajiv Gandhi followed the framework of Nehru's foreign policy decision-making.

Leadership and India's Foreign Policy:

S.R.Patel's book "Foreign Policy of India: An Enquiry and Criticism," examines the influence and dominance of personality factors in the formulation of a country's foreign policy. The author opines that the so-called extravagant foreign policy of India was dominated by one person, and it was a one man-show. It does not reflect the aims and aspirations of the common masses; it only reflects the likes and dislikes of a single person. Therefore, the author opines that India's foreign policy is formulated at the instance of a dominant personality keeping the large masses at bay.

The work of G.P.Ojha "Mrs. Gandhi's Foreign Policy Choice," deals with the leadership approach towards foreign policy. It also discusses the influence and role of personality characteristics of a leader in formulating and implementing the foreign policy of a country like India.

L.P.Singh, in his book titled "India's Foreign Policy: Shastri Period," discusses the role of Lal Bahadur Shastri's leadership in India's foreign policy formulation. The author has opined that though Shastri's leadership "lacked the unchallenged political power of Nehru. But he was a great manager of leaders and people. This quality enabled him to emerge as more than a first among equals among some of his cabinet colleagues who mattered on foreign policy issues."[12]

Michael Brecher, in his book "Nehru-A Political Biography" pointed out that Nehru was "the philosopher, the architect, the engineer, and the voice of his country's policy towards the outside world". He has further stated: "In no other state does one man dominate foreign policy as does Nehru in India."[13] This clearly shows that Nehru was unto himself and was all in the foreign policy matters of the country. The author has analyzed how Nehru dominated India's foreign policy and acted as a de facto leader.

A review of the literature on foreign policy studies reveals that there appears to be no systematic work on the role of leadership in shaping India's foreign policy. There are a few works on the leadership of Jawaharlal Nehru, Lal Bahadur Shastri, and Indira Gandhi. But there is no substantial work on Rajiv Gandhi's leadership and foreign policy. This study attempts to fill this gap to a considerable extent.

The Conceptual Framework:

It is essential to understand the various definitions of the key concepts in order to explain their significance and relevance to the present study.

---

12 L.P.Singh, India's Foreign Policy: Shastri Period, Uppal Publishing House, New Delhi, pp.108-109.

13 Michael Brecher, "Nehru – A Political Biography, Oxford University Press, London, 1959, p.564.

Foreign Policy:

It is the Americans who first used the term foreign policy. The main object was to establish friendly relations between the countries of the world, thereby lessening the conflicts and cold war tensions that plagued the globe during the Second World War.

According to the International Relations Dictionary, "foreign policy involves the dynamic process of applying relativity fixed interpretations of national interest to the highly fluctuating situational factors of the international environment to develop the implementation of policy guidelines."[14] Hugh Gibson defines foreign policy as "a well-rounded, comprehensive plan, based on knowledge and experience, for conducting the business of a government with the rest of the world". F.S.Northedge considers foreign policy "to be the use of political influence in order to induce other states to exercise their law-making power in a manner desired by the state concerned. It is an interaction between forces originating outside the country's borders and those working within them."[15] Frederick H. Hartmann writes that "A foreign policy consists of selected national interests presumably formulated into a logically consistent whole that is, then implemented. Any foreign policy can be viewed analytically in three phases: conception, content, and implementation."[16]

Cecil V. Crabb Jr, defines foreign policy as "reduced to its most fundamental ingredients, foreign policy consists of two elements: National objectives to be achieved and means for achieving them. The

---

14   The International Relations Dictionary, Holt Rinehart and Winston, New York, 1969, p.127.

15   A. Appadorai, Domestic Roots of India's Foreign Policy 1947-1972, Oxford University Press, New Delhi, p-1.

16   Frederick H. Hartmann., The Relations of Nations, Macmillan, 5th edition, New York, 1978, p. 69.

interaction between national goals and the resources for attaining them is the perennial subject of statecraft. In its ingredients the foreign policy of all nations, great and small, is the same."[17] The definition of Joseph Frankel reads that "the foreign policy consists of decisions and actions which involve to some extent relations between one state and others."[18]

According to Kurt London, "a nation's foreign policy determines its course vis-à-vis other nations. It is a programme designed to achieve the best possible position for the nation by peaceful means or by means short of war."[19] The definition of James N. Rosenau states: "A foreign policy might be roughly defined as a set of planned guidelines for expressing as much control as possible over existing, anticipated, or unforeseen circumstances in the international environment."[20] M. Ratnaswamy defines foreign policy" as "the bundle of principles and practices that regulate the intercourse of a state with other states."[21]

In general, foreign policy may be defined as the policy of a nation towards other nations aimed at not only achieving both short and long range national interests but also furthering its vital interests.

The Leadership:

According to Webster's Dictionary, the term leader is derived from the word "lxdere," which means a person or thing that leads; directing,

---

17   Quoted in S.S.Patagundi's, India's Foreign Policy: An Elitist Perception, Uppal Publishing House, New Delhi, 1995, p-7.

18   Joseph Frankel., The Making of Foreign Policy: An Analysis of Decision Making, Oxford University Press, London, 1971, p-1.

19   Bishweshwar Prasad., The Foundations of India's Foreign Policy 1860-1882, Ranjit Printers & Publishers, New Delhi, 1955, p-253.

20   A.P.Rana., The Imperatives of Non-alignment, The Macmillan Co. of India Ltd., New Delhi, 1976, p-265.

21   Quoted in A.M.Rajasekharaiah's "International Relations", Kartikeya Publication, Gulbarga, 1976, p-54.

commanding, or guiding head, as a group or activity. Leadership means the position or guidance of a leader."[22]

Historically, the concept of leadership was derived from leadership in a religious or sectarian setting or in groups with primary relationships. Sectarian followings inspired by prophetic figures have been at the genesis of many religious movements... The solitary, dramatic personality who mobilized and inspired masses to new goals and methods of religious salvation became an important prototype of leadership. This conceptual view was reinforced by research on historical and primitive governmental institutions, e.g., tribal chiefs and leaders of small city-states, vested with absolute authority."[23]

However, by the Twentieth Century, several intellectual trends and democratic revolutions had effected a change in the conception of leadership, and the term leadership was defined in many ways. In recent times, therefore, "a leader may be defined as someone whose orders are in fact obeyed by many other people, especially by the members of a group to which he belongs."[24] In the words of Joseph R Gusfield "a leader is a person who has to play a variety of roles, such as an educator, as a spokesman, as an expert, as a protector and also as a mediator, and all these roles."[25]

According to Narain I, leadership is essentially a sum total of the degree and extent of influence to which the rest of the members of a group are amenable. A leader's guidance and directions are supposed to be accepted by the rest because they consist of various factors

---

22 Webster's New 20th Century Dictionary., Collins World, Havana,1977, p-1030
23 International Encyclopaedia of The Social Sciences, Vol-6, The Macmillan Co & The Free Press , 1968, pp- 107-108.
24 Ibid., p- 261.
25 Joseph R. Gusfield., Functional Areas of Leadership in Social Movements., Quoted in L.P. vidyarthi (ed) Leadership in India, Asia Publishing House, Bombay 1967, p-22.

such as force, charismatic appeal, a sense of common good, influence, coercion, and so on."[26] F.A. Nigro and L.G. Nigro have observed that the essence of leadership is influencing the actions of others: "The essential quality of leaders is that they are convinced something must be done, and they persuade others to help them get it done."[27] As James Laundy, observes, "Leadership essentially involves the task of planning, coordinating, motivating, and controlling the efforts of others towards a specific objective."[28]

Considering all these definitions, we can generalize that leadership can be described as a person who influences the attitudes and behaviours of others through his charismatic appeal or image towards attainment of a specified goal or goals at a particular time.

The Inter-relationship between the Concepts:

Foreign policy and the leadership factor go hand in hand and are inseparable and inextricable and have become increasingly interrelated in the present international environment. The personalities of each country's leaders have an impact on its foreign policy. In a democratic system, the executive or cabinet is the ultimate policy-making authority. It is the leader of the ruling party in power, who represents the majority, will be the chief executive and head of the cabinet, and is the instrument in the country's policy-making. Therefore, the personality characteristics of a leader play a predominant role, unlike other factors, in the crucial policy decisions of the country. Perhaps it is the factor of leadership that determines a country's success and

---

26   Quoted in R.C.Swarankar ., Political Elite (A Sociological Study of Legislators in Rajastan) Rawat Publications, Jaipur, 1988, p-23.

27   S.P.Naidu., Public Administration, Concepts and Theories, New Age International Publishers, New Delhi, 1996, p-200.

28   SarojKumar Jena., Political Sociology a Realistic Approach, Anmol Publications (P) Ltd, New Delhi, 2002, p-95.

proper implementation of its foreign policy. Unquestionably, various elements influence a country's foreign policy, including geography, history, interaction of ideas, domestic affairs, economic policy, political parties, etc. As a result, there is a whole set of factors that significantly contribute to the development of a country's foreign policy. However, the influence of the leader's perception in making foreign policy decisions is very significant and paramount. Even though several countries in the world have different political systems and different forms of government, it is ultimately the leadership that determines the foreign policy of such countries. Therefore, a country's foreign policy is a projection of both its domestic policy and the perceptions of its leader. The leadership factor ultimately influences and guides the domestic policy of a country.

The pursuance of the right kind of foreign policy depends solely dependent on the leaders' ideology and beliefs. In fact, in the present world, the personal tendencies of the leadership will have a better say and an immense impact on the decision-making unit of foreign policy than the political affairs of a country. The study of India's foreign policy evolution reveals that the leadership alone plays a decisive role in a country's foreign policy decisions.

In a parliamentary democracy, the debate is a significant part of the country's policy-making process. The Parliamentarians, regardless of their party affiliation, participate in foreign policy debates in the House of the People initiated by the Prime Minister or External Affairs Minister, pose questions to them, and seek clarifications on issues of international importance to have a meaningful discussion. During the debate, the members of the House are likely to influence the policy and prevail upon the Prime Minister, the leader of the House, or the concerned Minister to manipulate decisions on particular issues in their favour or a specific direction. However, the final decision on the foreign policy matters rests with the cabinet, headed by the Prime Minister, the leader of the ruling party in power. As a result, the leaders who represent the government always have a say in the country's foreign policy decisions, which occasionally become one-sided. The leader sometimes assumes that he is the decisive factor in important foreign policy goals, disregarding the views expressed by the opposition leaders and the policy decision unit. There is little scope for the ideas and opinions expressed by the experts, advisors, diplomats, and bureaucrats entrusted with policy formulation in the External Affairs Ministry. If a foreign policy decision is influenced by a single personality or leader, such a policy may not achieve the desired goals in the challenging and changing international atmosphere.

The overall implementation and success of foreign policy are generally dependent on the personality of a leader. The approach of leadership to foreign policy issues is very significant. The perception of a leader, which influences national interests, is the primary factor guiding and influencing foreign policy decisions. It is sensible leadership that enhances the image and stature of the country in the international arena while making sound decisions on foreign policy matters.

The Objectives:

The main objective of this study is to contribute broadly to the field of foreign policy. We assume that leaders determine foreign policy decisions. No doubt, it is a fact that the changing perceptions of the different leaders will have a significant impact on the formulation of the country's foreign policy.

The purpose of this study is to analyze and assess the predominant and crucial role played by Rajiv Gandhi in formulating India's foreign policy. An assessment is made to understand whether Rajiv Gandhi has made any significant departure from the path of foreign policy established by his predecessors in so far as the basic principles of India's foreign policy are concerned.

The study also aims to learn about the efforts and measures undertaken by Rajiv Gandhi to improve India's relations with Sri Lanka and China and to maintain friendly ties with the world's superpowers and other countries. The study focuses attention on how Rajiv Gandhi was able to bring about peace in the international sphere by persuading the nuclear power countries of the world. His effort to bring about an agreed settlement between the superpowers of the globe on the I.N.F. Treaty (Intermediate Nuclear Force Treaty,) which aimed to destroy intermediate and short-range missiles, thereby saving the world from nuclear holocaust, has also been analyzed. Indeed, the role of the Six Nations Initiative on Disarmament and Peace is highly note-worthy and appreciative of statesmanship like Rajiv Gandhi as a representative of India. The role of Rajiv Gandhi as a vibrant and illustrious chairman of the non-aligned countries of the world is analyzed in greater detail. His role as the Chairman of the SAARC Association in promoting the ideas of peaceful coexistence and cooperation and as the Chairman of the AFRICA Fund in providing necessary financial assistance to the frontline African countries cannot be overlooked without adequate justification of the issues involved.

The study also intends to examine the contributions of Rajiv Gandhi to the world in general and to India in particular concerning disarmament, elimination of nuclear weapons, struggle against racial discrimination, resolution of ethnic conflict, peaceful relations with immediate neighbours concerning Sri Lanka and China, maintaining friendly and harmonious relations with the superpowers, and supporting the cause of world peace, which are some of the significant and outstanding contributions that helped to enhance the image of

Rajiv Gandhi in the international arena. However, an attempt is made not to lose sight of smaller events that may affect crucial issues in the future. It is impossible to examine thoroughly all aspects of India's foreign policy. This study attempts to analyze the vital concerns of India's foreign policy in the mid-1980s from the perspective of the leadership of Rajiv Gandhi. In other words, an attempt is made to assess Rajiv Gandhi's contribution to foreign policy decisions.

The primary goal of this study is to examine the challenging task set before Rajiv Gandhi by the non-aligned countries of the world. Under his multidimensional leadership, India chose to forge a common, united front under this body, which is working hard to stop the arms race and establish global peace. Finally, the implications of the role played by the power blocs, which are racing towards armament and conducting nuclear tests, thereby affecting international peace and security, have also been discussed. In this regard, the impact of the Six Nations Initiative Summits on disarmament and nuclear policy is noteworthy.

The Hypotheses:

The following hypotheses have been formulated in the study to analyze the crucial role played by Rajiv Gandhi in the formulation of India's foreign policy.

1. Rajiv Gandhi's leadership was mainly responsible for improving relations with the US.
2. The responsibility of formulating policy towards Sri Lanka under the leadership of Rajiv Gandhi became more difficult primarily due to the complex nature of ethnic problems in Sri Lanka.
3. The leadership of Rajiv Gandhi was primarily responsible for taking concrete policy initiatives to normalize India's relations with China.

The Methodology:

This study adopts historical and descriptive methods. It is historic in that it attempts to discuss some historical events that led to the formulation and implementation of India's foreign policy. The study also attempts to identify the significant foreign policy milestones during Rajiv Gandhi's tenure as Prime Minister of India. It is pertinent to mention here that the author has chosen only a few events that are considered the most crucial aspects of the leadership of Rajiv Gandhi, not only as head of the Indian government but also as head of the foreign policy mechanism. Further, the study briefly discusses Rajiv Gandhi's role, focusing on some of the events deemed essential for India's image development in the international sphere.

The study relies on primary and secondary sources of data. The study consults sources such as selected speeches and writings of Prime Minister Rajiv Gandhi, statements on foreign policy, Lok Sabha and Rajya Sabha debates, and so on. All the official foreign policy and party documents that were relevant and made available were referred to as primary source material.

The other source of data for this study includes all relevant writings of the leaders, members of the different political parties, scholars, and diplomats, published in news reports, editorials, and feature articles in newspapers, periodicals, and journals. Further, publications such as books that deal with the subject in some way have also been used as secondary source materials and enlisted in the bibliography.

The Outline of the Study:

The book is mainly divided into seven chapters.

The first chapter of this study deals with a brief introduction. An attempt has also been made to examine the statement of the problem, the scope of the study, the conceptual framework, the review of literature, the interrelations between the concepts, and the objectives of the study, the hypotheses, and the outline of the study.

The second chapter discusses India's foreign policy from a historical perspective. Its emphasis is on the influence of leadership factors in making India's foreign policy. It also discusses the role of the Indian National Congress and the various personalities, such as Mahatma Gandhi, Jawaharlal Nehru, Lal Bahadur Shastri, Indira Gandhi, Rajiv Gandhi, and others, in the formulation of foreign policy. There is also an attempt to discuss some theoretical dimensions of leadership.

The third chapter describes the dynamic role of Rajiv Gandhi in shaping the foreign policy of India as head of the nation. It also discusses the multifaceted roles as chairman of the Non-Aligned Movement, chairman of the SAARC, and chairman of the AFRICA Fund. The Major international concerns, including disarmament, nuclear testing, apartheid, and the Namibian issue, have all been discussed briefly from the perspective of Rajiv Gandhi's influence. Above all, his role as the leader of the Six Nations Initiative on Disarmament and Peace, Representative of the Common Wealth on Apartheid and persuader of the superpowers on the I.N.F Treaty has been emphasized.

The fourth chapter critically examines India's relations with the two superpowers in the world. Firstly, it discusses Indo-US relations in detail and the factors that led to the deteriorating relations between the two countries based on divergent perceptions. Further, the cooperation extended by the US in the field of Science and Technology and other areas, which paved the way for the strengthening of Indo-US relations, has also been discussed. The role of Rajiv Gandhi, who extended the hand of friendship to the West, which resulted in tilting towards the West without compromising any circumstances of India's national interests, has been highlighted.

The brief history of Indo-Soviet relations, which laid the foundation for the benign friendship between the two countries, has been elaborately discussed concerning the Indo-Soviet Friendship Treaty. Further, the role of Rajiv Gandhi, who strove hard to strengthen the bonds of friendship and the foundations of cooperation and coexistence between the two countries, has been analyzed. This study also includes the measures undertaken by Rajiv Gandhi to improve Indo-Soviet relations, thereby maintaining friendly relations and an amicable inclination towards the West, expressing dissatisfaction over the handling of the Afghanistan issue by the USSR.

The fifth chapter attempts to analyze the issues of Indo-Sri Lankan relations concerning the ethnic problem on the island. It evaluates the crucial role played by Rajiv Gandhi in the peaceful resolution of the Tamil issue without the involvement of superpowers. Further, it also discusses the role of Rajiv Gandhi in signing a historical agreement, i.e., the Indo-Sri Lankan Accord, which aimed at establishing peace and tranquility in strife-torn Sri Lanka, thereby resolving the vexed ethnic problem.

The sixth chapter deals with Sino-Indian relations, which were crucial in so far as the role of Rajiv Gandhi, who took the concrete initiative to normalize the strained relations, was concerned. He not only implemented several confidence-enhancing steps to normalize relations with China, the Asian giant but also served as a mediator and a stabilizing force between the two nations.

In chapter seven, the core argument of the study, which focuses on Rajiv Gandhi's varied contributions to the creation of India's foreign policy, is summarized.

CHAPTER – II

India's Foreign Policy: An Historical Perspective

India's foreign policy is mainly based on the principles of peaceful coexistence, friendship, and cooperation among all the countries across the globe, irrespective of their political systems. Foreign policy is concerned with promoting international peace and security and maintaining good and friendly relations with all the countries around the world. India, which was a colonial country under mighty British rule, experienced the power politics of the superpowers during the Cold War period and chose for herself the path of non-alignment and peaceful coexistence. While conducting its external relations with the superpowers, India avoided aligning itself with any of the blocs, thereby pursuing an independent foreign policy and maintaining its sovereignty. India's policy also maintained aloofness from the politics of the superpowers without taking sides. Thus, India always made just and independent judgements depending on the issues involved in the international arena. As a result, India's independence in international affairs enabled the concept of non-alignment, which became the guiding principle and the cornerstone of India's foreign policy. It was this foreign policy that started the Non-Aligned Movement, which later became one of the leading movements the world has ever seen, comprising more than one-third of the world's total population and covering a broad geographical and ideological spectrum.

Evolution of India's Foreign Policy

Pre-Independence Days:

The evolution of Indian foreign policy can be related to the pre- independence days of the Indian National Movement. Being a colonial country, India was under the dominant rule of the British government, which ruled this country for about 200 years. As a result, the British government managed and controlled India's external relations. The British Secretary of State for India was overall in charge of Indian foreign affairs. Therefore, India had no foreign policy of its own before 1947. However, the idea of foreign policy surfaced in the minds of the Indians during pre-independence days because of the articulated interests of the Indian National Congress leaders, like Jawaharlal Nehru. Further, Mahatma Gandhi's beliefs and the various resolutions adopted and endorsed by the Indian National Congress during British rule in India can be considered the basis of Indian foreign policy. However, the leaders of the Indian National Congress started taking more interest in foreign affairs only after the First World War.

The Indian National Congress played a crucial and essential role in shaping India's foreign policy, as its leaders adopted and passed several resolutions on foreign policy during its various sessions held in different locations across the country. Perhaps the exact origins of India's foreign policy can be traced back to the year 1921. The meeting of the All-India Congress Committee in New Delhi in 1921 was "a landmark in the history of India's foreign relations". For the first time, Congress passed a resolution on foreign policy, which included the statement that "the present government of India in no way represents Indian opinion". This resolution is crucial as much as it was the first significant declaration on the part of nationalist India that its interests in the field of foreign policy were diametrically opposed to those of Britain. It further laid down the basis of an independent India's foreign policy."[1]

Even under the British administration, the Congress leaders tried to establish external relations with several colonial and dependent countries. These relations were primarily to gain moral and sympathetic support for its ongoing struggle for independence. Further, India extended moral support to many colonial countries during their struggle for independence. Indian policy has always emphasized sympathy and support for other countries in their struggle for freedom. "Thus, in 1924, the Belgaum Congress Session conveyed a message of sympathy to Egypt against the British colonial policy. India also asked for the withdrawal of Indian troops from Mesopotamia as well as from other British colonies."[2] During India's struggle for independence, the All India Congress Committee passed another important resolution in its session held at Madras in 1927, which stressed the need to conduct independently the external relations of India with the rest of the world without the interference of the British government. The resolution protested against the use of Indian troops in China, Mesopotamia, and Persia and deplored the "extensive war preparations, which the British government was carrying on in India."[3] Indeed, the Congress session at Madras laid the foundations of India's foreign policy. "In 1928, the Congress assured the people of Egypt, Syria, Palestine, and Iraq of its full sympathy with them in their struggle to free themselves from the grip of Western imperialism, which in its view was also

---

1 Norman D.Palmer., Foreign Policy of the Indian National Congress Before Independence, in K.P.Misra.,(Ed) Studies in IndianForeign Policy, Vikas Publications, New Delhi, 1969, p- 22.

2 Quoted in N.M.Khilanani's Panorama of Indian Diplomacy, S. Chand and Co., New Delhi, 1981, p- 85.

3 K.P.Misra in Supra No-1, p.22.

a great menace to the Indian struggle."[4] In the same year, "the Congress declared that the Indian struggle was part of the general world struggle against imperialism and hence desired that India should develop contacts with other countries and peoples who were also combating imperialism. It also decided to open a Foreign Department in its office to develop such contacts".[5] This declaration of the Congress no doubt resulted in the solid foundation of India's foreign policy. Subsequently, in 1936, a full-fledged separate Department of Foreign Affairs was started in the Indian Congress Party under the able guidance and leadership of Jawaharlal Nehru.

The Congress resolution of 1930 condemned the acts of Nazis and Fascists, and that of 1939 disapproved of and dissociated itself from British foreign policy for its involvement in World War-II and the question of giving freedom to subject peoples. "The All India Congress Committee reaffirmed its determination to oppose all attempts to involve India in a war or to use Indian resources in such a war without the consent of the Indian people... It also advised the Congress Ministries in the provinces not to assist in any way in the war preparations of the British Government and to remain prepared to give up office if the Congress policy led to this contingency."[6] The Congress also passed some significant resolutions that substantially helped it take part in international affairs independently. Therefore, it is apparent from the discussion above that throughout the struggle for independence, Congress party resolutions on foreign policy played a crucial role in providing roots to concepts like anti-colonialism, anti-imperialism, anti-power politics, freedom, and good friendliness. These are some of the significant ideas that emerged during the struggle for

---

4   N.M.Khilnani in Supra No-2, p-85.

5   Quoted in Bimla Prasad's "The Origins of Indian Foreign Policy."Book Land Pvt. Ltd., Calcutta, 1960, p-85.

6   Ibid, P-157.

independence and became not only the guiding principles but also the basic principles of India's foreign policy.

However, during the Second World War, the British government dispatched Indian troops abroad without taking the Indian Legislative Assembly into confidence. These indifferent attitudes of the British government made the Congress leaders discontented and disassociated themselves from British foreign policy. Taking into consideration the British government's apathy towards the Congress and its leaders in foreign policy matters, Nehru declared in his broadcast on September 7, 1946, "India shall take full part in international conferences as a free nation with our own policy and not merely as a satellite of another nation."[7] This was regarded not only as a bold step but also as a serious attempt by India to formulate an independent foreign policy.

An assessment of the Congress resolutions from 1921 to 1947 reveals "an acute awareness of the dangers in the growth of fascism, a sympathetic approach to the aspiration of the Soviet Union, a consistent criticism of the continuation or expansion of Western imperial power anywhere in the world, and a sensitive exposure of all forms of racial, social, and economic discrimination."[8]

Apart from the Congress resolutions on foreign policy, the role of various leaders who significantly contributed to the development of India's foreign policy during the pre-independence days is also very crucial. Besides, geography, history, previous experience, the exchange of ideas, domestic issues, economic policies, political parties, and the leaders' perceptions all influence and determine foreign policy. These are the crucial factors that influence a country's foreign policy

---

7   T.N.Kual, Diplomacy in Peace and War, Vikas Publishing House, New Delhi, 1979, p-5.

8   Roy C. Macridis, "Foreign Policy in World Politics" 5th Edition, Prentice Hall of India (P) Ltd, New Delhi, 1979, p-321.

development. The latter aspect, i.e., the perception of the leaders' interests, played a significant role in determining the country's foreign policy. The history of India's foreign policy reveals that several political leaders and dominant personalities greatly influenced the formulation of India's foreign policy throughout its evolution. The words of some Congress leaders in designing the country's foreign policy were unquestionable and all-encompassing. To such an extent, the Congress leaders influenced India's foreign policy. Undoubtedly, the involvement of those personalities and their ideas in shaping foreign policy has provided a distinct approach for the country. In this framework, it is critical to assess the roles of various personalities who influenced India's foreign policy.

Mahatma Gandhi:

First and foremost, the influence of Mahatma Gandhi, the father of free India and the undisputed leader of the Indian struggle for independence, in shaping India's foreign policy was significant. Till the advent of freedom, Mahatma Gandhi dominated the Indian political scene. He advocated ideals such as peace, non-violence, and brotherhood, through which he achieved independence, and he used them as the greatest weapons against the mightiest British Empire the world has ever seen. These ideas, advocated by Mahatma Gandhi, were regarded as the governing principles of the Indian National Congress. Later, he recommended the application of these principles in formulating India's foreign policy. These ideas of Mahatma Gandhi became the cornerstone and guiding principle of India's foreign policy. Besides, Mahatma Gandhi also advocated the concept of peaceful co-existence with other nations of the world and the mutual settlement of various disputes amongst the countries without the interference of the superpowers, which were also taken care of while framing the foreign policy of an independent India.

In his address to Columbia University, Nehru very effectively captured the values of Mahatma Gandhi, in his address to Columbia University: "Means and ends are thus intimately and inextricably connected and cannot be separated. The great leader of my country, Mahatma Gandhi (under whose inspiration and sheltering care I grew up,)... always laid stress on moral values and warned us never to subordinate means to ends. After a generation of intense struggle with a great and strong nation, we achieved success, and perhaps the most significant part of this achievement, for which credit is due to both parties, was the manner of it. That revolution demonstrated to us that physical force need not necessarily be the arbiter of man's destiny and that the method of waging a struggle and the way of its termination are of paramount importance."[9]

Apart from the freedom struggle, Mahatma Gandhi also played a crucial role when Congress drafted several resolutions on foreign policy. He was a driving force behind such foreign policy resolutions formulated and piloted by Jawaharlal Nehru. In fact, Mahatma Gandhi was instrumental in moving the Congress resolutions on foreign policy matters, keeping in mind the aspirations of the Indian people. Therefore, foreign policy is not only the product of its immediate past but also the thoughts of Gandhi and the ideals proclaimed by Congress from time to time. Hence, India's foreign policy has its basis in Gandhism.

Post-Independence days:

As previously discussed, India had no foreign policy before 1947. India began to evolve its foreign policy in light of its requirements and the prevailing international situation only after gaining independence

---

9   K.P.Karunakaran., India in World Affairs, August 1947- January 1950, OxfordUniversity Press (London) Calcutta, 1952, p-24.

in 1947. As a result, it began to conduct its external relations with the rest of the world directly as a sovereign state. Several factors influenced post-independence foreign policy, including Congress party resolutions, national leader's ideologies, the power politics of the superpowers, the Cold War, colonial experience, imperialism, racial discrimination, and so on. India's foreign policy, ever since its independence, has advocated the principles of friendship and cooperation with most countries in the world, irrespective of their political systems. The establishment of friendly relations with neighbouring countries was the principal plank of India's foreign policy.

India has maintained cordial relations with almost every nation across the globe to achieve its national interests and objectives and promote world peace. When conducting foreign policy, India adheres to principles that include maintaining sovereign independence, pursuing an independent foreign policy without alignment with power blocs, mutual understanding and cooperation, and promoting international peace and prosperity. The post-independence foreign policy of India followed the path of non-alignment and peaceful co-existence to achieve these objectives. The policy of non-alignment advocated by both Mahatma Gandhi and Jawaharlal Nehru on the idea of non-involvement and non-entanglement became the cornerstone of independent India's foreign policy.

India achieved its independence at a time when the Cold War clouds were already looming large over the globe, and as a result, it not only underwent but also experienced the power politics of the superpowers. As a result, the post-Independence foreign policy was developed on the principle of non-alignment. Naturally, this led India to formulate her foreign policy along the lines of non-involvement and non-alignment, which became the basic principles of India's foreign policy.

Jawaharlal Nehru, the architect of India's foreign policy, who continuously held the External Affairs Ministry from 1947 to 1964, played a decisive role in shaping India's post-independence foreign policy. His contribution to India's foreign policy formulation and implementation was memorable and highly appreciable. Nehru's authority on foreign policy matters was all-encompassing, and his word was final in cabinet discussions, which several members of Congress and his colleagues in the government actively supported. In short, Nehru's role in Indian foreign policy matters was a one-man show.

Jawaharlal Nehru:

Apart from Mahatma Gandhi, Jawaharlal Nehru had a distinctive and significant role in shaping India's foreign policy. Indeed, Nehru, a hero of the liberation movement and a towering figure in Indian foreign policy, deserves credit for shaping India's foreign policy before and after independence. Nehru, who was instrumental in formulating and fashioning the foreign policy, was regarded as the sole architect of the foreign policy of independent India. Besides Mahatma Gandhi's principles, Nehru's ideological commitment greatly influenced the development of India's foreign policy. Nehru, who was Western educated, was deeply impressed by the liberal democratic ideology of the Western countries and also by the Soviet Union's economic policies. However, Nehru wanted to avoid both ideologies while formulating India's foreign policy. However, Nehru, on the other hand, followed H.J.Laski's philosophy, which was a synthesis of liberalism and Marxism. In a way, the policy of non-alignment was indirectly the result of the synthesis of Liberalism and Marxism.

Nehru, who took a keen interest in formulating and implementing India's foreign policy, influenced the West through his charismatic image, which considerably helped to change the discriminatory attitudes of foreign countries towards India. Taking into consideration the role played by Jawaharlal Nehru in the international field, Mahatma Gandhi wrote, "Pundit Jawaharlal Nehru is Indian to the core but, he being also an internationalist, has made us accustomed to look at everything in the international light instead of the parochial."[10]

Jawaharlal Nehru's sincere efforts in 1936 resulted in the opening of a separate Foreign Affairs Department in the Indian National Congress under his leadership. That paved the way to establish external contacts and organize the anti-imperialistic movement of the dependent people across the globe. The Foreign Affairs Department significantly helped Nehru while enacting the resolutions on foreign affairs and formulating a comprehensive and coherent foreign policy for India. During the struggle for independence, Nehru, as an internationalist, served as a bridge and balancing factor between the Indian National Congress and the anti-colonialist forces of the world. As a result of Nehru's efforts and articulated interest, India's foreign policy has occupied a unique place in the international sphere. Commenting on the role of Nehru in formulating India's foreign policy, V.B.Karnik opines that "the framework was provided from time to time by Nehru: his ideas and ideology, his aims and aspirations, his judgements and impressions, his desires and ambitions, his likes and dislikes, his passions and prejudices... constituted the timber of which went into the building of that framework."[11]

The abovementioned viewpoint undoubtedly has some truth. It is undeniable that Nehru was the one who formulated Indian

---

10   Quoted in A.B.Shah's (Ed), India's Defense and Foreign Policies, Manaktalas, Bombay, 1966, p-90.
11   Quoted in Tanveer Sultan, Indo-US Relations, Deep and Deep Publication, New Delhi, 1982, p-10.

foreign policy. However, India had to develop its foreign policy while considering concepts such as imperialism, colonialism, and power politics that evolved during the struggle for independence. Further, the historic declarations of the Congress and the principles advocated by Mahatma Gandhi were instrumental in providing roots to the anti-Cold War, anti-imperialism, anti-racialism, anti-power politics, and pro-neutralism, peaceful co-existence, and neighbourliness. India's foreign policy is evolutionary gaining inspiration from its history, past thought, and the teachings of Mahatma Gandhi rather than being created or established all at once. While commenting on foreign policy, D.C.Sharma in Lok Sabha observed, "Our foreign policy has the framework of our Indian culture and tradition, which has lasted for thousands of years. It is rooted in the philosophy which Mahatma Gandhi gave us and is also grounded in the theory and practice of the foreign policy which Pandit Nehru expounded to us and the whole world."[12] To summarize, India's foreign policy was not only moulded by a select few people or leaders but also by the interaction of several forces within and outside the country.

Jawaharlal Nehru had a long tenure as Prime Minister of India and made substantial contributions to the field of international relations, putting India on the diplomatic map of the world. During his tenure, certain events with far-reaching consequences, such as the beginning of the Cold War and the Sino-Indian War of 1962, heavily influenced Indian foreign policy. These developments undoubtedly influenced the formulation of post-independence foreign policy on the lines of non-alignment, test bans, non-proliferation, etc. It is now critical to comprehend these events, which significantly influenced India's foreign policy during Nehru's regime.

---

12   Quoted in Tanveer Sultan Supra No.11, p-10.

Beginning of the Cold War, 1950:

The events that occurred soon after the Second World War and had significant political repercussions led to a shift in the global environment. Firstly, the end of World War-II with direct-armed conflict and the beginning of the Cold War without armed struggle but with a diplomatic and ideological clash are considered significant events during the critical period. In short, it is a state of intense diplomatic, political, economic, and ideological struggle that does not involve armed belligerency or clash. Secondly, the emergence of newly independent countries marked the rapid decolonization. Thirdly, after the defeat of the Axis powers, namely Japan and Germany, in 1945, the rivalry between the US and the USSR, each trying to contain the other and, in the process, mustering friendly and subordinate nations on their behalf, came to dominate the international scene. "This state of affairs was known as the "Cold War"– the phrase was coined by Walter Lippmann – and was characterised by extreme hostility between the two factions, especially in public international organizations such as the United Nations, but with little actual fighting, and this, where it occurred, was mainly between one superpower, normally the United States, and an ally or client state of the other."[13]

a) Cold War:

There are divergent versions concerning the exact origin of the Cold War. Some say it was the Bolshevik revolution of 1917 in Soviet Russia that sowed the seeds of the Cold War. On the contrary, some opined that the Cold War had started soon after the Second World War, which was the widely prevalent and accepted version. Therefore, we may not go into the details of the origin of the Cold

---

13   F.S.Northedge and M.J. Grieve. A Hundred Years of International Relations, Gerald Duckworth and Co, Ltd., London, 1971, p- 249.

War, as it is beyond the scope of this study. Here, we are more concerned about the impact of the Cold War on newly emerged independent countries like India as part of the rapid decolonization process.

b) India and the Cold War:

By the time India gained its independence in 1947, the Cold War had already begun, and the world was being bifurcated into two hostile groups, namely, the American block and the USSR, block each jockeying for supremacy around the globe with conflicting ideologies. The world was virtually divided into two blocs, and a line was drawn in Europe "the crossing of which was recognized as *casus belli*."[14] During the Cold War era, the superpowers were busy consolidating their positions in the international arena. As a result, each group entered into military and political alliances with their respective supporters and followers. The US began organizing its friends and supporters into an American bloc through several alliances such as NATO, SEATO, etc. Similarly, to counter the American move, Russia entered the Warsaw Pact with Communist countries that owed allegiance and support to the USSR. International politics became chaotic and confused due to this tendency towards alliances and counter-alliances. These alliances greatly disturbed newly independent nations like India, which were looking forward to an era of peace and development. Despite the hostile circumstances of the international situation, India, which, like other countries, was inevitably moving towards the formation of peace and security, came under the heavy influence of superpower conflicts when it was stumbling in the dark to develop its independent foreign policy.

---

14 Quoted in K.Raman Pillai's., India's Foreign Policy: Basic Issues and Political Attitudes, Meenahshi Prakashan, Meerut, 1969, p-26.

Thus, it is clear that right from independence, India had to confront the problem of evolving a foreign policy consistent with its national interests at a time when the whole world was divided virtually into two blocs. As a result, India, which had just been liberated from the shackles of British colonialism, had to endure the impact of the politics of power blocs. In such an atmosphere, India wanted to achieve its rightful and honoured position on the international horizon, thereby drawing the attention of the superpowers with the idea of establishing peace and harmony around the globe.

To avoid foreign entanglements by joining either of the blocs, India decided to stay away from the power blocs aligned against one another. Explaining India's stand in the world, Jawaharlal Nehru declared, "We propose, as far as possible, to keep away from the power politics of groups aligned against one another, which had led in the past to world wars and which may again lead to disasters on an even vaster scale. We believe that peace and freedom are indivisible, and denial of freedom anywhere must endanger freedom elsewhere and lead to conflict and war. We are particularly interested in the emancipation of colonial and dependent countries and peoples."[15]

c) Cold War and Non-Alignment:

India, having suffered severely as a colonial country under dominant British rule, was resolved to maintain its hard-won independence by refusing to join either of the two blocs and ceding its right to make autonomous decisions in both domestic and foreign affairs to either of the blocs. To quote Jawaharlal Nehru, "What does joining a bloc mean? After all, it can only mean one thing; give up your view about a particular question, adopt the other party's view on that question in

---

15   Subash C. Kashyap., (Ed) National Policy Studies, Tata Mc-Graw Hill Publishing Company Ltd, New Delhi, 1990, p-250.

order to please it and gain its favour."[16] India felt that taking sides or joining one of the camps would cost her independence and lead to a new form of imperialism. As a result, India's opposition to alignment with the power blocs and opposition to imperialism and colonialism gave rise to the concept of non-alignment. India believed that the only way it could achieve its goal was to adopt a policy of non-alignment. Later, it expanded to include the foundation of India's foreign policy besides the guiding concept. Perhaps non-alignment, which played a significant role during the Cold War, enabled India to identify and maintain its power status and position in the international arena.

India was subject to the decisions of the British Government as a colony because she felt excluded from actively participating in world affairs. It also resented it twice for its involuntary involvement in two world wars at the behest of Great Britain. Therefore, this involvement with Great Britain and its allies during times of war undoubtedly contributed to the development of India's foreign policy along the lines of non-alignment with power blocs, especially with Western alignment, with which she had been familiar all along. In short, India decided not to join either of the two blocs in the interest of economic development, to maintain independent judgement in evaluating and choosing foreign affairs, to pursue autonomous foreign policy, to safeguard its interests, and to promote international peace.

Therefore, India had to evolve its foreign policy by considering all the primary factors discussed above, such as Cold War conflicts, superpower alliances, imperialism, colonialism, etc., which greatly influenced the formulation of India's foreign policy along the lines of non-alignment.

16　A. Appadorai and M.S.Rajan., India's Foreign Policy and Relations, South Asian Publishers , New Delhi, 1985, p-43.

The 1962 Indo-China War:

The history of Sino-Indian relations reveals that the two countries disagreed on several post-independence issues that had far-reaching effects. Since the two countries enjoy a strategic position in the South Asian region, the international community and the smaller nations on the Asian continent were closely observing the developments that were taking place in the area. It became critical for the two countries to preserve amicable relations in the interests of the South Asian region and the rest of the world. The two countries' hostile ties and tension have consistently had an enormous effect on the South Asian countries. Therefore, the leaders of both countries strove hard to restore normal relations between the two countries, thereby keeping the region a zone of peace despite certain conflicting ideologies and inherent differences. However, the significant incidents after 1949 resulted in deteriorating relations between the two countries. We can now explore the issues surrounding the 1962 China War.

a) The Tibetan Issue:

The Tibetan dispute was one of the most significant issues that led to the deterioration of relations between China and India. In a short time, after the installation of the new government, the Chinese leaders, with their expansionist nature, thought of annexing Tibet to China. As a result, in October 1950, China attacked eastern Tibet and occupied Chamdo. India, a nation that values peace, strongly objected to China's invasion of Tibet and offered to mediate in response to Tibet's appeal. Besides, India lodged another protest with a note saying that the incursion by Chinese troops in Tibet was highly deplorable and lamentable. Instead of resorting to force, China's government should have resolved the issue peacefully. In response to India's protest, China replied, "Tibet is an integral part of the Chinese territory. The problem of Tibet is entirely a domestic problem of China. The Chinese People's Liberation Army must enter Tibet, liberate the Tibetan people and defend the frontiers of China...The problem of Tibet remains a domestic problem of the People's Republic of China, and no foreign interference will be tolerated."[17]

Protests and counter-protests went on between India and China over the Tibetan issue, but these did not yield the desired results in normalizing relations. On the contrary, they further worsened the situation despite sincere efforts to normalize relations. Despite protests from India and the rest of the world, China claimed Tibet as an integral part of its territory. Even Tibet's request for the mediation of the UN did not help resolve the issue.

b) The Korean Issue:

The Korean War was another significant issue that led to deteriorating relations between India and China. From 1950 to 1953, a war broke out between North Korea and South Korea, and China backed North Korea, resulting in its troops' participation in the Korean War in 1953. When the Korean War ended, a sizeable contingent of troops moved into Tibet. Naturally, this led to a tense situation in Sino-Indian relations. Further, the large-scale deployment of Chinese troops along the Indo-Tibetan border posed a grave threat to India's security and integrity. India, through its position as the Chairman of the Neutral Nations Repatriation Commission (NNRC) of the war prisoners, had to undertake the job of repatriating the war prisoners in Korea. China alleged that India, being partisan, sided with the Americans on the prisoners of war in Korea. As a result, the gap between China and India widened even further, and tensions escalated.

---

17 Quoted in G.P.Ojha., Mrs. Indira Gandhi's Foreign Policy Choice, Mrinal Book House, Meerut, 1982, p-104.

c) The Tibetan Revolt:

In 1959, a dramatic event occurred when Tibetan guerrillas suddenly revolted against Chinese belligerence and wanted to safeguard their territorial interests. The main object behind the revolt was to liberate Tibet from the Chinese clutches and regain its lost autonomy. But China soon realized that it was the handiwork of India, without which the Tibetans would not have dared to revolt against the Chinese army. Besides, China also claimed that India, which was sympathetic towards the cause of Tibetans, not only extended her help but also allegedly supported the Tibetan rebellion. This hostility took a different shape through paramilitary patrol clashes, culminating in the 1962 border war between the two countries.

It is pertinent to note that during the 1962 war, India lost substantial miles of its frontier to China. The Chinese aggression in 1962 did not lead to any shift in India's foreign policy. Despite the initial setback, India managed to deal with that aggression and its sequel without significantly altering its foreign policy. That was the most fitting tribute to the soundness of Nehru's leadership in foreign policy. Even the Indian leaders who relentlessly opposed Chinese policy towards Tibet, at last, conceded the accession of Tibet, to which China's "New Agency" wrote, "the Chinese People's Army will hoist the Red Flag over the Himalayas."[18]

The Post-Nehru Era:

The golden era of India in world affairs ended soon after the glorious role of Jawaharlal Nehru. The successor of Nehru, Lal Bahadur Shastri, had little experience as far as external affairs were concerned, unlike

---

18   S.R.Patel, Foreign Policy of India: An Inquiry and Criticism, N.M.Tripathi, Pvt. Ltd Publishers Bombay, 1960, p-162.

his predecessor. Shastri followed in Nehru's footsteps concerning non-alignment, the basic principle strategy of India's foreign policy. In his first speech as Prime Minister in June 1964, Shastri affirmed, "Non-alignment will continue to be the fundamental of our approach to world problems and our relations with other countries. On his arrival in London on December 14, 1964, for talks with the British Prime Minister, he went even further and reiterated that there would be "no deviation" from the lines of policy laid down by Nehru."[19]

However, Lal Bahadur Shastri influenced India's foreign policy in his own way. As a result, the Jan Sangh leaders sought clarification regarding any deviation from Nehru's declared policy and the surrender of Indian land to China or Pakistan. Similarly, Communists claimed that foreign policy was veering to the right. But Shastri, disarming the charges, gave a reference to Tilak, Gandhi, and Nehru and said, "...Mahatma Gandhi deviated completely from Lokmanya Tilak, Aurobindo Ghosh, and Lajapat Rai. In a way, Gandhiji was the preceptor of Jawaharlalji, his Guru. But did Jawaharlalji always agree solely with Gandhiji? No. And yet, could you find a more loyal and devoted follower of Gandhiji than Jawaharlalji?.[20]

As Prime Minister, Shastri made some noticeable contributions to foreign policy, which elevated India's position in the international sphere. Though Shastri's tenure as Prime Minister was brief, it was significant in the history of India's foreign relations. During Lal Bahadur Shastri's shot period, India faced two crucial issues: China's nuclear test in October 1964 and the war between India and Pakistan in 1965. These two developments had a significant impact on India's foreign policy.

---

19   Quoted in Tanveer Sultan's, Supra No-11, p-29.
20   Quoted in L.P.Singh's India's Foreign Policy: The Shastri Period, Uppal Publishing House, New Delhi, 1980, p-21.

China's Nuclear Explosion, 1964:

During Shastri's tenure, China successfully exploded an atom bomb in October 1964, conducting its first nuclear test and becoming the world's fifth nuclear club member. (The USA, UK, USSR, and France are also members.) Indeed, the Chinese bomb announced to the world, with a bang, the emergence of China as a great nuclear power. However, the Chinese Prime Minister "assured that though China stood for the complete prohibition and thorough destruction of nuclear weapons, it was compelled to conduct nuclear testing. China's production of nuclear weapons was entirely for the purpose of protecting the Chinese people from the US nuclear threat. He solemnly reiterated that at no time and under no circumstances would China be the first to use nuclear weapons."[21] In addition to India, the smaller South Asian countries also experienced a sense of unease following the explosion of an atomic weapon. Even the detonation of the bomb drastically altered the operational environment of India's nuclear policy.

Taking into consideration the gravity of the explosion, Shastri said, "The Chinese atomic blast had caused shock not only to him but to the whole of humankind, as it cut across the general desire of humanity to live in peace. He hoped that the voice of the peace-loving people in all the countries of the world would be raised against it and that the world conscience awakened to fight against this aggression on peace and security."[22] Even some leaders cutting across party lines expressed grave concern over the Chinese development and wanted a fitting reply to China. As a result, a faction of leaders within the ruling Congress party put pressure on Shastri and demanded the immediate production

---

21   Quoted in Shri Ram Sharma's Lal Bahadur Shastri, An Era of Transition in Indian Foreign Policy, Kanishka Publishers, New Delhi, 2001, p-57.

22   Ibid., p-102.

of a nuclear bomb to counter the Chinese threat. On the other hand, a group that opposed the use of bombs supported Shastri and argued that creating bombs went against the values of Nehru, who strongly advocated for universal disarmament both within and outside of the United Nations, as well as the principle of non-alignment. However, the Cold War between the two factions was blown out of proportion and split the party along the lines of anti-bomb and pro-bomb, just like the moderates and the extremists during the struggle for independence. Even Atal Bihari Vajpayee, the Jan Sangh leader, proudly declared, "The only reply to the Chinese bomb was an Indian bomb."[23] Above all, H.J.Bhabha, then Chairman of the Indian Atomic Energy Commission, in his broadcast on United Nations Day claimed "India could explode a nuclear device within 18 months."[24] Thereby, India will join the bandwagon of nuclear nations and become the sixth member of the nuclear club.

Shastri had to deal with increasing pressure not only from within the Congress party but also from the opposition parties. Shastri did not explicitly declare that India would never develop a bomb. However, due to the altered circumstances caused by the Chinese bomb and the changes in domestic policy, Shastri and his colleagues began to introduce some deviations from Nehru's policies. In fact, at one point, Shastri considered pursuing the development of a nuclear bomb due to pressure but was ultimately prevented from doing so by the opposing faction. Commenting on the production of nuclear bombs to give a fitting reply to the Chinese bomb, Shastri himself declared in parliament that "the government policy was not rigid or static and that it would change according to circumstances."[25]

---

23   L.P.Singh, Supra No-20, p-30.
24   Shri Ram Sharma in Supra No-21, p-104.
25   L.P.Singh, Supra No-20, p-31.

From the above discussion, it is evident that in the post-Nehru era, the influence of Nehru started declining when the two pro-and anti-bomb-factions started gaining momentum within the Congress party. Despite Nehru's categorical statement, "No man can prophesy the future. I would like to say on behalf of my government, and I think I can say with assurance on behalf of any government of India, that whatever might happen and whatever the circumstances, we shall never use this atomic energy for evil purposes."[26] But on the contrary, during Shastri's period, the pro-bomb lobby forced India to go in for a nuclear bomb, which was against the wishes and ideas of Nehru, who was one of the world's leading opponents of such weapons. Therefore, it appears that there was a departure from Nehru's foreign policy on nuclear weapons during Shastri's tenure, despite his claims that he has not strayed from Nehru's original path.

The 1965 Pakistan War:

The 1965 war was a significant event in India's foreign relations as it occurred during the post-Nehru era and posed a difficult challenge for Lal Bahadur Shastri's leadership. Although the 1965 War was intended to improve Indo-Pak relations, it did not solve the Kashmir issue.

The Kashmir issue has been a significant point of contention between India and Pakistan since India gained independence in 1947. Further, the two-nation theory that became the dividing line of India's partition continues to be a principal plank of conflict between Pakistan's Islamic ideology and India's secular nationalism. The division gave rise to many disputes and problems with far-reaching political consequences. Discussions and agreements between the two countries led to the resolution of numerous issues over time. Nevertheless, the

---

26 L.P.Singh, Supra No.20, p-28.

Kashmir issue remains unresolved despite several rounds of untiring talks, dialogues, and attempts by international organizations to mediate. Both countries place great importance on Kashmir, making it difficult for either to relinquish control. "India sees in Kashmir not only an important link in its geographic line of security and its economy, but also a largely Muslim area possession of which tends to justify India's secular political philosophy. Pakistan, in turn, sees Kashmir as advantageous to her military security, as a predominantly Muslim area of some economic value and as a land contiguous to Pakistan.[27] Because of Pakistan's aggressive and hostile attitude towards India, the two warring countries were unable to reach an amicable settlement and find a lasting solution to the Kashmir issue.

As a result, the United Nations Security Council eventually agreed to arbitrate the situation. The United Nations Security Council passed a resolution urging joint negotiations between India and Pakistan to resolve the Kashmir dispute and suggesting the option of a referendum. However, India categorically rejected any outside intervention in resolving the Kashmir issue and unequivocally refused the UN Security Council's recommendation for a vote. Since there was no breakthrough in resolving the vexed issue and disgust over the Security Council's resolution, Pakistan decided to acquire Kashmir by waging an undeclared war against India and resolved to resort to methods other than peaceful to achieve its aims. It was in "October 1958 that then President Ayub Khan declared: The first thing to note about Kashmir is that, apart from any other consideration, from the purely security point of view, we have to continue the struggle for the liberation of the state of Jammu and Kashmir. In no circumstances can we give up that struggle...We shall be infinitely glad to have a settlement through peaceful means. But if we are forced to adopt

---

27   Roy C. Macridis. Supra No.8, pp-332-333.

means other than peaceful, the blame will surely lie at the doorstep of India."[28] Pakistan, which was determined to acquire Kashmir using violent methods, hatched a conspiracy and incited communal violence along the Line of Control on the Indian borders to do so. The aggression began in early August of 1965.

During this period, some significant developments occurred in the international arena that not only strengthened Pakistan but also instilled confidence in it. The first and foremost development is that China has developed close relations with Islamic Pakistan. The international observers viewed this as an unusual alliance between the two countries to isolate India.

Further, taking advantage of the hostile relations between India and Pakistan, China gave an ultimatum to India in September 1965 to remove all the "aggressive military structures" on the Sikkim-China border within three days,"[29] which, according to China, were illegally constructed by India. Though China did not participate in the war, her moral and material support was sufficient to heighten security tensions in India. Above all, America openly supported Pakistan with sophisticated arms and ammunition in the ensuing war. During times of severe crisis with Pakistan, this proved to be a fatal blow to India's interests. The formation of military alliances with the US and China disrupted the regional power structure and presented a potential security risk to India's domestic and international political aspirations.

The Tashkent Declaration:

When the Indo-Pakistan war was on, the Prime Minister of the Soviet Union, Kosygin, wrote a letter to Ayub Khan and Lal Bahadur

---

28   Quoted in A. Appadorai and M.S.Rajan's, Supra No.16, p-96.
29   Quoted in Bidanda M. Chengappa, India–China Relations, Post-Conflict Phase to Post-Cold War Period, A.P.H. Publishing Corporation, New Delhi, 2004, p-109.

Shastri. The letter stated, "The parties should enter into negotiations for the peaceful settlement of the differences that have arisen between them. As for the Soviet Union, both sides could count on its willing cooperation or, to use the accepted expression, on its good offices in this matter."[30] Accordingly, both parties accepted the invitation and signed the Tashkent declaration. "The agreement called for both sides to withdraw their forces to position held prior to August 5 and to repatriate prisoners of war. Both sides pledged not to have recourse to force and to settle their dispute through peaceful means."[31]

However, the Tashkent declaration failed to resolve the core issue of Kashmir despite the agreement between the two countries. From the Indo-Pak war, two things were clear "One was that no country, except Malaysia and Singapore, was prepared to come out openly to support India...Even the Soviet Union, after reiterating that Kashmir was an integral part of India chose to assume, like several other countries, a posture of neutrality when it came to pulling up Pakistan."[32] Though India was committed to friendship and peaceful co-existence with its neighbours, it was forced to fight with them due to circumstances that went against its interests. For every country, national interests hold greater significance than any other issue. Therefore, to protect its vital interests, India had to retaliate against Pakistan's action despite compromising with the basic principles of India's foreign policy, such as friendship, peaceful co-existence, and non- alignment. Naturally, this greatly influenced India's foreign policy and necessitated a review of its policy in light of the Indo-Pak War.

---

30   A.Appadorai and M.S.Rajan in Supra No-16, p-98.
31   Quoted in George Perkovich's, India's Nuclear Bomb, The Impact on Global Proliferation, Oxford University Press, New Delhi, 2000, p-110.
32   Quoted in Shri Ram Sharma.Supra No-21, p-2.

Indira Gandhi's Period:

After the sudden death of Shastri in January 1966, Indira Gandhi emerged as the leader of the Congress Party after its factional politics. Like her father, Jawaharlal Nehru, she established a glorious record and became a landmark in Indian foreign policy history. Indira Gandhi had moved away from Shastri's little India posture. However, she deviated slightly from the intended path set forth by her father, Jawaharlal Nehru, concerning India's foreign policy. She continued to strengthen the policy of non-alignment founded by her father. But her approach was more realistic than idealistic.

Indira Gandhi received much credit for enhancing foreign policy during the post-Nehru era. The ideals of Nehru greatly influenced Indira Gandhi as far as the foreign policy of India was concerned. As Nehru's daughter, she had opportunities to travel to most countries by holding talks with the world's leaders. The main objective of Indira Gandhi was to put India on the diplomatic map of the world. The active involvement of Indira Gandhi in Indian diplomacy substantially helped her become familiar with almost all the leaders of the world. As a result, her international stature grew, and she became recognized as one of the world's most influential leaders. Indira Gandhi was greatly influenced by her father, Nehru, in all of this. Indira Gandhi, in her statement on foreign policy "on January 26, 1966, categorically said that Nehru's principles would continue to guide her: The fundamental principles laid down by my father, to whom he and Shastriji dedicated their lives, will continue to guide us. It will be my sincere endeavour to work for the strengthening of peace and international cooperation so that people in all lands live in equality, free from domination and fear."[33]

---

33   Quoted in A.Appadorai and M.S.Rajan, Supra No-16, pp-48, 49.

In shaping India's foreign policy, Indira Gandhi, a vibrant figure in international politics, consistently prioritized national objectives over international considerations, and she never sacrificed India's interests. As head of the government, "she always carried overall responsibility for foreign policy, but her direction was more than institutional. She concentrated decision-making in her own hands."[34] Indira Gandhi profoundly affected Indian foreign policy and dealt with several global political issues throughout her sixteen years as Prime Minister. The issues she dealt with and the international developments that had a significant impact on India's foreign policy, such as the beginning of détente, the signing of the Simla agreement, the revival of diplomatic relations with China and Pakistan, the dialogues between America and the USSR in the 1980s, etc., are regarded as the significant events of Indira Gandhi's period.

Détente in the 1970s:

During the late sixties, the Cold War conflicts between the two superpowers gradually decreased, and the tensions reduced. Further, there was also a shift in East-West relations from Cold War tensions to compulsions, especially in military strategy and security. The end of the Cold War and the advent of détente, which ensued a period of international security and peace, were significant events during this era. In the words of Northedge and Grieve, "the superpowers had, by 1962, come to respect each other's sphere of interest, and hence 1962, when the Cuba crisis occurred and quickly subsided, may be regarded as the true beginning of the end of the Cold War, or the start of the East-West détente, though some would date this from the construction of the Berlin wall in August 1961 and the

---

34 Surjit Mansingh, India's Search for Power: Indira Gandhi's Foreign Policy 1966-1982, Sage Publications, New Delhi, 1984, pp-26, 27.

Soviet-American agreement of that year not to place weapons of mass destruction in outer space."[35]

As a peace strategy and diplomatic doctrine, "détente was designed, in the words of Henry A. Kissinger, to create an environment in which competitors can regulate and restrain their differences and ultimately move from competition to cooperation."[36]

Meaning of Détente:

"Détente is a French term, meaning relaxation of tension, with a watering down of antagonism and hostility between the superpowers, an atmosphere of relaxation that found expression in the term détente."[37] In the current global scenario, the superpowers decided on their own to abandon rivalry and begin to contemplate mutual trust and collaboration. As a result, in 1970, resentment and hatred between the superpowers began to fade, and an era of peaceful cohabitation and cooperation came to dominate the international scene. In the words of Baral, "Détente means an effort by both superpowers to develop goodwill, understanding, and cooperation between them, which may gradually help in increasing the identity of the Cold War conflict."[38]

Role of Non-Alignment:

India became the leader of the third force, known as the non-aligned group, which consisted of newly emerged independent nations. In a way, this group compelled the superpowers to adopt the policy of peaceful co-existence, as they were pursuing a policy of conflict

---

35 F.S.Northedge and Grieve, A Hundred Years of International Relations, Gerald Duckworth & Co. Ltd., London, 1971, p-268.

36 Quoted in Vinay Kumar Malhotra's, International Relations (Second Edition), Anmol Publications Ltd., New Delhi, 2001, p-229.

37 Vinay Kumar Malhotra, Supra No.36, p-242.

38 Vinay Kumar Malhotra, Supra No.36, p-243.

and contradiction. Most of the colonial countries that achieved their independence by 1963 became active members of the non-aligned movement and followed in the footsteps of India. These non-aligned countries were able to mobilize global public opinion in their favour as far as international issues were concerned. Naturally, this made it extremely difficult for the superpowers to go against the interests of the non-aligned countries and cold-shoulder their (NAM) opinion. By the time the Non-Aligned Movement assumed significance on the international horizon; the superpowers were not in a position to withstand its growing influence and, as a result, decided to mend their attitudes slowly. Given the crucial role played by the members of the non-aligned movement, the Cold War between the two superpowers ended, paving the way for peaceful co-existence.

The Simla Agreement of 1972:

The Simla Agreement between India and Pakistan is regarded as a watershed moment in the history of Indo-Pak relations because, following the 1971 Indo-Pak war, it allowed both the warring countries to settle long-standing disputes amicably without the intervention of third parties, including the issues of the 1971 war. Besides, several foreign policy experts and statesmen also predicted that there would be a sea change in Indo-Pak relations and that there would be hope for a resolution in Kashmir. But things began to change when Pakistan stuck to its stand on Kashmir and persisted in bringing up the vexed issue again in nearly all the international forums, despite the Simla Agreement, which called for a peaceful resolution of the conflict.

Factors responsible for the Simla Agreement:

The Indo-Pak War of 1971 and the changes that had taken place in East Pakistan (now Bangladesh) led to the Simla Agreement. Since East Pakistan was under the dictatorial government of West Pakistan

(Present-day Pakistan), it chose to revolt to attain independence. India, a crusader against imperialism and colonialism and a champion of dependent people decided to support East Pakistan in the noble cause of freedom. As a result, the Indian government provided moral, material, and political support to the people of East Pakistan. Naturally, this upset Pakistan and relations between India and Pakistan continued to drift until they reached a stalemate. In the 1970 general elections, the Awami League of East Pakistan secured a full majority, leading to the invitation of Sheikh Mujibur Rahaman to form the government. But Bhutto "advised Yahya not to follow up the result of the elections held in April 1970, in East Pakistan by allowing Mujibur to become the Prime Minister of the whole of Pakistan."[39] Then Mujibur pushed autonomy for East Pakistan, which West Pakistan also rejected. As a result, in March 1971, the military leadership, at the insistence of Bhutto, started an unprecedented massacre of Bengalis. However, this resulted in a massive influx of Bengali refugees into India. According to Bangabandhu Mujibur Rahaman, this genocide "resulted in the killing of about 30 lakhs, and refugees of about one crore into India."[40] Further, the Pakistani army also fanned communal tensions along the Indian border and conducted raids on India. Naturally, this made India retaliate against Pakistan. Before entering the war, India accepted Bangladesh as an independent nation. The war between India and Pakistan broke out with the support of Bangladesh on December 4, 1971, and finally, Pakistan surrendered for its debacle in the war. India declared a ceasefire on December 17, 1971, which paved the way for the dialogue. After the truce, India started efforts to normalize its relations with Pakistan. Samer Sen, the Indian delegate to the U.N., stated in a note to the Secretary-General, Kurt Waldheim, on January

---

39   T.N.Kaul, Supra No-7, p-179.

40   B.K.Shrivastava, Indo-US Relations: Search for Mature and Constructive Ties, Quoted in India Quarterly, 41 (1) Jan-March 1985, p-44.

12 that India was ready to start bilateral negotiations with Pakistan on mutual troop withdrawal on the Western and Kashmir fronts.[41]

In July 1972, Indira Gandhi and Z.A.Bhutto, Pakistani President, signed the Simla Pact, a document that was part of repairing ties between the two countries. "The importance of the Simla Summit consisted in the fact that for the first time, Indo-Pakistani negotiations went beyond a particular problem or a specific set of issues. From the Indian perspective, it meant the working out of a new arrangement for peace on the subcontinent, taking into account the power equations in South Asia."[42] The Simla Agreement presented an opportunity for countries to resolve their differences amicably, ending the conflict and confrontation that have hitherto marred their relations and thereby promoting harmonious relations and establishing long-lasting peace in the subcontinent.

Though there was widespread criticism of the Simla Agreement from various political groups, Indira Gandhi dismissed the claims brought against her as unfounded. "But it was she who consolidated India's relations with Pakistan through the Simla Agreement and thus began the process of normalization by re-opening diplomatic relations between countries in 1976. Though the principles followed by Nehru and Indira Gandhi were identical, the latter implemented them more dynamically and courageously. As a result, India's prestige in the world rose. More to the point, the prospects of peace in the Indian subcontinent improved."[43] Both the leaders and the people of Bangladesh acclaimed the crucial role played by Indira Gandhi in achieving independence and extending support to the people of East Pakistan. After the 1971

---

41   Quoted in S.S.Patagundi's "Political Parties, Party System And Foreign Policy of India, Deep and Deep Publications, New Delhi, 1987, p-131.

42   Ibid, p-132.

43   S.S.Patagundi, Supra No-41, p-146.

Bangladesh War, India emerged as the dominant power in the South Asian region. For achieving a glorious victory in the war, Indira Gandhi was nicknamed "Durga" and "Kali" (the War Goddess), and she was also conferred with the "Bharat Ratna", the highest civilian award of the government of India.

Lack of mutual trust was the root cause of the strained relations between the two countries. However, by signing the agreement, Indira Gandhi played a crucial role in improving Indo-Pak ties, thereby removing the doubts that had previously existed. She also took the initiative to create an atmosphere of mutual trust by improving Indo-Pak relations and aiming to establish international peace and security.

Reviving Diplomatic Relations with Pakistan and China:

Even though India has initiated various measures to normalize the strained relations, those between India and China have remained frozen. It was mainly because of the absence of direct contact and positive responses from the Chinese side, especially after the 1962 war. However, by 1976, it had become essential for India to normalize Sino-Indian relations for various reasons. "Post-1962, India demonstrated her relative power in the 1971 Bangladesh war, the 1974 nuclear explosion, and the merger of Sikkim in 1975. It was from this relative position of strength that Indira Gandhi sought the normalization of relations with the Peoples Republic of China (PRC) in 1976."[44] This was to reduce India's dependence on Moscow following the Indo-Soviet Treaty of 1971. Similarly, China also wanted to reduce Soviet influence in South Asia, anticipating the probable threat to their occupation of Tibet. These advancements in both countries culminated in the normalization of Sino-Indian relations.

---

44   Dawa Norbu, India and Tibet in Lalit Mansingh and Others (Eds) Vol-2, Indian Foreign Policy, Konark Publishers, New Delhi, 1998, p-270.

A far-reaching development took place in the spring of 1976 when the government of India unilaterally proclaimed its decision to restore full diplomatic relations with China, and accordingly, Indira Gandhi designated K.R.Narayanan as its ambassador as a result. However, this was considered one of the most daring steps towards normalizing the two countries' long-standing strained relations. But at the same time, China also decided to reciprocate by restoring diplomatic ties with India, and India welcomed its move to improve its relations with China. This period also corresponded with the resumption of trade and cultural cooperation between the two countries. Perhaps the initiative that India took in 1976 in normalizing relations with China was a sign of maturity, suggesting that Indian diplomacy did not change its direction with the change of governments in the country.[45]

India's relations with Pakistan, like China's, have been strained and frozen since the 1965 Indo-Pak War. However, the 1972 signing of the Simla Agreement between India and Pakistan under the leadership of Indira Gandhi and President Z.A.Bhutto paved the way for the normalization of strained relations and the revival of diplomatic relations between the countries. The efforts made by both leaders in this regard were highly appreciated and welcomed by the leaders of the South Asian countries, who were in favour of establishing peace in the region.

As a result, under Indira Gandhi's leadership, India was prepared to take the risk of resuming diplomatic relations with China and Pakistan. Due to Indira Gandhi's efforts, the Asian region, which had previously been mired in domestic disputes, eventually experienced peace.

---

45 Quoted in Shri Ram Sharma., India-China Relations, 1971-1991, Part-II, Discovery Publication House, New Delhi, 2003, p-8.

Super Powers' Dialogues in the 1980s:

In 1980, the détente process began a declining trend and led to the resurgence of the Cold War. During this period, the ideological frictions and differences between the US and the USSR on various international issues started again. The re-emergence of Indira Gandhi in 1980 on the Indian political horizon coincided with Russia's intervention in Afghanistan and the emergence of Ronald Reagan as President of America. In the first four years of his administration, American foreign policy remained aggressive, assertive, exceedingly conservative, and combative. As a result, Ronald Reagan's tenure took a tough stand against the Soviet Union. Consequently, super power relations took a nosedive.[46]

The following concerns arose between the two superpowers that affected India's security and integrity. The primary source of contention between the two super powers has been the Afghanistan crisis, the Supply of highly sophisticated weapons to Pakistan, the Diego Garcia issue, and so on.

The Afghanistan Crisis:

The Afghan issue was an important source of contention between the two superpowers because the US did not like the Russian intervention in Afghanistan and termed it illegal, immoral, and contrary to the rights and wishes of the Afghan people. Further, the US also regarded Russia's move as an attempt to encircle China, pressure Pakistan, and reach the warm waters of the Persian Gulf. Therefore, America condemned and opposed Russia over the Afghanistan issue and criticized its support for a puppet regime. When the ideological differences between the superpowers began to take on a different shape, India, under the leadership of Indira Gandhi, decided to

---

46   B.K.Shrivastava, Supra No. 40, p-2.

adopt a wait-and-see approach. The Soviet Union's intervention in Afghanistan had created a piquant situation for her government. "She could not endorse the Soviet action in Afghanistan as it was against the professions of Indian foreign policy. At the same time, she could not condemn the Soviet Union, as it would benefit countries like Pakistan, China, and the US, whose clandestine support for the insurgents in Afghanistan only made the Soviet intervention possible.[47] However, India did not condemn Russia because it felt Russia's intervention in Afghanistan was to prevent some forces from trying to install an anti-communist and anti-Soviet regime in Afghanistan. Naturally, this made Americans consider India's stance to be supportive of the Soviet Union.

US Arms Supply to Pakistan:

To undermine the Soviet Union, America opted to give economic and military aid to Pakistan. It was during this period that India faced some implications as a result of American policy. America evolved a strategic consensus in which Pakistan came to occupy a very significant position. "It served as the conduit through which US assistance reached the Afghan rebels, provided recruits for the insurgency operation from the Afghan refugee camps, and extended them training and other facilities. It played a significant role in lining up Islamic countries against the Soviet presence in Afghanistan. Besides, it was assigned an important place in the scheme for the defence of American interests in the Middle East."[48] The American policy was no doubt a matter of great concern for India. Because America's arms supply to Pakistan increased its military capability, which heightened India's threat perception.

---

47   Quoted in Shri Ram Sharma, Indo-Soviet Relations 1972-91 A Brief Survey Part-II, Discovery Publishing House, New Delhi, 2003, p-54.
48   B.K.Shrivastava, Supra No.40, p-2.

Besides, America offered help to China in purchasing sophisticated arms. Accordingly, China seized the opportunity to modernize its army. Naturally, this led to a climate of insecurity and altered the balance of power in South Asia in general and the Asian region in particular. Further, the American policy indirectly encouraged Pakistan and China to pursue their anti-India policies. As a result of the worsening relations between the US and the USSR, India had to suffer politically and economically.

Rajiv Gandhi's Period:

Rajiv Gandhi assumed the mantle of India's leadership at a critical juncture after the tragic assassination of Indira Gandhi. During this period, India suffered a tremendous crisis both within and outside, and the situation was grave across the country. Internationally speaking, Rajiv Gandhi also had to brave many storms.

Rajiv Gandhi followed in the footsteps of his grandfather, Jawaharlal Nehru, and his mother, Indira Gandhi, who served as India's foreign policy guiding spirits and prominent global figures. However, Rajiv Gandhi's approach differed from his predecessors. Rajiv Gandhi's inclination towards the West to get technological know-how is a classic example of his differences from his predecessors, who inclined more towards the East than the West. Under his leadership, India's foreign policy began improving relations with the West without deviating from the actual path set by his predecessors.

Rajiv Gandhi, the youngest Prime Minister of the largest democracy in the world, had a significant impact on the development of India's foreign policy. Being a newcomer on the international horizon, he demonstrated dynamism and enthusiasm in India's foreign policy formulation. However, some significant events that showed Rajiv Gandhi's ability to lead in resolving fundamental issues, such as

Pakistan-backed terrorist activities along the Indian border, improved relations with superpowers, tense relations between India and China, and most importantly, the ethnic problem in Sri Lanka, can be examined in the context of his role in developing India's foreign policy. In fact, these issues are dealt with separately in the next chapter.

The Coalition Era: National Front Government.

Soon after the end of Rajiv Gandhi's glorious era in the Indian political system, the period of coalition government began in the late 1990s. V.P.Singh formed a coalition administration, with support from both right and left, involving other minor parties with divergent ideologies. Because it was a coalition government, the Prime Minister could not devote much time to foreign affairs because he was busy managing the coalition partners and also because of his weak leadership. On August 2, 1990, Iraq invaded Kuwait, a Gulf country, with the avid intention of controlling the oil resources. However, this irritated the USA, which had an interest in Kuwait. Instead of condemning the attack, India assumed a neutral stance on Iraq's invasion of Kuwait. It naturally raised several questions in the international community about the propriety of India's silence, which had all along fought for the sovereignty and supremacy of the non-aligned countries. As the leader of the Non-Aligned Movement, India, failed to uphold its legal obligations for the first time in the history of its foreign policy. Even India's credibility at the international level suffered due to its policy stance on Iraq's invasion of Kuwait.

When V.P.Singh lost power due to internal conflicts at the end of 1990, Chandra Shekhar became the Prime Minister of India for a short span. Chandra Shekhar opposed the invasion of one non-aligned country by another and joined the international community's call for Iraq to vacate Kuwait. The most significant issue that Chandra Shekhar addressed was the Gulf War in January 1991, which had a bearing on India's foreign policy. During this period, a dramatic development occurred when America attacked Iraq in January 1991 without provocation. However, some leaders condemned India's inactivity for its passivity and for remaining a silent spectator without objecting to the Americans' smugness. The most controversial decision during the regime of Chandra Sekhar was allowing refuelling facilities for the American aircraft involved in the Gulf War. Commenting on India's stance, the then Foreign Secretary, J.N.Dixit said, "There has been much ado about India diluting its non-aligned and neutral position by having allowed this facility to the US. One has to analyse this decision in terms of India's interests and compulsions."[49] Therefore, during the regime of the National Front government India's foreign policy was in great shambles owing to mishandling of the issues.

P.V. Narasimha Rao's Period:

The tenure of P.V.Narasimha Rao as Prime Minister of India was one of the most glorious and crucial moments in India's foreign policy history. During this period, he placed a high value on the country's economic prosperity, which he considered an essential requirement for sound foreign policy. He was considered the architect of Indian economic reforms introduced in the 1990s. As a result, Prime Minister Rao and Dr. Man Mohan Singh, the then Finance Minister, are mainly responsible for India's present economic boom.

P.V.Narasimha Rao assumed the reins of the country when the economy was on the verge of collapse due to low foreign exchange reserves and when the country's foreign policy was in shambles. Soon after assuming office, he introduced several reforms in the Indian economy to tide over the Balance of Payments (BOP) crisis. He was

---

49 J.N.Dixit, Across Borders, Fifty Years India's Foreign Policy, Picus Books, New Delhi, 1998, p-366.

the only Prime Minister after Rajiv Gandhi who opened up Indian economic policies to integrate with the global economy. Even though liberalization began in the early 1980s, it was only during P.V.Narasimha Rao's regime that the process of globalizing the economy accelerated.

At the same time, he also turned his attention to bringing foreign policy back on track. He made genuine attempts to strengthen India's foreign policy, thereby improving India's relations with all countries in the world, including her immediate neighbours. P.V.Narasimha Rao's most significant achievement in foreign policy was the signing of the peace talks with China to end the long-standing border dispute between the two countries.

The United Front Government:

H.D.Deve Gowda became Prime Minister in June 1996 by heading the United Front coalition government. The foreign policy plank of the United Front government reiterated the continuation of the approach as enunciated by his predecessors. I.K.Gujral was appointed the Minister for Foreign Affairs of the country. He was an able statesman who could diplomatically handle the River Ganga sharing water issue. Gujral was instrumental in sorting out the Ganga water problem with Bangladesh and also dealt firmly with the issue of signing the Comprehensive Test Ban Treaty (CTBT). He was given a free hand in dealing with matters of external affairs during Deve Gowda's regime.

Signing of the Draft CTBT:

During H.D.Deve Gowda's regime, there was tremendous pressure from certain quarters to sign the Comprehensive Test Ban Treaty (CTBT). However, India refused to sign the CTBT since it was discriminatory. When asked about India's foreign policy, H.D. Deve Gowda stated that the country would resist international pressure to sign the CTBT. Before reaching any agreement on a nuclear test ban,

India would have to keep in mind the overt and covert nuclear activity by our neighbours."[50] In July 1996, Russia proposed negotiating with India to encourage it to sign the CTBT, followed by US pressure to sign the treaty and not to block it. Considering the pressure from the US, I.K.Gujral, the then External Minister, asserted unequivocally in a Lok Sabha reply on August 2, 1996, "We will not dilute our stand– not at all. The question of revising our position on the present draft does not arise."[51] Further, India's stand was reaffirmed, emphasizing that the world needed nothing less than global nuclear disarmament, to which India remained committed. It was also stated that India would stick to its nuclear policy despite pressure from other nuclear countries.

Sharing of Ganga Water:

During the UF government's regime, the sharing of Ganga water became a bone of contention between India and Bangladesh. However, Foreign Affairs Minister I.K.Gujral took the initiative to resolve the long-standing issue on a priority basis. Accordingly, in September 1996, the foreign ministers of both countries met in Dhaka, and agreed on the broad principles for an agreement for the permanent sharing of Ganga water. It was decide at the meeting to iron out the details of the quantum of water sharing between the two countries. The UF government's determined efforts resulted in an agreement on the issue of sharing water.

The Foreign Policy of the National Democratic Alliance (NDA) Government:

In 1998, a new coalition government was formed under the leadership of A. B. Vajpayee. He made significant contributions

---

50   Attar Chand., Prime Minister DeveGowda: The Gain and Pain, Gyan Publishing House, New Delhi, 1997, p-189.

51   Indian Recorder, Vol-III, September 16-22, 1996, p-2257.

to India's foreign policy as Prime Minister of India. The first and foremost development was the carrying out of nuclear tests, which was a surprising development. In 1998, the NDA government led by A.B.Vajpayee shocked the world and many of his country's citizens by detonating five nuclear weapons in the desert of Rajasthan. It was crucial to note that the NDA government established a record by exploding nuclear weapons at a time when 149 countries had signed a ban on nuclear testing. It also became the first non-Congress government to abandon decades of nuclear restraint.

The conduct of nuclear tests caused a great deal of concern, not only regarding global security but also the security of the neighbouring countries. Nuclear weapon testing had an unavoidable impact on power dynamics in the South Asian region. The Indian government, like China, clarified that the atomic explosion was not intended to harm any country but rather to protect its interests. The nuclear tests were the result of the nuclear power countries' hegemonic policy, involved in perpetuating their nuclear dominance and preventing other countries from acquiring nuclear capability. As a result, India always claimed that the CTBT and NPT (1968) were discriminatory because the nuclear nations always refused India's proposal for universal disarmament.

Further, the issue of nuclear tests became a debatable issue in the international arena when the world was moving towards the abolition of nuclear weapons. Perturbed by the developments that had taken place in India; the international community strongly criticized its actions. Besides, several countries, including America and its ally, Japan, imposed economic sanctions on India for its nuclear explosions, which went against the principles of the NPT and CTBT. However, India boldly faced the consequences arising from the economic sanctions. Speaking in the parliament, A.B.Vajpayee said, "There is also a consensus that if attempts are made to impose unreasonable restrictions on our economic sovereignty and if the inflow into our country of the aid coming from world organizations is stopped, then we will face the situation unitedly."[52] As a result, India withstood all the economic sanctions imposed by various countries and emerged as one of the strongest countries in the world. However, the nuclear tests brought structural changes to Indian foreign policy.

Bus Diplomacy:

Bus diplomacy played a significant role in promoting cordial relations between India and Pakistan. To strengthen people-to-people contact and the bond of friendship between the two countries, A.B.Vajpayee came up with the innovative idea of introducing a bus service from New Delhi to Lahore. As part of bus diplomacy, Vajpayee travelled to Lahore and signed the Lahore Declaration on February 21, 1999. In fact, Vajpayee took concrete steps in bus diplomacy.

Lahore Declaration:

As part of the declaration, both countries agreed to work on the principle of cooperation and coexistence and agreed to reduce their forces along the Line of Control. There was optimism that the two countries' relations would improve. However, things did not move on the expected lines when intruders from Pakistan were found occupying strategic locations along the Line of Control, especially in the Kargil sector of Kashmir, in mid-May 1999.

Kargil Conflict:

The Lahore Declaration catalyzed for the preparations for the Kargil intrusions, but India was unaware of these developments. However, the Indian leadership continued to deny the intrusions that had taken place in the Kargil sector. Even though "the intrusion

---

52   Vajpayee A.B., Lok Sabha Debate 29th May 1998 Vol-II, No.3, 1998, pp-387-388.

was detected on May 3rd, 1999, by "shepherds," who are occasionally retained by the Brigade Intelligence team for forward information gathering."[53] The intruders were not terrorists, as previously assumed, but Pakistani army soldiers backed up by the Pakistan government. When the situation went out of control, the Indian military launched its offensive under "Operation Vijay" to flush out the intruders in the high terrain of Kargil. Even though a "war-like situation" was developing in the Kargil region of Kashmir, it was only after Farookh Abdullah, the then Chief Minister of Jammu and Kashmir briefing, that Vajpayee realized the gravity of the situation. Then, immediately, the brave Indian soldiers retaliated and drove out the Pakistani intruders from Kargil. During the Kargil crisis, Pakistan even threatened to use nuclear weapons against India. However, Pakistan did not stick to its stand, possibly because of India's nuclear capability.

Even though India's military acted quickly to drive out the intruders, many people believed an intrusion could have been avoided much earlier, before the government's intelligence agencies were alerted. According to the Kargil Review Committee Report, the main reason for widespread intrusion was the glaring shortcomings in the country's surveillance capability and intelligence agencies. Therefore, opposition parties, including the Congress Party, criticized the NDA government for handling the Kargil issue.

The Foreign Policy of the United Progressive Alliance (UPA) Government:

Under Man Mohan Singh's government, India's foreign policy became one of the most contentious, with the US insisting on voting

---

53 From Surprise to Reckoning "The Kargil Review Committee Report, Govt. of India, National Security Council Secretariat, Sage Publication, New Delhi, 2000, p-229.

against Iran on its nuclear programme. Because the left parties, which are partners in the UPA government, strongly opposed India's move to vote against Iran in the International Atomic Energy Agency (IAEA) meeting. The Communist Party of India (Marxist) held Prime Minister Man Mohan Singh responsible for adopting a significant decision that affected the country's independent foreign policy and status in the Non-Aligned Movement. It is only natural for the leftist parties to oppose the West. In fact, the left party's stance was an embarrassing situation for the UPA government at the Centre. Undoubtedly, the UPA government voted against Iran in the Security Council to appease the United States. By voting with the US against Iran, India became engaged in yet another "infamous exercise in intimidation and coercion" against a country with which it had friendly relations and vital energy stakes.

As a signatory to the Nuclear Non-Proliferation Treaty (NPT), Iran deserves to enrich uranium and develop nuclear technology for civilian purposes. The United States, three European countries, and Russia have all demanded that Tehran give up uranium enrichment. Though, India, which had entered into an agreement with Iran concerning the supply of natural gas through pipelines, decided to vote against Iran when the issue came before the International Atomic Energy Commission of the UN Security Council. Since the beginning, the US opposed the Iran-Pakistan-India gas pipeline on several counts, with the idea that "the pipeline would help anchor friendly ties among Iran, Pakistan, and India. This would greatly undermine US strategic leverage with India and Pakistan against Iran in the future."[54]

The George W. Bush Visit to India:

The pro-left parties strongly manifested public opinion against George W. Bush, the American president, during his visit in the

---

54   Atul Aneja, India and Iran: A Time for Reflection, The Hindu, 25 August 2005.

first week of March 2006. George W. Bush was in India to sign the "historic" nuclear civilian agreement. The nuclear deal between India and the United States evoked strong protests again, and the issue became debatable and controversial for the pro-left Parties. Because the Left parties were supporters of the UPA government, they strongly opposed the deal as a "bad bargain" and termed it detrimental to the country's commercial and strategic interests. Even CPI (M) Polit Bureau Member Brinda Karat criticized the deal, saying, "The UPA government, by agreeing to the pre-determined framework of the U.S. is pushing India into a relationship which will not serve the interests of the Indian people."[55] However, Man Mohan Singh, in reply to V.P.Singh the former Prime Minister of India, said, "The Government was fully conscious of the imperative need that nothing should be done that can harm our national security interests or cast a shadow on the requirements of our Minimum Credible Nuclear Deterrent. Further, there will be no negative effects on research and development in the nuclear field."[56]

The study of India's foreign policy evolution demonstrates that its foreign policy has gone through several ups and downs and is not inflexible but rather adaptable. Besides, there was no clarity when dealing with specific issues, such as Sri Lanka, China, etc. India's foreign policy proved beyond doubt that it is not static but adjustable in the case of its tilt towards the West. India leaned towards the West during Indira Gandhi's tenure (1980-84), which has been proven in the case of America. As a result, India's relations with the Soviet Union began to take a different shape. India's inclination towards this is considered a deviation from the approach set by foreign policymakers. Nonetheless, there were structural shifts in Indian foreign policy when fresh

______

55 The Hindu, March 6, 2006.
56 Ibid.

developments occurred in the international environment. Therefore, India's foreign policy is an admixture of both tilt and upright.

Some Theoretical Dimensions of Leadership:

Understanding Rajiv Gandhi's leadership in India's foreign policy formulation is pertinent to understand some theoretical dimensions of leadership. Numerous theorists have proposed various theories in the study of leadership. It is endeavoured to comprehend some of the leadership theories in this situation. Among the following leadership theories, a few that are more relevant to the present study have been examined. Trait theory (Great-Man theory), behavioural theory, situational leadership theory, and participative theory of leadership have been relied upon to explain and analyse the leadership of Rajiv Gandhi. These theories have been selected for their broader dimension and universal relevance because they are more appropriate for understanding leadership in the context of India's foreign policy formulation under the able leadership of Rajiv Gandhi.

Trait Theories of Leadership:

The trait theory of leadership identifies various traits, characteristics, abilities, behavioural patterns, or skills that leaders must demonstrate. Further, this theory deals with different characteristics of the leader, such as charisma, ethics, goal-orientedness, initiative, inspiration, and empowerment, among others. The term 'traits' may be taken to mean the personal characteristics of a leader. Stogdill identified the following traits as critical to leaders, viz, adaptable to situations, alert to social environment, ambitious and achievement-oriented, assertive, cooperative, decisive, dependable, dominant, tolerant of stress, willing to assume responsibility."[57] The

---

57   http://www.changingminds.org/disciplines.

theory states that persons who possess these leadership traits are presumed to be psychologically better adjusted to display better judgment and participate in various political and social activities. A person who has these traits would be considered a potential leader. This theoretical approach is seeks to answer the vital question of what are the characteristics or traits that make a person a leader?. To which, Fred Luthans states that "the earliest theories, which can be traced back to the ancient Greeks and Romans, concluded that leaders are born, not made."[58] Similarly, Dessler discovered that "some leaders are characterized by certain traits; they were initially inspired by a "great man" concept of leadership."[59] According to Worchel and Cooper, "certain individuals are born to lead has been labelled the "great man" theory of leadership. In its simplest form, it states that history is shaped by a few men in leadership positions, and these men possess certain unique traits that qualify them for the leader's role."[60] The implication is that leaders are born with unique traits or have some unique background. Adair has listed certain inborn qualities "such as initiative, courage, and intelligence, which together predestine a man to be a leader. By the exercise of willpower itself seen as an important leadership trait, or by the rough tutorship of experiences, some of these qualities might be developed."[61] All of these definitions assume that leadership characteristics are inherited.

Many great leaders of the world are born with certain unique traits that make them leaders. If the same analogy applies to Rajiv

---

58 Fred Luthans., Organisational Behaviour (5th Edition), Mc Graw-Hill Company, Singapore 1989, p-457.
59 Dessler Garry., Management Fundamentals: Frame Work Reason, Reston Publishing Company Inc, Reston, 1977, p-261.
60 Worchel S and Cooper J., Understanding Social Psychology, The Dorsey Press, Homewood Illinois, 1976, p-360.
61 Adair John., The Skill of Leadership, Wildwood House Ltd., West Mead, 1994, p-5.

Gandhi's leadership, it is proven beyond doubt that he, too, was a natural leader. Rajiv Gandhi came from a family of eminent freedom fighters such as Motilal Nehru, Jawaharlal Nehru, and Indira Gandhi, who fought for the independence of India. Rajiv Gandhi cultivated leadership qualities right from an early age, having grown up under the influence of such great leaders. Rajiv Gandhi's father, Feroze Gandhi, who was a leading journalist, played a significant role during the struggle for India's independence by writing articles in prominent journals. He was a disciplined and hard-working man. Rajiv Gandhi's mother, Indira Gandhi, was a freedom fighter and a social worker like her father, Jawaharlal Nehru. She was also the most courageous leader the country had ever seen. The rest of the country knew Rajiv Gandhi's parents for their selfless service, discipline, and courage. He inherited all the qualities of his parents and his grandfather, such as discipline, courage, inspiration, etc., and emerged as an able leader.

Apart from his family, Rajiv Gandhi also came under the influence of a Dane named "Anna" in his early days. He grew up under the care of "Anna", as his mother was busy with attending the dignitaries at Teen Murthi Bhavan, the official residence of Prime Minister Jawaharlal Nehru that became the hub of political and administrative activities of the country soon after independence. Anna, who possessed a rare blend of unique characters, was one of the leading personalities in India. Commenting on the qualities of "Anna" Krishna Hatheesing said that "She (Anna) was a strict disciplinarian, an ardent believer in cold showers, sunbathing, and exercise, and a vegetarian."[62] It was this Dane under whose care Rajiv Gandhi had to grow and spend his fruitful childhood. The environment in the home enabled Rajiv

---

62   Krishna Hatheesing. Dear to Behold: An Intimate Portrait of Indira Gandhi, IBH Publishing Company, Bombay, 1969, p-129.

Gandhi to learn discipline, cleanliness, and strictness right from his early days. However, this immensely helped Rajiv Gandhi in shaping his future personality. Later on, young Rajiv Gandhi proved himself a strict disciplinarian and Mr. Clean when he assumed the office of Prime Minister of India.

Rajiv Gandhi studied at the Wellham School, also known as the Doon School, and is one of the most prestigious schools in the country. The Doon School is known for its academic quality and has produced several generals, politicians, bureaucrats, Scholars, etc. Rajiv Gandhi also happened to be one of the products of such an esteemed institution. Rajiv Gandhi, who enjoyed the company of such eminent students, emerged as one of the most complete personalities.

Another "trait" often associated with leadership is charisma. "Max Weber used the term to mean the "gift of grace". Charisma has almost supernatural qualities, which are difficult to describe and may be impossible to study. Weber felt that a leader's charisma is especially evident in times of crisis and that situational events seem to "draw it out."[63] Further, charisma can refer to the magnetic pull that some leaders appear to have. This theory is more relevant in the case of Rajiv Gandhi, who was a charismatic leader like Jawaharlal Nehru. In a short period, he proved himself an able leader soon after he entered the Congress party. His charisma was tested when he contested the by-election to the Lok Sabha in June 1981 from Amethi, once represented by his brother Sanjay Gandhi. Due to his popularity and charismatic qualities, he got elected with a thumping majority by defeating his nearest Lok Dal candidate. Commenting on his victory and attractiveness, R.Venkatraman, the then Defence Minister, said," Rajiv has achieved what Jawaharlal Nehru could not achieve in his

---

63 Worchell S and Cooper J., Understanding Social Psychology, The Dorsey Press, Homewood Illinois, 1976, p-365.

lifetime. All his opponents lost security deposits."[64] It demonstrated Rajiv Gandhi's popularity as the youth leader of this country who had the quality of influencing the common masses of this country. Indeed, the emergence of Rajiv Gandhi on the Indian political horizon as a leader of the Congress party has marked the beginning of a new era in modern Indian politics, particularly in the lives of the youth.

Rajiv Gandhi became a source of inspiration and a role model for the youth, and it was under his leadership that the country's youth began to organize. As a charismatic leader, he took the initiative to organize rallies and motivated the youth to combat the country's most pressing issues, such as poverty, illiteracy, unemployment, etc. However, he became a source of inspiration to the modern youth, and under his leadership, youngsters began to organize across the country. Being a mass leader, he made a tremendous impact on the economic and political development of the country. He possessed the ability to influence and inspire the people of this country, especially the young Turks.

Behavioural Theory of Leadership:

The emergence of leadership can also be studied based on the behavioural patterns of the leaders. Behavioural theories of leadership do not seek inborn traits or capabilities. Instead, they look at what leaders actually do. In other words, this approach emphasizes what a leader actually does and how he behaves while carrying out his leadership responsibilities. According to the theory, an individual who displays appropriate behaviour will emerge as the leader in whatever group situation he is in. Thus, McGinnie summarized that "leadership is the result of effective role behaviour,

---

64   Devender Khanna., "Mother and Son", Affiliated East-West Press Pvt Ltd., New Delhi, 1986, p-51.

and it is shown by a person more by his acts and behaviour than by his traits."[65] McGinnie's behavioural theory of leadership is relevant in the case of Rajiv Gandhi's leadership. He was a humble leader who was always concerned about world peace and the abolition of nuclear weapons, which endangered human life on earth. Therefore, Rajiv Gandhi's ardent efforts saved the world from the nuclear holocaust. His unique behaviour was a model not only for the entire country but even for the world as well. He was a man of action and never tolerated injustice against the oppressed and suppressed people of the world community. As a result, he waged a relentless war against the inhumane practice of apartheid prevailing in South Africa against blacks. In fact, in his struggle against apartheid, Rajiv Gandhi inspired world leaders by gaining moral and material support and mobilizing public opinion against the dreaded practice of apartheid. Rajiv Gandhi was also a humanist to the core. It was proven when he ventured into raising funds to assist South African frontline countries in their struggle against colonialism and imperialism. Rajiv Gandhi was responsible for the economic prosperity of the South African frontline countries and Namibia's independence. However, this obviously earned him good dividends from the global community. Rajiv Gandhi's leadership thus was recognized by his courageous acts opposing all forms of dominance, oppression, hegemony, racial discrimination, the proliferation of nuclear weapons, and so on.

To Tannenbaum, "The behavioural approach emphasizes what the leader is leading. An important contribution of this theory is that a leader neither behaves the same way nor takes identical actions in every situation he faces. He is flexible to a degree because he feels he must take the most appropriate action for handling a particular problem.

---

65 McGinnie.C.Elliot., Social Behaviour, Houghton Mifflin Company, Boston, 1970, p-228.

This suggests a leadership continuum whereby the leader's actions and amount of authority are related to the decision-making freedom or participation available to the subordinates."[66] The theory expounded by Tannenbaum aptly applies to Rajiv Gandhi's behaviour, who used different techniques to deal with different situations while formulating foreign policy against a particular country. For example, while dealing with the Sri Lankan ethnic problem, he adopted a different approach wherein his involvement was direct, i.e., a participatory role rather than a mediator role, unlike the Chinese border issue and normalization of relations with the USA. However, concerning ethnic problems, he entrusted the task of preparing the groundwork for the India-Sri Lankan Accord to J.N.Dixit, the then Indian High Commissioner to Sri Lanka. Besides, he also sent special emissaries such as Bhandari, the then Foreign Secretary, P.Chidambaram, and K.Natwar Singh, the then Ministers, to deal with the Tamil situation in Sri Lanka. Indeed, the signing of the Indo-Sri Lankan Accord, the brainchild of Rajiv Gandhi, is considered a significant step towards ending the ethnic violence in Sri Lanka.

Further, Tannenbaum's leadership continuum concept, which deals with the amount of authority and freedom given to subordinates, also applies to Rajiv Gandhi's leadership. Rajiv Gandhi decided to constitute a Policy Planning Committee to delegate authority to his colleagues in formulating foreign policy. Accordingly, a committee under the chairmanship of G.Parthasarathy "was constituted for the first time nearly 15 years ago, both to assess the security environment in the world, especially in the immediate neighbourhood and to make suggestions for tailoring India's foreign policy to meet new stresses and strains and to exploit new opportunities."[67] By appointing

---

66 Quoted in Terry G.R., *Principles of Management*, (6th edition), Richard.D.Irwin, Inc, Homewood-III, 1972, p-468.
67 Tribune (Chandigarh) 15 October 1985.

G.Parthasarathy as Chairman of the Policy Planning Committee, Rajiv Gandhi demonstrated that he allowed his subordinates to frame India's foreign policy. As a result, he was instrumental in constituting the PPC and delegating the authority to various wings of the Policy Planning Committee to formulate the country's foreign policy. As head of the foreign policy mechanism, Rajiv Gandhi solicited advice and suggestions from the personnel of the External Affairs Ministry, including the External Affairs Minister, while framing the foreign policy. He even took his colleagues and bureaucrats into confidence while making the final decision on foreign policy matters. However, Rajiv Gandhi had the final say as far as decisions on foreign policy matters were concerned.

Situational Leadership Theory:

After increasing disillusionment with the "great man" and trait approaches to understanding leadership, some researchers shifted their focus to situational factors responsible for producing a leader. According to Fred Luthans, a situational approach was initially called *Zeitgeist* (a German word meaning 'spirit of the times'); a leader is viewed as a product of the times and the situation. The person with the particular qualities or traits that a situation requires will emerge as the leader."[68] "Most psychologists have found out that the situational leadership theory can help to predict the emergence of a type of leadership."[69] Koontz and O'Donnell have also found out that "a large number of studies have been made on the premise that leadership is strongly affected by the situation from which the leader emerges and

---

68　Fred Luthans., Organizational Behaviour, (8th Edition), Mc Graw-Hill Book Company, Singapore, 1998, p-383.
69　Worchell S and Cooper J., Understanding Social Psychology, The Dorsey Press, Homewood III, 1976, p-367.

in which he or she operates."[70] According to Fiedler, people become leaders not only because of the attributes of their personalities but also because of various situational factors and the interaction between the leaders and the situation."[71]

The situational theory can very well be attached to Rajiv Gandhi's leadership, who emerged as a leader due to situational factors. Indeed, he was not interested in politics since he loved flying. However, the circumstances were such that he had to give up his pilot's profession and join politics against his will and wishes. All this happened when Rajiv Gandhi's younger brother Sanjay Gandhi, who was projected as the legal heir to the Nehru-Gandhi family and the future Prime Minister of India, died "in an air crash on 23 June 1980."[72] Therefore, Indira Gandhi persuaded Rajiv Gandhi to fill the vacuum created by Sanjay Gandhi, and this obviously made him quit his job as a pilot and join politics. Rajiv Gandhi, while replying to the debate on the Thakkar Commission Report in the Lok Sabha, said,- "She (Indira Gandhi) called out to me in her loneliness. I went to her side. At her instance, I left my love for flying. At her instance, I sacrificed my family life. At her instance, I joined her as a political aide."[73] At the insistence of Indira Gandhi, Rajiv Gandhi entered politics and soon became the leader of the Congress party when the situation demanded. Hence, Rajiv Gandhi emerged as the leader due to the situational factor.

---

70   Koontz H and O'Donnell C., Management: A Systems and Contingency Analysis of Managerial Functions, (6th Edition) Mc Graw-Hill Kogakusha Ltd., Tokyo, 1976, p-592.

71   Ibid., p-593.

72   J.N.Dixit., Across Borders, Fifty Years of India's Foreign Policy, Picus Books, 1998, p-167.

73   National Herald, 11th April 1989.

Participative Theories of Leadership:

This theory involves other people in the leadership process. However, the leader retains the right to give or deny the subordinate a say in the leadership process. Rajiv Gandhi, as Prime Minister, provided an opportunity for the people of India to take an active part in the democratic process of the country. He was responsible for introducing the Panchayat Raj system in the country to decentralize the system's concentrated powers. By taking part in the democratic process, Rajiv Gandhi was able to reach out to the grossly disadvantaged and make them recognize his leadership. As the leader of the Congress party, he travelled extensively, visiting every nook and cranny of the country to spread the ideals of the Congress party and the government.

Leadership of Rajiv Gandhi:

After reviewing the various leadership theories, it was found that Rajiv Gandhi's personality as the charismatic leader of the nation is a blend of the trait theory of leadership and the situational theory of leadership. So far as trait theory is concerned, Rajiv Gandhi imbibed leadership qualities right from his early days and grew up under the influence of his grandfather, Jawaharlal Nehru, followed by his mother, Indira Gandhi. Therefore, the trait theory is rightly applicable in the case of Rajiv Gandhi. In a sense, the situational theory of leadership presupposes that Rajiv Gandhi was the leader of the situation. Perhaps Rajiv Gandhi, a pilot with Indian Airlines, was fond of flying and loved the profession very much. To God's disgrace, he had to quit the pilot post at Indira Gandhi's behest to enter turbulent Indian politics to fill the vacuum created by his younger brother Sanjay Gandhi, who died in an air crash in 1979. However, this makes it abundantly clear that Rajiv Gandhi, a pilot by profession, had to enter Indian politics reluctantly, which was accidental. Therefore, the developments that led to Rajiv Gandhi's entry into Indian politics indicate that he was the leader of the situational factors.

CHAPTER – III

Rajiv Gandhi's Foreign Policy

The characteristics of the personality of a leader play a significant role in the making of a country's foreign policy, irrespective of the nature of its political system. Therefore, leadership determines the strength and direction of a country's foreign policy. In a parliamentary system of government, the leader plays a decisive role in making foreign policy. However, in any political system, the leader significantly influences the decision. Hence, the study of leadership has acquired immense importance and has become one of the most crucial domestic determinants in foreign policy formulation. Because of the increasing significance of the study, several scholars and researchers are taking up such studies with great enthusiasm and interest. Therefore, in this chapter, an attempt is made to discuss the leadership of Rajiv Gandhi in India's foreign policy formulation.

Rajiv Gandhi became the youngest Prime Minister of the biggest democracy on October 31, 1984. The year 1984 heralded the beginning of a new era in the history of modern Indian politics, particularly in the political life of Rajiv Gandhi. He assumed the office of Prime Minister at a critical juncture following the assassination of Indira Gandhi. In that hour of uncertainty and confusion, the situation was pretty dire across the country, and Rajiv Gandhi accepted the responsibility of steering the Indian ship in the right direction. Naturally, in that period uncertainty, he had to deal with several internal and external issues. The internal problems, like language problems, communal rights, the Khalistan Movement, border disputes (states) and separatist tendencies in the north-eastern States of India, were challenges to the leadership of Rajiv Gandhi. Above all, the crisis of centre-state relations, where states were demanding more autonomy, became another irritant. On the international front, Rajiv Gandhi encountered numerous issues, including terrorist activities along the Indian border supported by Pakistan, the refugee crisis in Bangladesh, China's strained relations with India, the complex ethnic issue of Tamils in Sri Lanka, and so on. These issues, especially the ethnic issue, posed a significant challenge to the leadership of Rajiv Gandhi.

With his charismatic leadership and multi-faceted personality, Rajiv Gandhi significantly influenced domestic and foreign policy decisions. To make the country's foreign policy sound and strong, he decided to resolve all the domestic problems. Since a country's foreign policy is a projection of its domestic policy, it should be stable and robust. There can be no sound foreign policy unless the domestic policy is solid. The British Prime Minister, Gladstone, has rightly said that "the first condition of a good foreign policy is a good domestic policy".[1] Therefore, Rajiv Gandhi, being a newcomer on the international horizon, showed a great deal of dynamism and enthusiasm in resolving most of the domestic and international issues.

Apart from internal challenges, he was also determined to deal with some international problems that had arisen, primarily to undermine his prominence among the non-aligned countries and the Commonwealth. The leaders of the hostile countries retaliated against him in the form of Khalistan, the Tamil crisis in Sri Lanka, Gorkhaland demands in Bengal, and, most importantly, the Chinese incursion in Arunachal Pradesh. Rajiv Gandhi worked tirelessly to find solutions to domestic and global problems despite all odds. Even as the Chairman of the Non-Aligned Movement, he had to deal with various issues, such

---

1   A.Appadorai & M.S.Rajan, India's Foreign Policy and Relations, South Asian Publishers, New Delhi, 1985, p-3.

as the South African problem of apartheid, the liberation of Palestine, the Iran-Iraq war, campaigning for nuclear disarmament, etc. Naturally, this made Rajiv Gandhi an internationalist. However, some people criticized him for his active role in international affairs and opined that the country's foreign policy should be distinct from its domestic policy. However, Rajiv Gandhi, brushing aside the criticisms, said that, "the domestic policy was interlinked with our foreign policy. Unless India played an important role in international sphere, our domestic policy of internal unity and integrity could not be strengthened." He further said, "India is to play a very important role in international diplomacy. It could not confine itself only to Southeast Asia. Today, India is enjoying a very high reputation in the country of nations all over the world, because from the very beginning India had pursued a policy, which had been enunciated by Jawaharlal Nehru."[2]

Despite being a newcomer on the international horizon, Rajiv Gandhi has established himself as an internationalist. In a short period, like his mother, he had gained a unique familiarity with most countries through Indian diplomacy. He strove hard to diffuse international conflicts and tensions and tried to achieve harmony among the countries to promote world peace. As head of the nation, Rajiv Gandhi travelled widely, met leaders, and addressed international summits and gatherings to promote global peace and cooperation. His visit to all the continents, both Communist and non-Communist, was an event extraordinaire in the history of India's foreign policy. What Rajiv Gandhi did in a short span of five years as Prime Minister, Jawaharlal Nehru in his seventeen years in office, and Indira Gandhi in her sixteen years in office could not do in so far as the visits to foreign countries were concerned.

---

2   Hindustan Times, 7th November 1987.

Rajiv Gandhi carried on the legacy of his mother, Indira Gandhi, and his grandfather, who served as guiding spirits in pursuing foreign policy objectives. In this context, Rajiv Gandhi once said, "There was no shift in the foreign policy of India. India was following the foreign policies which late Jawaharlal Nehru and Indira Gandhi had formulated and pursued."[3] However, the approach of Rajiv Gandhi was somewhat different from that of his predecessors. His leaning towards the West to get technological know-how was the best instance, wherein one can find that he had slightly deviated from his predecessors, who were more inclined towards the East than the West. But this may not be construed as a change in India's foreign policy or a deviation from the actual path set forth by his predecessors. Therefore, J.N.Dixit, then High Commissioner to (Colombo) Sri Lanka, has rightly pointed out that "the policies of a country like India did not change with leadership because the country's interests remained unchanged. There could be different policy interpretations, but the basic directions and content remained the same."[4] He was commenting on the reports that there has been a change in India's foreign policy.

Rajiv Gandhi as Head of the Foreign Policy Mechanism:

Rajiv Gandhi influenced the world on international issues through his pragmatic approach as head of the foreign policy decision-making mechanism. As Prime Minister, he exercised his authority more directly in matters of state-to-state relations. Rajiv Gandhi, like Jawaharlal Nehru, kept foreign affairs and diplomacy mostly under his control and guidance. Rajiv Gandhi, who had been taught the art of conducting foreign policy since the days of his mother, enjoyed the power of both the External Affairs Ministry and the Prime Minister. (Brief period as

---

3   Hindustan Times, 7th November 1987. (Delhi)
4   Hindustan Times, 22nd October 1985.

External Affairs Minister) In his five-year term as Prime Minister, he has kept the foreign affairs portfolio to himself for nearly two years, with five external affairs ministers. It is evident that Rajiv Gandhi played a dominant role in foreign policy decision-making. Commenting on Rajiv Gandhi's role in the formulation of India's foreign policy, P. Shivashankar, then External Affairs Minister in Rajiv Gandhi's cabinet, made it clear that "External Affairs claims a good deal of attention from the Prime Minister, who chalks out the policies. The Ministry implements them".[5]

Rajiv Gandhi, as a leading foreign policy maker, made substantial contributions to India's foreign policy. The principal plank of Rajiv Gandhi's foreign policy was to maintain friendly relations with all countries in the world, including India's immediate neighbours. Rajiv Gandhi, during his first-ever broadcast address to the nation on October 31, 1984, after assuming the office of Prime Minister, said that "India's traditional foreign policy, with its commitments to non-alignment, co-existence, and friendly relations with all, will remain unchanged."[6]

It is important to note that, in addition to managing foreign policy, Rajiv Gandhi was instrumental in resolving several international issues, which helped to strengthen amicable relations with India's immediate neighbours and superpowers. Further, his multifaceted roles as the Chairman of the Non-Aligned Movement, Chairman of the SAARC countries, Chairman of the Africa Fund, Crusader against apartheid, persuader of the Super Powers on the INF Treaty, Leader of the Six-Nation Initiative on disarmament and peace, etc., demonstrate what kind of leader he was. His role as a great statesman in transferring technological know-how from the US was highly noteworthy. Above all, his role in normalizing Sino-Indian relations and signing the Indo-Sri

---

5   Hindustan Times, 28th July 1986.
6   Amrit Bazar Patrika, 2nd November, 1984.

Lankan Agreement was crucial in developing Indian foreign policy. These developments helped Rajiv Gandhi prove his leadership on the international horizon. As a result, these three significant developments have been dealt with separately in the following chapters.

a) Rajiv Gandhi and the SAARC:

Rajiv Gandhi has been a driving force behind the South Asian Regional Cooperation movement since its inception. It was an honour for him to be present at four SAARC Summits in a row, including as its Chairman during his tenure as Prime Minister of India. Due to the principles of cooperation and coexistence, his leadership enabled the forum to achieve a unique position not only in the South Asian region but also in the international domain. Rajiv Gandhi, a dynamic leader, assumed the Chairmanship of South Asian Association of Regional Cooperation (SAARC) in 1986-87 when the forum was experiencing internal bickering among its leaders. It was he who instilled a sort of enthusiasm in the SAARC regional forum with the object of achieving all-round development of the member countries. Under his leadership, the SAARC forum quickly rose to prominence as one of the world's most important regional forums in a short period. Besides, it became a forum for promoting mutual understanding and coexistence. The SAARC forum consisted of non-aligned countries as its members, whose main objective was to strengthen mutual understanding and cooperation. Further, as a body of seven nations, SAARC allowed the regional heads of state to meet each other, sort out bilateral differences, and promote regional cooperation.

Origin and Development of SAARC:

The SAARC Association, which emerged in the second half of the 1980s, is one of the most significant events in the history of South Asian countries. Like other countries, India thought of having a regional forum for the all-round development of the South Asian countries on the model of the ASEAN Forum. Accordingly, "the South Asian Regional Cooperation (popularly known as SARC) scheme was formally launched in August 1983 by the first joint meeting of foreign ministers of the seven South Asian states".[7] SAARC was launched primarily as a result of the efforts of these countries and the preparations made by the secretaries of the respective countries since 1980. The formation of the SAARC is undeniably beneficial to South Asian countries and will advance the cause of friendship, cooperation, and coexistence among the member countries. Indira Gandhi, the then Prime Minister of India, and Ziaur-Rahman, the then President of Bangladesh, made commendable efforts in this regard. The main object of the two leaders was to resolve the problems amicably between the South Asian countries, thereby creating an atmosphere of cooperation, mutual understanding, and friendship. Therefore, the credit for launching the SAARC Forum goes to these leaders. The forum emerged as an agency for promoting economic and cultural cooperation among its member countries.

Initially, the forum identified specific areas of cooperation, taking pains to handle regional intricacies carefully. The SAARC included nine areas of cooperation: agriculture, rural development, health and population, transport, scientific and technological collaboration, telecommunication and meteorology, postal services, sports and arts and culture."[8] In addition to this, study groups came into existence to identify other areas of cooperation among the SAARC members.

However, the efforts of Ziaur-Rahman, the then president of Bangladesh, when he proposed a South Asian regional forum

---

7   Lok Raj Baral, SARC, But No "SHARK", South Asian Regional Cooperation in Perspective, Pacific Affairs, 58(3), fall 1985, p-411.

8   Lok Raj Baral, Supra No.7, p-411

consisting of Bhutan, Bangladesh, India, the Maldives, Nepal, Pakistan, and Sri Lanka in December 1980 may be credited as the origins of SAARC. Initially, India was reluctant to join the forum because its relations with Pakistan and Bangladesh, the two major countries, were going through a difficult phase. Further, ties with Sri Lanka were not cordial due to the ethnic crisis.

Under the turn of events Indira Gandhi, anticipated that 'the grouping would be more an arrangement to exert various kinds of pressure on India rather than as an instrumentality to forge regional cooperation."[9] Despite the reservations, India, under the leadership of Indira Gandhi, agreed on principle to join the forum. Though the SAARC was launched at the initiative of Ziaur-Rahman, the then President of Bangladesh, with the idea of cooperation and coexistence, India, under Indira Gandhi's leadership, was instrumental in developing the forum into one of the most powerful regional forces in South Asia.

The SAARC forum, founded on the principle of mutual understanding, has considerably helped to further the cause of friendship, cooperation, and coexistence among its members. In this regard, the initiative taken by Ziaur-Rahman, to establish a regional forum was significant and deserved appreciation. His main object was to solve the problems that South Asian countries were facing, thereby creating an atmosphere of cooperation, friendliness, and mutual understanding. Further, the formation of the SAARC was thought to reduce tensions and conflicts in the South Asian region, where conflicting views and divergent strategies are ever-present. Naturally, this paved the way for stronger ties among SAARC member countries. Sensing the gravity of regional conflict, Rajiv Gandhi said during his visit to the USSR in May 1985 that "world peace and tranquillity were closely linked, and a regional

---

9   J.N.Dixit, India and Regional Development Through Prism of Indo-Pak Relations, Gyan Publishing House, New Delhi, 2004, p-76.

conflict could easily turn global, and we must all be concerned about this. India had initiated discussions with its neighbours to improve the total environment of regional peace and cooperation. We desire South Asian Regional Cooperation (SAARC) to make a contribution to a better, mutually beneficial relationship among the countries of the region".[10]

The formation of SAARC provided moral support to members of South Asian countries. Despite the inherent differences among its member countries, perhaps SAARC was regarded as a watershed moment in regional cooperation. It also allowed the member countries in the region to settle their differences amicably without the interference of outside forces. The following are the crucial objectives of the SAARC.

1. "To promote the welfare of the peoples of South Asia and to improve their quality of life.
2. To accelerate economic growth, social progress, and cultural development in the region and to provide all individuals the opportunity to live in dignity and to realize their full potential.
3. To promote and strengthen collective self-reliance among the countries of South Asia.
4. To contribute to mutual trust, understanding, and appreciation of one another's problems.
5. To promote active collaboration and mutual assistance in the economic, social, cultural, technical, and scientific fields.
6. To strengthen cooperation with other developing countries.
7. To strengthen cooperation among themselves in international forums on matters of common interest; and
8. To cooperate with international and regional organizations with similar aims and purposes".[11]

---

10   Asian Recorder, 31(25), June 18-24, 1985, p-18370.
11   Commerce, Jan-Feb, 1987, p-27.

The First SAARC Summit:

The First SAARC Summit Conference was held in Dhaka on December 7 and 8, 1985. Gen. Irshad hosted the first summit conference. "The Dhaka Summit was a historic event in South Asian history as it provided a unique opportunity for the first direct contact among the leaders of the region at the summit level."[12] The leaders also described the first meeting as a 'tangible manifestation of their determination to cooperate regionally, to work together towards finding solutions towards their common problems in a spirit of friendship, trust, and mutual understanding, and to the creation of an order based on mutual respect, equity, and shared benefits."[13]

The summit adopted a declaration for establishing SAARC, with Bangladesh's President H.M.Irshad as its first chairman. The seven South Asian countries "reaffirmed their commitment to the UN Charter and the principles governing sovereign equality of states, peaceful settlement of disputes, non-interference in internal affairs, and non-use or threat of use of force against the territorial integrity and political independence of other states. The leaders reaffirmed their deep conviction in the continuing validity and relevance of the objective of the non-aligned movement as an important force in international relations."[14]

Organisational setup:

The technical committees are at the bottom of SAARC, supported by study groups and expert teams. The technical committees shall be responsible for monitoring the programme in their respective

---

12   Nancy Jetly, SAARC: Looking Ahead, (Eds) Lalit Mansingh and others, Indian Foreign Policy: Agenda For the 21st Century, (vol-1), Konarak, New Delhi, 1998, p-4.

13   http://www.saarc-sec-org/

14   http://www.saarc-sec-org/

areas of cooperation. Standing Committees comprising the Foreign Secretaries have the responsibility of monitoring and coordinating the cooperation programme. The Council of Ministers, consisting of the Foreign Ministers of the countries, is primarily responsible for formulating the policies of the Association. At the apex of the SAARC institutional framework is the summit".[15] The Charter also provides the creation of the Secretariat with a Secretary General, Directors, and General Services Staff. The significant feature of the SAARC Charter is that the heads of state would meet once a year or more, if necessary.

The Dhaka Summit not only gave the "Charter of the Association but also set up two study groups – one to examine the problem of terrorism and the other of drug trafficking and abuse. It further agreed to convene conferences of ministers to consider the issues of the New International Economic Order and the improvement of the World Trading System through GATT, taking particularly into account the interests of the least developed among the developing countries and the participation of women in development".[16]

Rajiv Gandhi's Stance:

The first-ever SAARC Summit held in Dhaka was one of the most significant events in the history of South Asian countries. The Dhaka Summit heralded a new era of regional cooperation among South Asian countries despite the hostile atmosphere in the region. The bilateral concerns among the member countries were the major obstacles to strengthening SAARC. However, Rajiv Gandhi, while addressing the first Summit meeting, said, "Certainly we have problems and difficulties, and these impose constraints on us. Enduring cooperation is cooperation adapted to the realities of our conditions. The model we

---

15   http:// www.nipa-khi-edu.pk.
16   Quoted in Suman Sharma., India And SAARC, Gyan Publishing House, New Delhi, 2001, p-89.

have evolved for ourselves is one that is in accord with our realities. Our compulsions are our genius. We have not sought to melt our bilateral relationships into a common regional identity but rather to fit South Asian cooperation into our respective foreign policies as an additional dimension. We have evolved modalities which do not allow bilateral stresses and strains to impinge on regional cooperation. Our cooperation tempers enthusiasm with pragmatism and initiative with consensus. At the same time, in light of our experience in the recent past, we have every reason to hope that the practice of regional cooperation will have a beneficial impact on bilateral relationships.[17]

Further, commenting on the unique culture and character of the South Asian people, Rajiv Gandhi said, "The South Asian region has been one of the great crucibles of human creativity. Here, an indigenous civilization, whose origins stretch back into unfathomed antiquity, interacted with peoples and races who poured in from distant parts of the world. Out of the intermingling of their ideas, philosophies, and ways of life grew the nobler heritage to which all our seven countries can lay claim."[18]

The Dhaka Summit established the framework for cooperation and coexistence among South Asian countries. The formation of the SAARC was considered an extraordinary event in the history of South Asia, whose endeavour was to establish a regional forum for cooperation among South Asian countries. The first SAARC Summit generated high hopes and expectations among the member countries concerning regional collaboration and coexistence. Above all, the summit paved the way to foster peaceful and good-neighbourly relations between the

---

17   Rajiv Gandhi, Selected Speeches and Writings, Vol-I, 1984-85, Publication Division, New Delhi, 1987, p-401.

18   Ibid., p-400.

member countries. Further, the Dhaka Summit also decided to broaden the areas of cooperation by considering a few more subjects.

The Second SAARC Summit:

Rajiv Gandhi hosted the Second SAARC Summit in Bangalore in November 1986, which was attended by the heads of all member countries. The said summit was no doubt a significant event in the history of India that dealt with several issues of both regional and global interest. Further, the Bangalore Summit assumed special significance because the summit meeting was not only confined to economic, technical, and cultural issues but also dominated issues such as terrorism, drug trafficking, and bilateral political disputes. During the summit, Rajiv Gandhi took over as Chairperson of the SAARC from President H.M.Irshad of Bangladesh. While taking over the chairmanship, Rajiv Gandhi reaffirmed the commitment of all seven countries to make SAARC a success.

The Bangalore Declaration:

The Bangalore Summit Declaration called for "increasing involvement of the people for ensuring the success of regional cooperation. It focussed on the need for promoting greater contact among the people through such actions as the regular and frequent interchange of scholars, academics, artists, authors, professionals, and businessmen. The Declaration welcomed the establishment of the Technical Committee on Women in Development and on the Prevention of Drug Trafficking and Drug Abuse.[19] On global issues, 'the summit called for an end to the nuclear arms race and early conclusion of a Comprehensive Nuclear Test Ban Treaty. It called for the adoption of a regional approach for obtaining favourable terms of trade and assistance from the developed world and the revival of the North-South

---

19   http:// www.mofa.gov.bd/

dialogue. It emphasized closer SAARC consultation and cooperation at relevant international economic conferences and institutions.[20]

Rajiv Gandhi's Stance:

As discussed above, the Bangalore Summit emphasized global issues such as drug trafficking, terrorism, etc. Therefore, on the eve of his inaugural address at the Second SAARC Summit, Rajiv Gandhi expressed deep concern over the growing menace of terrorism in the South Asian region and urged the leaders of the world to curb all types of terrorism, and said that "terrorism must be severely condemned and that each of us must do nothing that condones terrorism or gives aid and comfort to terrorists. As responsible members of the international community and as good neighbours within our region, each of us must ensure that our territory is never used as a sanctuary or launching pad for terrorism anywhere in the region".[21] But, on the contrary, Pakistan and Bangladesh, the two members of the SAARC, were indirectly supporting terrorist activities and also allowed training camps for terrorists across the borders, including sheltering the terrorists on their land, which is a mockery of the principles of cooperation, coexistence, and mutual understanding on which the forum founded.

Rajiv Gandhi, in his addresses on the objectives of SAARC, said, "Ours is not a political association. We have much to gain from peace, progress, and stability in our neighbourhood. This is the logic of our working together. Bilateral relations have their difficult moments. SAARC reminds us that at such moments, we should seek what unites us and not what divides us. We have consciously decided not to burden SAARC with our bilateral concerns.[22] As a result, it was decided to

---

20   Suman Sharma, Supra No.16, pp-93.94.

21   Rajiv Gandhi, "Selected Speeches and Writings", 1986, Vol-II, Publication Division, Ministry of Information and Broadcasting, New Delhi, p-320.

22   Rajiv Gandhi, Supra No.21, Vol-II, 1986, p-318.

keep bilateral issues out of the SAARC forum. Even the SAARC, at the insistence of India, had "two important pre-conditions" – no bilateral and contentious issues were to be discussed at SAARC and the principle of unanimity for decision-making was incorporated in the SAARC Charter as "General Provisions."[23]

However, on the eve of the Second SAARC Summit in Bangalore, the SAARC offered a chance for informal bilateral discussions among the leaders of the member countries on the fringes of the Summit. As a result, the SAARC Summit has developed into a platform for discussion of regional cooperation issues and informal bilateral concerns among member countries. Rajiv Gandhi and J.Jayewardene used the summit fringes to informally discuss Indo-Sri Lankan relations, which later resulted in the signing of the Indo-Sri Lankan Accord to find a lasting solution to the ethnic problem. Further, during this time, the informal talks between India and Pakistan led to the diffusion of tensions between the two countries to some extent. Indeed, the Bangalore summit laid the foundation for informal bilateral political discussions among the leaders of the member countries in its realm. Even Rajiv Gandhi in Kathmandu acknowledged that "the summits also provide annual opportunities for meetings outside the conference premises. These are by no means confined to questions of regional cooperation but range freely over bilateral and international issues. None of us underestimate the value of these meetings. The SAARC Summit has become an important fixture in our calendar for bilateral discussions and the exchange of views".[24]

However, countries such as Pakistan and Sri Lanka are opposed to holding the bilateral talks on the fringes of the summit forums. However,

23 Suman Sharma., Supra No.17, p-87.

24 Rajiv Gandhi, Selected Speeches and Writings, Vol-III, 1987, Publication Division, Govt. of India, New Delhi, p-407.

taking into consideration the tension between India and Sri Lanka, President Jayewardene said at the Bangalore summit, "We cannot build this association if we allow bilateral issues to grow. If we bring bilateral issues to this forum, then, maybe, we would be crippled before we could walk. The SAARC ship has set sail and has started its journey. There should be no mutiny on board.[25] Contrary to this, Jayewardene himself discussed the Tamil issue in the realm of the SAARC Summit at Bangalore, as reported in one of the newspapers: Sri Lankan President Jayewardene's arrival some three hours ahead of others made it possible for him and Prime Minister of India to exchange views on the airport itself.[26] Therefore, the bilateral discussions, which took place between the countries on, some occasions, were certainly outside the SAARC Forum. Even Rajiv Gandhi, while replying to a question during the debate in Parliament, once again reiterated that" SAARC is not a bilateral forum, and we will not use it to sort out bilateral issues. We have direct contacts, and we deal directly on bilateral issues.[27]

However, the bilateral discussions during the Bangalore Summit significantly helped to decrease the political tensions and inter-state rivalries among the SAARC countries, including Sri Lanka. Rajiv Gandhi made substantial efforts to normalize and strengthen bilateral relations between India and her smaller neighbours through SAARC. It is proven beyond doubt that the South Asian countries, despite internal bickering, have stood united for the cause of regional cooperation, thereby upholding the principle of mutual understanding and peaceful coexistence. In this regard, Rajiv Gandhi played an important role in diffusing regional tensions and keeping the SAARC forum out of inter-state rivalries.

---

25   http://www.southasianmedia.net.Magzine
26   The Hindu, 16 Nov 1986.
27   Prime Minister Rajiv Gandhi, Statement on Foreign Policy, April-June1988, Ministry of External Affairs, p-8.

Further, the second SAARC Summit in Bangalore also took a significant step towards institutionalizing SAARC by establishing a Secretariat to coordinate the proper implementation of SAARC programmes. In this regard, the third SAARC Summit in Kathmandu was to establish the Secretariat, as outlined in a memorandum of understanding signed by the SAARC Foreign Ministers. This document also outlined the role, functions, and Secretariat's funding. The Bangalore Summit, therefore, will be remembered for the early decision to set up the SAARC Secretariat.

Perhaps the SAARC Summit at Bangalore demonstrated to the rest of the world that India remains on a high pedestal of leadership, particularly as an architect of non-alignment. India also continued to swear by anti-terrorist and anti-racial postures. As SAARC leader, Rajiv Gandhi played a significant role in strengthening regional cooperation. He took the initiative to introduce several new areas of collaboration wherein the member countries had an opportunity to participate and interact as far as issues of regional cooperation were concerned. At the summit, he also sought greater cooperation among the member countries to tackle drug trafficking and terrorism.

The Third SAARC Summit: Kathmandu

The Third SAARC Summit held in Kathmandu in November 1987 under Rajiv Gandhi's chairmanship was undoubtedly a path-breaking event in the history of South Asian countries. At the summit meeting, it was decided to introduce new areas of cooperation and expand existing ones. Further, the Kathmandu Summit was unique in so far as issues of far-reaching implications and regional issues were concerned. The summit meeting resolved to pursue the areas of cooperation adopted in previous summits with great vigour, apart from the introduction of new areas of collaboration. The summit meeting witnessed the signing of two important agreements: "one on establishing the SAARC Food

Security Reserve and another for a SAARC Regional Convention on Suppression of Terrorism. The summit also decided to commission a study on "Protection and Preservation of the Environment and the Causes and Consequences of Natural Disasters in a Well–Planned Comprehensive Framework.[28] The permanent SAARC Secretariat creation in Kathmandu was an important decision at the summit meeting.

In Kathmandu, the summit leaders emphasized the need for strengthening inter-governmental efforts with increased people-to-people cooperation as well as greater participation of non-governmental organizations (NGOs), including professional bodies in the private sector, in the process of promoting socio-economic and cultural development as envisaged in the SAARC Charter. On international issues, the leaders welcomed the understanding reached between the United States and the Soviet Union on Intermediate Nuclear Forces (INF)... and called for the early conclusion at the Geneva Conference on Disarmament of a Comprehensive Test Ban Treaty and Convention to Ban Chemical Weapons.[29]

The summit leaders also expressed satisfaction with the launch of the SAARC Audio-Visual Exchange Programme, which coincided with the opening of this summit. While taking note of the dates for the institution of the SAARC Chairs, Fellowships, and Scholarships and the commencement of organized tourism among SAARC member countries, they directed that the schemes for the SAARC Documentation Centre and the SAARC Youth Volunteer Programme be implemented at the earliest. They welcomed the first annual review of the situation of children in SAARC member countries.[30]

---

28   Quoted in Suman Sharma., Supra No.16, p-97.
29   www.saarc-sec-org/main.
30   Ibid.

Rajiv Gandhi's Stance:

As previously stated, the Kathmandu Summit introduced new areas of cooperation, wanted to expand the scope of cultural collaboration, and brought the issue of cooperation in trade and industry onto the SAARC agenda. Rajiv Gandhi, addressing the summit, said, "There is also much more we can do in the area of culture, especially forms of culture that draw in large numbers of people as participatory spectators. We might consider a South Asia Festival, which brings together from all parts of our region a diversity of arts and crafts, poetry and songs, dance and drama, and traditional sports. Further, he said, "Our planning experts have foreseen the advantages of cooperation in trade and industry, money, and finance. It would be useful to authorize studies on the scope and modalities of cooperation in these sectors. We would make an objective determination later as to whether the balance of advantage lies in our entering the fields.[31]

Rajiv Gandhi raised the issue of terrorism and drug trafficking at the Bangalore Summit, which became a focal point at the Third Summit. Regardless of their differences, the leaders expressed concern over the growing menace of terrorism and sought immediate action. Taking note of the terrorist activities sponsored by certain member countries (without naming Pakistan) against other states, President J. Jayewardene of Sri Lanka took a strong exception and warned that those who adopted violence against other states should be "outside the pale of our friendship and protections". At the same time, he also commended the agreement his country had signed with India to usher in peace in a country which, he painfully recalled, had struggled with groups of terrorists calling themselves separatists for years until the signing of the agreement "through the good offices of India"[32] In fact,

---

31   Rajiv Gandhi, Supra No.17, p-406. (Vol-1)
32   Asian Recorder, 33(51) Dec 17-23, 1987, p-19789.

Jayewardene lauded the role played by Rajiv Gandhi in bringing peace to war-torn Sri Lanka by signing the Indo-Sri Lankan Accord.

The Third Summit was notable for its focus on the contentious political issues that India desired to discuss at the summit. These issues were India's move to support Afghanistan's application for membership in SAARC and to welcome the Indo-Sri Lankan Accord in the summit declaration. Most of the SAARC countries, including Pakistan, opposed Afghanistan's application for membership. However, Pakistan, a bête noire of India categorically stated that "the issue of giving admission to Afghanistan was a political one".[33] Further, Pakistan also objected to the second move, questioning the principle as to "whether SAARC, under the provisions of the Charter, could discuss a bilateral and contentious issue and, in the context of the presence of Indian Forces in Sri Lanka (and) also draw a parallel between Afghanistan and Sri Lanka".[34] However, there was a lack of unanimity among the members of the SAARC on ethnic issues. However, the SAARC Standing Committee received instructions to examine the question of new members' admission since the Charter contained no such provision.

The Kathmandu Summit was mainly responsible for introducing new areas of cooperation at Rajiv Gandhi's initiative and expanding the existing sphere of collaboration to achieve greater cooperation among South Asian countries. The summit also stood as a model for its greater unity despite certain misperceptions and sharp differences among the member countries.

The Fourth SAARC Summit:

The Fourth SAARC Summit held in Islamabad in December 1988 assumed significance in light of certain significant developments.

---

33   Asian Recorder, 35(51) Dec 17-23, 1987, p-19791.
34   Suman Sharma, Supra No.17, p-99.

"Firstly, it was held against the backdrop of the signing of the INF Treaty by the USA and the USSR, aimed at eliminating nuclear weapons. Secondly, Pakistan, the host country, restored democracy just before the summit, which coincided with "Benazir Bhutto's electoral victory and coming to power in November 1988".[35] Thirdly, the signing of the Indo-Sri Lankan Accord and change of guard in the Sri Lankan political system with Premadasa becoming President.

The Islamabad Declaration:

The Fourth SAARC Summit witnessed several crucial declarations on social, economic, and cultural issues. "The heads of state expressed satisfaction at the progress so far made in the development of the SAARC integral Programme of Action and took note of the measures to streamline and re-orient various SAARC activities to make them more action oriented. They welcomed the establishment of the SAARC Agricultural Centre (SAC).[36]

The decision to designate 1989 as the "SAARC Year for Combating Drug Abuse and Drug Trafficking" was taken by the Summit leaders in Islamabad, allowing the Technical Committee concerned to examine the possibility of a Regional Convention on Drug Control. The leaders also agreed to declare 1990 the "SAARC Year of the Girl Child". The Summit made a point to expand the new areas of cooperation, and it was emphasized" that all Member States should identify areas of core interest in their national perspective plans and consolidate them into a regional plan to be called "SAARC–2000: A Basic Needs Perspective", with specific targets to meet by the end of the century.[37]

---

35   J.N.Dixit, Across Borders, Fifty Years of India's Foreign Policy, Picus Books, New Delhi, 1998, p-197.

36   www.saarc-sec-org.

37   Ibid.,

Rajiv Gandhi's Stance:

The summit in Islamabad began with certain political disputes, sensitive issues, and contentious points. Further, some adversaries were noticed on the summit's periphery. When Ranasinghe Premadasa became the President of Sri Lanka, relations between India and Sri Lanka reached their lowest ebb. He demanded the immediate withdrawal of the IPKF troops stationed on the island, which Rajiv Gandhi refused under the guise of upholding the terms of the Indo-Sri Lankan Agreement. The demand of Premadasa and the refusal of Rajiv Gandhi about the withdrawal of IPKF obviously plunged the region and the SAARC process into a crisis. However, Premadasa criticized India's stance, and as a mark of protest, he decided not to host the Fourth Summit until the withdrawal of the IPKF from Sri Lanka. Though initially he "offered to host the Fourth (SAARC) Summit in 1988 in Sri Lanka,"[38] which was accepted by the leaders at the Kathmandu Summit.

Despite the political dispute between India and Sri Lanka, the venue of the Fourth Summit in Islamabad witnessed a friendly atmosphere concerning Indo-Pak relations when Rajiv Gandhi and Benazir Bhutto signed three important bilateral agreements on the periphery of the summit in December 1988. These related to an agreement against attacking each other's nuclear installations, avoiding double taxation, and promoting cultural exchanges between the two countries."[39] Further, both countries decided to settle the vexatious Kashmir issue with bilateral discussions and also to respect the Line of Control in mutual interest.

The most sensitive issue at the Islamabad summit was trade cooperation. At the summit meeting, Rajiv Gandhi expressed concern

---

38   www.saarc-sec-org.

39   Asian Recorder, 35 (8), Feb 19-25, 1989, p-20450.

about the lack of collaboration in core economic areas, particularly trade, and suggested adding it to the SAARC agenda. In one of his speeches, he said, "We also need to strengthen linkages between ourselves to give us strength, individually and as a region. This calls for increased economic exchanges within our region, covering the gamut of economic activities from agriculture to industry-infrastructure, technology, and human resource development. Economic cooperation must lie at the heart of regional cooperation. There has to be a degree of harmonization to ensure that complementarities in our economies are matched to give strength to our respective economies and strength to our voice and influence in world forums.... Yet we shy away from trade and economic cooperation.[40]

However, Pakistan expressed its reservations on the issue of economic cooperation, particularly "trade," among the SAARC countries and considered it a sensitive issue. Further, the smaller countries in the region feared that, due to its size and vast economic potential, India would obviously dominate trade in the South Asian region. However, "the proponents of South Asianism suggested that there might be some small costs in the short and medium term, but all countries of the region, including India, would stand to gain from trade and economic cooperation".[41]

Rajiv Gandhi, in his address to the summit, pointed towards the 'momentous events' that had taken place and were "fundamentally altering the world and the world order". He pointed out in this regard the following events:

I. The treaty concluded between US President Reagan and Soviet President Gorbachev on the dismantling of nuclear weapons systems;

---

40   Quoted in Suman Sharma, Supra No.16, pp-100, 101.

41   Ibid.,

II.   Geneva Accord on Afghanistan, which could lead to the establishment of a government based on national consensus, ensuring a sovereign, independent, and non-aligned Afghanistan

III. end of the Iran-Iraq war

IV.   proclamation of the Palestinian state by Yasser Arafat and the Commencement of dialogue between the United States and the PLO;

V.   possibilities of a solution to the conflict in Kampuchea, promise to the Namibian people for implementation of the Independence Plan adopted by the Security Council ten years ago;

VI.   revival of cooperation between India and China in working towards a new world order based on the Panchsheel, the Five Principles of peaceful coexistence;

VII. progressive defusion of the tension between the Soviet Union and China; and

VIII. Indian response to the request for assistance from the Maldives to thwart the invasion by foreign mercenaries aimed at subverting the democratic will of the people; and democratic elections in Pakistan leading to the installation of a new government in that country".[42]

Despite the developments that had taken place in the international arena, the Summit in Islamabad was a mixture of tensions, conflicts, and cooperation and had to bear the brunt of the political disputes among the member countries. Even during the summit meeting, many political leaders and analysts expressed the concern that the SAARC would split over the ethnic issue of Sri Lanka. However, the SAARC summit in Islamabad survived its first test and demonstrated that

---

42   Foreign Affairs Recorder, 34 (12), December 1988, pp-423-24.

it was still committed to the founding principles of cooperation and mutual understanding. Therefore, the credit for smooth travel and the survival of the SAARC to a greater extent goes to Rajiv Gandhi, who was instrumental in convincing and bringing an agreed settlement on the contentious issues of the member countries at the Islamabad Summit.

b) Origin and Growth of the Non-Aligned Movement:

The concept of non-alignment emerged in the second half of the twentieth century and is considered one of the most recent political developments. The policy of non-alignment, which took birth in those days of alignment and the Cold War, was a product of historical processes and circumstances. The end of the Second World War is said to be the turning point in the history of non-alignment. Soon after World War-II, the superpowers began their rivalry for supremacy by expanding their spheres of influence in global politics. The socialist bloc, led by the USSR, and the capitalist bloc effectively divided the world into two ideologically opposed camps. The bipolar world order posed a significant threat to India's hard-won independence. As a result, the newly independent countries, led by India, were determined to remain aloof from the power blocs to assert their political and economic independence and end the colonial hegemony of the imperialistic powers. Further, India rejected the Cold War paradigm, whose shadows were already appearing on the horizon, and instead of aligning with either of the blocs, chose the thorny path of non-alignment.

The sincere efforts of India's first Prime Minister, Jawaharlal Nehru, can be traced back to the origins of non-alignment. His role as the non-alignment architect was a novel development. However, the concept of non-alignment was not new to India, as it had roots in the philosophy of Buddha, Ashoka, and Mahatma Gandhi, who preached peace, tolerance, compassion, and universal brotherhood. Therefore, "non-alignment is the translation in international affairs of the Gandhian concept of tolerance, for it connotes constant efforts towards peaceful co-existence and cooperation," as Indira Gandhi said in a speech in Mauritius in October 1976.[43] Therefore, non-alignment was not new to India. It was in the history, culture, and tradition of India. However, the term "non-alignment" was coined by Jawaharlal Nehru in his speech in 1954 in Colombo, Sri Lanka"[44] when he came across superpower rivalry in world politics. Later, the idea of non-participation, non-commitment, non-entanglement, and non-alignment with the blocs found expression in the name of non-alignment. Explaining India's stand, Nehru said," We have sought to avoid foreign entanglements by not joining one bloc or the other. The natural result has been that neither of these blocs looks upon us with favour".[45]

Rajiv Gandhi as Chairman of the NAM:

India was NAM's chairperson for over three years, with Indira Gandhi leading the movement from March 1983 to October 1984. After her assassination, Rajiv Gandhi, India's new Prime Minister, assumed the NAM's chairmanship and his period was one of the most important and extraordinary events in the history of the NAM. As chairman, Rajiv Gandhi played a multi-faceted role in resolving most of the complicated issues the NAM confronted that hampered the international community's development. Considering Rajiv Gandhi's contribution to the movement, Prime Minister Mugabe paid a handsome tribute to Rajiv Gandhi for the "dynamism and prudent manner in which (he)

---

43   Quoted in M.S.Rajan, The Goals of India's Foreign Policy, The International Studies,35(1), Jan-Mar 1998 , p-76.

44   Times of India, 18 September 2006.

45   Quoted in K.Raman Pillai, India's Foreign Policy: Basic Issues and Political Attitudes, Meenakhsi Prakashan, 1969, p-28.

you steered the movement... with dignity and skill". He also said that he was inheriting the chairmanship of the NAM after it had been given India's "healing touch".[46]

Rajiv Gandhi, a staunch supporter of Nehru and Indira Gandhi's principles, reaffirmed his commitment to non-alignment as India's foreign policy, as it had been since pre-independence days. During his broadcast address on September 12, 1984, he said, "Jawaharlal Nehru bequeathed to us a foreign policy which Indira Gandhi so creatively enriched. I shall carry it forward. I reaffirm our adherence to the United Nations, the Non-Aligned Movement, and our opposition to colonialism, old or new. We are determined to work towards narrowing international economic disparities".[47]

Rajiv Gandhi was India's youngest Prime Minister to become Chairman of the Non-Aligned Movement, the world's major political force with a membership of more than 100 countries representing nearly two-thirds of the human race. Rajiv Gandhi, like Jawaharlal Nehru, was a charismatic leader determined to lead the caravan of the Non-Aligned Movement; the most responsibility fell on him. When there was a threat to international peace and security, he accepted the task of leading the movement. The non-aligned countries disagreed during Rajiv Gandhi's Chairmanship on issues such as apartheid and the imposition of sanctions against the racist Pretoria regime. As a result, Rajiv Gandhi took decisive action to resolve the differences and come to a consensus. As chairman of the Non-Aligned Movement, Rajiv Gandhi played multiple roles in resolving several complex international issues, including apartheid, the Iran-Iraq war, the Palestine problem, and nuclear disarmament.

---

46 Quoted in K.P.Misra, Nonaligned Movement India's Chairmanship, Lancers Books, New Delhi, 1987, p-82.
47 Rajiv Gandhi., Supra No-17, (Vol-1), pp-7, 8.

Besides, Rajiv Gandhi, through his multi-faceted charismatic personality, influenced world leaders to join the Non-Aligned Movement, whose main object was to establish international peace and security on the one hand and reduce the global arms race on the other. As a result, Rajiv Gandhi's period as chairman of the NAM was extraordinary in resolving the most complex issues that the globe confronted.

India, a non-aligned country, has remained too distant from the two power blocs to join any of them. Rajiv Gandhi maintained the same distance from the global superpowers as his predecessors. However, he took a slight deviation from the actual policy of non-alignment, thereby influencing India's foreign policy. During his tenure, Rajiv Gandhi gave the impression that he was friendlier towards the West than the East due to his liberalised policies. Besides, he endeavoured to get sophisticated technological know-how from the US for economic advancement and had a great vision to lead India into the 21st century. But Rajiv Gandhi, while acquiring technological know-how from the United States, did not compromise India's interests or the interests of the Non-Aligned Movement in exchange for the said technology. He even refuted the allegations levelled against him by the leaders of the Non-Aligned Movement at the Harare Summit that the Non-Aligned Movement is tilting more towards the West. Rajiv Gandhi, in his address to the Congress-I Parliamentary Party meeting in New Delhi, refuted the criticisms and said, "It was a matter of amusement that certain other countries of the world had become so enamoured by India's foreign policy that they had started emulating it. Further, he said," We have indeed not shifted even an inch from our foreign policy, which has been followed ever since India became independent".[48]

---

48   Hindustan Times, 7 November 1987.

c) Eighth NAM Summit: 1986

The Eighth Summit conference of the non-aligned countries, held in Harare, Zimbabwe, in September 1986, brought together heads of state and other political leaders from over a hundred countries of the world, of which more than half were African, and should go down in history as having signified Africa's qualitative as well as quantitative dominance of the movement.[49] Further, the summit in Harare, the capital of Zimbabwe, a frontline African country, was said to be a historical event in the history of the Non-Aligned Movement. The Non-Aligned Movement celebrated its silver jubilee year and completed 25 years since its founding during the period in question, making the holding of the 8th summit meeting of the movement at the start of September 1986 a significant event. The first summit of the non-aligned nations was held exactly 25 years ago, i.e., on September 1, 1961, in Belgrade, Brussels. In Harare, more than 100 members, with several other nations as observers, attended the summit meeting. Rajiv Gandhi happened to be the chairperson of the said summit, and he transferred the chairmanship of the NAM to the Prime Minister of Zimbabwe, Robert Mugabe. India led by Rajiv Gandhi, made a significant contribution to the success of the Harare Summit.

Several issues of international importance were discussed at the Harare Summit, leading to possible solutions. Some of the problems dealt with at the meeting were delicate and posed a threat not only to global peace but also to the economic development of the respective countries. For example, the Kampuchean issue, the Iran-Iraq war, the question of Palestine, the attack on Libya, the problem of apartheid, Namibia's independence, etc., were the major ones. However, during the summit meeting, apartheid and economic assistance to the

---

49   K.Mathews, Africa and Non-Alignment, India Quarterly, 42 (1), January-March1987, p-40.

frontline countries dominated the agenda without losing sight of others. Unlike previous summits, which commenced with tensions, the Harare Summit began with great confidence, optimism, and a desire for fresh thinking on crucial issues. But there were also some pressures and pulls from disgruntled elements outside the movement. Despite all this, the summit meeting was fruitful, satisfactory, and successful. Important issues such as disarmament, the nuclear holocaust, apartheid, and independence for frontline African countries dominated the deliberations.

Rajiv Gandhi's participation in the non-aligned summit in Harare, the capital of Zimbabwe, from September 1-6, 1986, definitely earned him good dividends. The leaders of the member countries appreciated his speech at the special session to commemorate the NAM's silver jubilee. The Harare Summit undoubtedly built on the Delhi Summit of 1983; the NAM in 1986 was a more united body and had regained momentum. The general belief was that India's leadership was the main reason for the possibility of achieving unity. However, India faced an embarrassing situation during the summit meeting when it asked to chair a sub-committee on Afghanistan in Harare despite having made clear its stand on Afghanistan.

The Harare Summit brought out "Rajiv Gandhi's statesmanship, which unquestionably placed India at the helm of the comity of nations; it also secured India's position on substantive issues. It helped frontline states get ready to tackle with confidence the issue of economic sanctions against South Africa. The summit also consolidated India's position in the peace movement, and Rajiv Gandhi's contribution was recognized by general consensus.[50] Prior to the summit meeting, even in the preparatory meeting in New Delhi, the non-aligned foreign ministers had taken a significant step

---

50   Asian Survey, 37, (2), February 1987, p-41.

to defuse tension in the Mediterranean by vociferously condemning terrorism. In April 1986, even Rajiv Gandhi, as Chairperson of the NAM, strongly condemned the US bombing of Libya, including the Presidential Palace in Tripoli. The decisions made at the summit level and the preparatory meetings significantly helped India emerge as a consensus builder, and its chairmanship applauded these decisions.

As chairman of the Non-Aligned Movement, Rajiv Gandhi made genuine efforts to resolve most international issues, which resulted in defusing tensions and conflicts and thereby establishing peace to some extent around the globe. The contentious issues, such as Palestine, apartheid, and Namibian independence, have progressed to the point of finding a long-term solution. However, the intricate problems of international importance, such as the Middle-East crisis, the Iran-Iraq war, and the Kampuchea, reached a stalemate due to a lack of cooperation from the parties involved in resolving them peacefully. However, Rajiv Gandhi left no stone unturned in persuading Iran and Iraq to negotiate and end the war. Rajiv Gandhi led the NAM, which significantly aided in preserving world peace, safeguarding independence and sovereignty, and combating racism, colonialism, imperialism, hegemony, and other forms of oppression. Commenting on the achievements of the NAM, he stated, "We have moderated areas of conflict and forestalled a scramble for allies. Without the NAM, disaster might have already overcome the world".[51] As a result, the NAM had significant influence in world affairs, primarily due to the dynamic role played by Rajiv Gandhi as its chairman.

The Summit Declaration:

Before the summit meeting, the leaders at the Harare Summit unanimously adopted the Harare Declaration on several complicated

---

51   Quoted in K.P.Misra Supra No. 46, p-55.

issues with far-reaching consequences. The summit's political declaration "called upon the superpowers to refrain from taking any measures aimed at developing, testing, or deploying weapons and weapons-systems in outer space pending negotiations and the conclusion of an agreement preventing the extension of an arms race into this area... The declaration welcomed the six-nation appeal and the offer to lend their good offices for the establishment of verification mechanisms to monitor the moratorium".[52] Further, the summit's political declaration strongly condemned the United States for attacking Libya and described the US involvement in Angola as aggression.[53]

The Economic Declaration called for the development of a new international economic order, for whose creation the movement had fought so hard. It urged the industrialized countries to join in efforts to restart global negotiations. It laid particular stress on the need for South-South cooperation.

In addition to making political and economic commitments, the summit meeting decided to impose sanctions on South Africa's racist government and also insisted the UN Security Council adopt comprehensive mandatory sanctions without further delay. The summit meeting resolved to establish the AFRICA Fund, the idea mooted by Rajiv Gandhi to help the frontline African countries in their economic war against colonialism and imperialism. The Summit also decided to set up a standing Ministerial Committee to review and harmonize the policies and programmes of non-aligned and other developing countries concerning international issues.

---

52   K.P.Misra, Non-aligned Movement India's Chairmanship, Lancers Books, New Delhi, 1987, p-73.
53   Asian Survey, 27(2), Feb 1987, p-191.

d) Ninth NAM Summit, 1989:

Rajiv Gandhi had the privilege of attending and addressing the Ninth Summit of the Non-Aligned Movement in Belgrade, the capital of Yugoslavia, in September 1989. The Belgrade Summit had the honour of holding the Ninth Summit of the NAM on its land, which was responsible for giving birth to the movement "exactly 28 years ago when Jawaharlal Nehru, Josip Broz Tito, Gamel Abdel Nasser, Kwame Nkrumah, and Ahmed Sockarno met, along with twenty other colleagues, to chart an alternative vision of the world order".[54]

The Belgrade Summit mainly focused on various unaccomplished global tasks discussed at the Harare Summit, such as apartheid, colonialism, imperialism, the Afghan question, disarmament, the superpower's dominance over the world's economy, early independence for Namibia, and so on. However, "the summit called for a political solution to the Afghanistan problem, resolution of the Kampuchean question, early independence for Namibia, democratization of Latin America, and restoration of the legitimate rights of the Palestinian people. The racist Pretoria regime came in for severe criticism for its policies of apartheid and aggression against the frontline African countries".[55] The summit level meeting also focused mainly on the issues discussed at the Harare Summit to find a lasting solution.

The highlight of the inaugural session in Belgrade was the presentation of a report on the AFRICA Fund by Rajiv Gandhi in his capacity as Chairman of the Fund. Rajiv Gandhi, who presented the AFRICA Fund report at the summit, reaffirmed his commitment to the cause of the frontline African countries by helping them financially in

---

54   M.K.Rasgotra., (Ed) Rajiv Gandhi's World View, Vikas Publishing House, New Delhi, 1991, p-48.

55   Asian Recorder, 35 (46), November, 12-18, 1989, p-20866.

their struggle against colonialism and imperialism and the abolition of apartheid. In his address to the summit, he said, "When Southern Africa was to come face-to-face with one of the most crucial moments of its history; at this critical juncture we carried forward the struggle against invasion, colonialism, and apartheid with renewed vigour. He added that there must be no wavering at the moment when the people of southern Africa urgently needed NAMs support and assistance".[56]

Rajiv Gandhi, at the Belgrade Summit in September 1989, highlighting the growing concern over global pollution, "proposed the establishment of a Planet Protection Fund, under the aegis of the United Nations. The Fund will be used to protect the environment by developing or purchasing conservation-compatible technologies in critical areas, which can then be brought into the public domain for the benefit of both developing and developed countries".[57]

The Summit Declaration:

On the political side, the agreed formula on Afghanistan reiterated that the non-aligned countries should continue to support the UN efforts in seeking a just and long-lasting solution. On the Iran-Iraq issue, the declaration stated that the Movement actively supported the UN Secretary-General in his efforts to reach a comprehensive, just, honourable, and durable settlement. "On the economic situation, the declaration said that, as 15 years ago, the new international economic order remained a difficult but valid goal. The declaration called for structural changes in the global economic order to the conflict between affluence and poverty. On terrorism, the declaration said that all forms of it, including state terrorism, violated the fundamental rights of the individual, threatened stability within and among nations, and

---

56   Asian Recorder, 35(46) Nov,12-18, 1989, p-20867
57   M.K.Rasgotra, Supra No-54, p-64.

deserved to be universally condemned and countered by every legal means possible. The principle of shared responsibility was necessary for combating drug trafficking".[58]

e) Rajiv Gandhi's Contribution to the AFRICA Fund:

Rajiv Gandhi, as Chairman and frontline leader of the Non-Aligned Movement, was instrumental in mobilizing resources for the economic development of South African frontline countries in their struggle against colonialism and imperialism. As a crusader against apartheid, he provided all possible assistance to frontline countries to make them economically and politically strong enough to withstand the pressure and hegemony of the racist South African government. Rajiv Gandhi, who was committed to the abolition of apartheid, launched a relentless campaign against South Africa for its cruel apartheid policy. His visit to Zambia, Zimbabwe, Angola, and the United Republic of Tanzania in May 1986 was widely welcomed as "a timely gesture of solidarity with the frontline states and support for their relentless struggle against the apartheid regime".[59] It was due to his relentless efforts and ambition that the frontline countries in South Africa were able to see economic prosperity and Namibia's independence. Rajiv Gandhi, who spearheaded the global movement against the South African colonial regime, was a source of inspiration and the voice of the people of the South African frontline countries.

The Eighth Harare NAM Summit resolved to establish the AFRICA Fund with the avid intention of assisting frontline African countries economically in their fight against colonialism and racial discrimination perpetrated by South Africa's racist regime, which practised apartheid. Rajiv Gandhi was primarily responsible for proposing the AFRICA

---

58   Asian Recorder, 35(46) November 12-18, 1989, pp-20868, 69.
59   Quoted in K.P.Misra, Supra No.46, p-60.

Fund, which was unanimously endorsed at the summit meeting. It was a matter of credit to India when Robert Mugabe, the then Prime Minister of Zimbabwe and the incoming Chairman of the Non-Aligned Movement, announced the name of Rajiv Gandhi as the Chairperson of the AFRICA Fund (Action For Resisting Invasion, Colonialism and Apartheid) and the President Kenneth Kaunda of Zambia elected as the vice-chairman of the AFRICA Fund. The principles laid down at the summit meeting were that the prime duty of the fund would be to assist the frontline countries and freedom fighters in South Africa. Further, the summit designed the fund as the "Solidarity Fund for Southern Africa."

On January 25, 1987, Rajiv Gandhi, declared at the Africa Fund Committee meeting in New Delhi, "The Fund will provide emergency assistance to the liberation movements in South Africa and Namibia. It will strengthen the economic infrastructure of the front-line states. It will help them resist the blackmail of the racist regime. The AFRICA Fund will supplement the activities of SADCC (Southern African Development Co-ordination Conference) and other organizations engaged in promoting the long-term development of Southern Africa". The Fund will also promote political and diplomatic initiatives in support of the struggle for dismantling apartheid and establishing a truly multi-racial democratic government in South Africa".[60]

Rajiv Gandhi, who ventured into mobilizing funds for frontline African countries, made Herculean efforts to achieve the same. He pledged "Rupees 500 million in kind to the Fund as the first contributor to the Fund".[61] Therefore, India had the honour of making the first contribution. Further, he appealed to all countries, such as developing and developed members and non-members of NAM,

---

60   Rajiv Gandhi, Supra No. 24, p-354.
61   http:www.anc.org.za/ancdocs/historysolidarity

to contribute generously to the AFRICA Fund. In response to his appeal, all the countries in the world, irrespective of their economic position, contributed generously to the cause of the frontline states in the fight against colonialism and imperialism. Even the nations with severe resource constraints, such as Peru and Ecuador, Nicaragua and Venezuela, Ghana and Kenya, Congo and Cameroon, and Guyana and Vietnam, had contributed to their might. Rajiv Gandhi said at the Belgrade NAM Summit in response to the massive donation to the AFRICA Fund, "I am happy to inform you that the world at large has responded to our appeal in a most heartening manner. Fifty-four nations and several international organizations have pledged to our cause the equivalent of almost half a billion US dollars–476 million dollars to be exact – in cash, kind, and technical assistance".[62] However, at a summit-level meeting of the Fund Committee in Belgrade, wealthy nations, like the United States, Britain, West Germany, and Japan came in for sharp criticism for not making any contribution to the Fund.[63] Despite the lack of cooperation from Western countries, Rajiv Gandhi, as Chairman of the AFRICA Fund, worked categorically to build up a substantial resource for the envisaged purpose.

Rajiv Gandhi's role in bringing the frontline African countries under one banner for a common cause, i.e., dismantling apartheid, was highly appreciated by all the member countries of the Non-Aligned Movement. Naturally, this put Rajiv Gandhi's name on the diplomatic map of the world. Further, the international community praised his role in mobilizing the resources for the Fund to improve the basic infrastructure in the domains of communication and transportation to substantially reduce the dependence of frontline African countries on the South African racist government. It is because of Rajiv Gandhi that

---

62   M.K.Rasgotra, Supra No.54, p-223.
63   Asian Recorder, 35(46) Nov 12-18, 1987, p-20869.

the frontline countries of South Africa became economically strong enough to withstand the hegemony of South Africa's racist regime. Perhaps the economic assistance to the frontline countries helped them achieve their independence and stand on their own to dismantle colonialism and imperialism. Therefore, it is because of Rajiv Gandhi's efforts that the last bastion of colonialism began to disappear from the South African continent.

Rajiv Gandhi correctly predicted and stated in his speech as Chairman of the AFRICA Fund at the Belgrade Summit in September 1989, "The curtain is finally beginning to be drawn over the era of humiliation, racial discrimination, oppression, and exploitation to which Africa has been subjected. We must continue to stand together. The AFRICA Fund is our earnest commitment to stand by the people of South Africa as destiny carries them to a famous victory.[64] Further, Rajiv Gandhi said, "Since the Fund was created at the Harare Summit, Southern Africa had witnessed important changes. The process of Namibia's independence was gathering momentum".[65]

f) The Crusader against Apartheid:

Apartheid in the modern world is unquestionably a curse on human civilization and a crime against humanity. The obnoxious practice of apartheid is a heinous crime against humankind in a society of equality, fraternity, and brotherhood. Therefore, apartheid needs condemnation from all sections of the international community, wherever it exists. India, a land of great philosophers and spiritual leaders, preached non-violence, equality, fraternity, and other causes to eradicate all forms of discrimination in some parts of the world. Since pre-independence, India has been the chief exponent of the cause of apartheid. Mahatma

---

64   M.K.Rasgotra., Supra No.54, p-227.
65   Asian Recorder, 35(46) Nov 12-18, 1989, p-20867.

Gandhi, the father of the nation, spearheaded the movement against racial discrimination and was a victim of the said practice when he was in South Africa to defend a case. Commenting on the horrifying conditions, Mahatma Gandhi said, "When I went to South Africa in 1893, I knew nothing about that country, yet, within seven days of my reaching there, I found that I had to deal with a situation too terrible for words".[66] Since then, Mahatma Gandhi vowed to fight against the inhuman practice of racial discrimination and succeeded in drawing the attention of the world community, thereby mobilizing the opinion against apartheid in order to eradicate it.

Apart from Mahatma Gandhi, leaders like Jawaharlal Nehru and Indira Gandhi also made significant efforts to end racial discrimination in South Africa during the post-independence period. Nehru took a keen interest in the abolition of apartheid; it was on his initiative that India donated to the Organization of African Union (OAU) Assistance Fund to help the African frontline countries in the struggle against colonialism and apartheid. Above all, as Prime Minister, Indira Gandhi was instrumental in promoting global awareness among the world community about racial prejudice and its impact on modern civilized society. Further, she also believed that racial inequality in the world, especially as a system of apartheid, was a constant threat to international peace and security.

Given the gravity of the situation in South Africa, in August 1985, the Indian Parliament unanimously adopted a resolution condemning apartheid and urging all countries to impose mandatory sanctions against the South African regime. Intervening in the discussion, Rajiv Gandhi said, "There was no other answer to the present struggle in that country except the freedom of blacks. The struggle in South Africa was not only the struggle of a few million people in South Africa.

---

66   Rajiv Gandhi., Supra No.21, p-261.(Vol-II 1986).

It was a struggle for all humanity".[67] India was a pioneering campaigner against racial inequality for many years because of this fundamental condition and dread. It was not only the blacks of South Africa but also the people of Indian origin who happened to be the victims of racial discrimination in South Africa or Fiji. Indira Gandhi, a staunch believer in equality, once, while inaugurating the One Asia Assembly in New Delhi in February 1973, remarked that she believed in the "one world" concept but pungently asked if the Vietnam War or the savage bombing that had taken place in Vietnam would "have been tolerated for long, had the people been European".[68] In other words, India was concerned not only with the causes and symptoms of non-peace but also with violations of human rights, racial discrimination, narrow national interests, and so on.

During Rajiv Gandhi's tenure, apartheid became a much more serious problem than it had been under his predecessors. He was determined to fight against apartheid, a societal evil, and eradicate it from the earth. The issue of apartheid has been raised at several international forums, and the global community has been alerted to its gravity and impact on civilization. He considered apartheid a bane to the world community and humankind and waged a crusade against it in all forums. Rajiv Gandhi, while addressing the global preparatory meeting of parliamentarians for the removal of apartheid, said, "apartheid is a blot on our civilization. It is a crime against humanity. It has become a structure of institutionalized terror sustained by racist domination and economic exploitation. Apartheid means a small bigoted minority overwhelming and holding a majority by bondage, keeping thousands in prison every year".[69] Therefore, Rajiv Gandhi, as

---

67   Asian Recorder, 31(41), Oct 8-14, 1985, p-18545.
68   Quoted in M.S.Rajan, Supra No.43, p-88.
69   Rajiv Gandhi, Supra, No.24, Vol-III, p-392.

the leader of the Non-Aligned Movement, spared no pains to eradicate the dreaded practice of apartheid from the African continent.

Rajiv Gandhi, who spearheaded the movement to eradicate the dreaded practice of apartheid, convinced the world's leaders to impose some restrictions on the discriminatory, racist Pretoria regime. As the frontline leader of the non-aligned movement, he proposed comprehensive, mandatory sanctions against the South African government to end apartheid. In his speech in New Delhi on November 25, 1986, Rajiv Gandhi, stated unequivocally, "One way to limit future bloodshed and dismantle apartheid is through comprehensive, mandatory sanctions. There is worldwide popular support for sanctions. But action is slow and halting on the part of these governments, which are in a position to make sanctions effective. The march of history cannot be halted. Apartheid will crumble. Freedom and racial equality will triumph.[70] However, the efforts of Rajiv Gandhi at the Eighth Summit, which contributed systematically to arriving at a consensus on sanctions, made him emerge as a successful leader.

Before the Harare Summit, the members of the Non-Aligned Movement differed on the agenda of imposing sanctions against the South African racist regime. Because there was no agreement among NAM and Commonwealth leaders on modalities to impose sanctions on South Africa, some leaders, particularly radicals, suggested that military action would be the best way to end apartheid. However, several black leaders in South Africa were against any armed conflict. Commenting on the military solution to apartheid, "then Commander-in-Chief of the military wing of the African National Congress, Joe Modise, said in Harare: "We have a very good reason for working very hard to prevent this struggle from becoming black-versus-white. We need these whites; we need all the people of South Africa to develop

---

70   Rajiv Gandhi, Supra No.21, (1986, Vol-II), p-327.

that country".[71] Therefore, it is believed that a military solution to the apartheid issue was not advisable because the frontline countries were no match for South Africa's military capability, which was well equipped with sophisticated weapons.

In contrast, a group of leaders of the NAM proposed comprehensive mandatory sanctions against the Pretoria regime to abolish apartheid, to which most agreed, with the exception of a few Western countries, especially the United Kingdom. The Western countries opposed imposing sanctions against South Africa, which had economic and military interests in the South African regime. Therefore, Rajiv Gandhi, in his speech in August 1987, rightly said, "Apartheid survives because of economic infusions from some developed countries. It survives because Pretoria is integrated into the global political and defence strategies of certain countries. It survives because conscience has been subordinated to other considerations. All countries, all over the world, must realize that by not cooperating in ending apartheid, they are not, in the long run, serving even their own geo-political, military, or economic ends. They are jeopardizing those very interests by their support to Pretoria today".[72] Even the Commonwealth Group of Eminent Persons gave an unambiguous answer; "The termination of apartheid with relatively less upheaval is possible provided all economic and military sustenance to Pretoria ceases".

Like Western countries, the United Kingdom, a member of the Commonwealth, was also reluctant to impose sanctions against South Africa because of its close contacts with the Pretoria regime. However, it favoured only limited sanctions against South Africa. As a result, Britain also differed on the issue of imposing sanctions

---

71   Quoted in K.P.Misra, Supra No.46, p-64.
72   Rajiv Gandhi, Supra No.24, (Vol-III), pp- 392,393.

against South Africa. In fact, this was proved at the Commonwealth Summit held in Vancouver in October 1987, when "the Programme of Action relating to sanctions on South Africa, was adopted by all Commonwealth countries with the exception of Britain.[73] The isolated stand of then British Prime Minister, Mrs. Thatcher on the sanctions evoked strong resentment from the leaders of the world, particularly NAM and the Commonwealth. Before this, even Rajiv Gandhi, as a mark of protest against the United Kingdom, which was perpetuating apartheid, boycotted the Commonwealth Games held in Scotland in 1986, by not allowing the Indian team to go to the Commonwealth Games.[74]

When the world leaders differed and started treading different paths on imposing sanctions against South Africa. Rajiv Gandhi anticipated danger for the movement and warned that there would be attempts by the South African government and its Western allies to divide the NAM at the eighth summit. Taking into consideration the delicate nature of apartheid and the urgency of imposing sanctions against South Africa, Rajiv Gandhi declared in his address to the Harare Summit that "freedom in South Africa was going to "brook no further delay". He said the options were "liberty now, with innocent lives saved, or liberty later, in a welter of blood".[75] As a result, he urged the world's leaders to impose sanctions immediately against the Pretoria regime to dismantle apartheid. However, at the end of the Harare Summit, a consensus emerged on the urgent need to put a swift end to the racist regime in South Africa. Further, majority of the leaders of the non-aligned countries believed that practical measures were necessary in support of the African frontline countries, which were likely to be worst hit by the impending sanctions. Thus, deciding to

---

73   Rajiv Gandhi, Supra No.24, p-415.
74   Rajiv Gandhi, Supra No.21, (Vol-II) p-348.
75   Quoted in K.P.Misra, Spra No.46, p-63

impose sanctions against South Africa required careful consideration. After extensive consultations, the summit advanced on issues relating to Southern Africa. This was evident from the 13-point programme adopted by the conference dealing with sanctions against South Africa. These were:

"Prohibition of the transfer of technology to South Africa;

- Cessation of exports, sales, or transport of oil products to South Africa;
- Cessation of further investments in and financial loans to South Africa or Namibia and of any government insurance guarantee of credits to the racist regime;
- An end to all promotion of the sale of or support for trade with South Africa, including governmental assistance to trade missions;
- Prohibition of the sale of Krugerrands and any other coins minted in South Africa;
- Prohibition of imports from South Africa of agricultural products, coal, uranium, iron, steel, etc;
- Enactment of legislation or adoption of other measures to comply with United Nations Decree No.1 for the Protection of natural Resources of Namibia enacted by the United Nations Council for Namibia in 1974;
- Termination of any visa, free entry privileges, and the promotion of tourism to South Africa;
- Termination of air and shipping links with South Africa;
- Cessation of all academic, cultural, scientific, and sports relations with South Africa and of relations with individuals, institutions, and other bodies endorsing or based on apartheid;

- Suspension or abrogation of agreements with South Africa, such as agreements on cultural and scientific cooperation;
- The termination of double taxation agreements with South Africa; and
- A ban on government contracts with the majority owned by South Africa;"[76]

However, Rajiv Gandhi played an important role in persuading world leaders to arrive at a consensus on the issue of comprehensive sanctions against the Pretoria regime.

Rajiv Gandhi, who all along waged an unrelenting struggle against racial discrimination, reiterated that comprehensive mandatory sanctions were the only effective peaceful means left to force Pretoria to dismantle apartheid. Accordingly, he, as the leader of NAM, went all out to pressure South Africa to accomplish the task of removing apartheid from the African continent itself. After a certain period, South Africa realized the pressure from the non-aligned countries and started mending its attitude towards frontline countries. Therefore, addressing the Ninth NAM Summit in Belgrade, Rajiv Gandhi said, "Within South Africa, there were stirrings of change and indications that at least some sections of the white community had begun to realize the need for fundamental political reforms leading to the dismantling of apartheid."[77]

Therefore, Rajiv Gandhi, who waged a crusade against the obnoxious practice of apartheid, succeeded in accomplishing the laborious task of removing the inhuman practice from the South African continent. Rajiv Gandhi's tireless efforts have resulted in racial equality in a land plagued by racial discrimination and inequity.

---

76   K.P.Misra, Supra No.52, pp-64, 65.
77   Asian Recorder, 35(46) Nov 12-18, 1989, p-20867.

g) Leader of the Six-Nation Initiative on Disarmament and Peace:

The age of nuclear weapons dawned just before India achieved its independence. Since then, India has been at the forefront of the worldwide campaign for complete disarmament across the globe. "In fact, in 1954, Jawaharlal Nehru was the first to bring the problem of the proliferation of nuclear weapons to the attention of the world and also of the World Organization".[78] Further, the issue has also been discussed in most of the forums both within the country and abroad, i.e., the United Nations, the NAM Conferences, the Commonwealth Forum, and so on. India, which has consistently opposed the proliferation of nuclear weapons, also criticized the Great Powers, particularly the nuclear weapon powers, for producing and stockpiling nuclear weapons and encouraging the arms race among non-nuclear nations. This obviously jeopardized not only the global peace but also the stability and security of the developing countries in the modern world. Furthermore, with the advent of nuclear weapons, the very survival of the human race has been in jeopardy. Therefore, disarmament, especially nuclear disarmament, is currently the most urgent requirement in the world.

Rajiv Gandhi advocated for international friendship, cooperation, and goodwill with all countries to eliminate nuclear weapons and reduce the global arms race. Therefore, the role played by Rajiv Gandhi as the persuader of the superpowers to sign the INF Treaty, thereby saving the world from nuclear holocaust, was one of the most unique contributions to world peace, and was greatly appreciated by the most peace-loving leaders of the world. Rajiv Gandhi's unrelenting efforts to banish nuclear weapons contributed to the establishment of peace on a conflict-torn globe. However, the superpowers engaged in the proliferation of arms were reluctant to reduce their nuclear arsenals

---

78   qouted in M.S.Rajan, Supra No.43, p-82.

and reach an agreement because each expected the other to take the initiative. No one came forward in the process due to superiority complexes and egoism. However, under Rajiv Gandhi's leadership, the group of Six-Nations took the initiative to bring the two superpowers to terms and conclude an early agreement on Intermediate Nuclear Weapons. As a result, in December 1987, President Reagan of United States and General Secretary Gorbachev of the USSR signed the historic INF Treaty.

The First Summit on Disarmament:

Rajiv Gandhi took the initiative to convene the meeting of the nations because he wanted to establish world peace by attempting to destroy nuclear weapons in mass. As a result, on July 28, 1985, a meeting of the heads of state representing Argentina, Greece, Mexico, Sweden, Tanzania, and India was held in New Delhi. This meeting was attended by, among others, the distinguished African statesman and former Tanzanian President Julius Nyerere, who launched what came to be known as the Six-Nation, Five-Continent Initiative on Nuclear Disarmament. The initiative, which was very much in keeping with the grand old tradition of Indian opposition to nuclear weapons and their destructive consequences for the normalization of international relations, urged the nuclear weapon states to halt testing and conclude an early comprehensive test-ban treaty. It also called for the prohibition of development and the use of all weapons in space. It urged that outer space must be for the benefit of humankind as a whole, not as a future battleground.[79] Even the leaders at the meeting unanimously urged the nuclear powers (countries) to end the destructive arms race and effectively eliminate the threat of nuclear war.

79　Quoted in M.S.Rajan, Supra No.43, pp-90-91.

In this context, a summit meeting of the President of the United States and the General Secretary of the Communist Party of the Soviet Union was held in Geneva in November 1985 to deliberate on the nuclear disarmament issue. After the meeting, both declared that "their objective was "to prevent an arms race in space and terminate it on earth, ultimately to eliminate nuclear arms everywhere". A nuclear war can never be won, they said, and so it must never be fought".[80] The Geneva Summit Meeting was held in high regard and even the leaders of the Six-Nation Group anticipated a positive and constructive outcome on the subject. But the anticipation of the leaders went wrong when the nuclear arms race continued unabatedly in spite of the summit meeting of the two leaders. "In fact, in the form of the Strategic Defence Initiative, a new and far more dangerous dimension was added to the already explosive situation".[81]

The Delhi Declaration: 1986

India believed in "a nuclear-weapon-free" and a "non-violent world".[82] As a result, Rajiv Gandhi made no compromises in completing this monumental assignment, which fell on his shoulders both as the head of the Non-Aligned Movement and the leader of the Six Nations Initiative on Disarmament. Even while pursuing multilateral efforts, the Soviet Union, a trusted ally of India, appreciated its efforts and urged the need for a nuclear-weapon free world. "On the occasion of President Gorbachev's visit to New Delhi in November 1986, Prime Minister Rajiv Gandhi and the Soviet President spelt out (in the "Delhi Declaration") specific and immediate action for disarmament through, among other things, complete destruction of nuclear arsenals before the end of the century, banning all weapons from outer space, banning

---

80   Rajiv Gandhi., Supra No.21, p-280.Vol-II.

81   K.P.Misra, Supra No.46, p-51.

82   M.S.Rajan, Supra No-43, p-92.

all nuclear weapons tests, banning chemical weapons, and reduction of the levels of conventional arms and armed forces". Taking advantage of the occasion, the two leaders proclaimed: "A nuclear war should never be fought and can never be won".[83] This is the crowning achievement of Rajiv Gandhi's efforts in the field of disarmament, and it naturally added a feature to his cap.

The Second Summit on Disarmament:

Not relenting in his efforts, Rajiv Gandhi sought an opportunity to raise the issue of disarmament at the Second Summit of the Six Nations held at Ixtapa, Mexico, in August 1986. The meeting of the Six Nations coincided with the 41st anniversary of the Hiroshima tragedy. In his address to the conference, Prime Minister Rajiv Gandhi spoke strongly against nuclear weapons, branding them a "crime against humanity" and reiterated that the earlier (1985) declaration had called for a binding international agreement, which would outlaw every use of the weapons. Rajiv Gandhi restated the demand for a comprehensive test ban and commended the Soviet Union for unilaterally accepting a moratorium on nuclear tests and extending it twice. He repeated the group's proposal to undertake verification of the moratorium by all nuclear weapons states. He also opposed the lodging of nuclear weapons in outer space, which is "the common heritage of all humankind".[84]

To bring about world peace, Rajiv Gandhi took several initiatives to achieve the same. He even succeeded in bringing the repercussions of the nuclear war and its impact on humankind to the attention of the whole world. Commenting on the magnitude of the probable destruction of humanity in the event of nuclear war, he expressed the

---

83   M.S.Rajan, Supra No.43, p-92.
84   M.S.Rajan, Supra No-43, p-91.

view that "nuclear death will not inspect people's passports. It will not care for nationality as much as it will not care for life. There are no winnable wars or impregnable defences against nuclear weapons". As such, none of us, while safeguarding the interests of our nations, can overlook our duty to the human race".[85]

Because of Rajiv Gandhi's tireless efforts, both Ronald Reagan, former President of the US, and Gorbachev, former General Secretary of the USSR, signed the historic INF Treaty in December 1987, putting an end to the arms race, albeit not entirely but gradually, in a war-torn world. In response to the agreement, Rajiv Gandhi said, "It represents a truly momentous development. It is true that it envisages the elimination of only around three per cent of the combined nuclear arsenals of the United States and the USSR. But its historic significance is that it is the world's first nuclear arms reduction agreement. It is also the first time that the United States and USSR have agreed to eliminate the entire category of nuclear weapons".[86] As expected, the method of eliminating arms was slow. Therefore, Rajiv Gandhi renewed his efforts and compelled the nuclear-power countries to destroy nuclear weapons in a time-bound manner. In light of this, he devised a strategy for the gradual destruction of weapons in a phased manner.

In light of ongoing trends in the proliferation of weapons of mass destruction, Rajiv Gandhi proposed a specific time frame. It was in June 1988 that Rajiv Gandhi, in his address to the UN General Assembly (9 June 1988) on disarmament in New York, made comprehensive proposals for general, complete, and non-discriminatory disarmament. The essential features of the action plan are as follows,

---

85   Asian Recorder, 31 (25), June 18-24 1985, p-18730
86   Rajiv Gandhi, Supra No.24, (Vol-III), p-425.

1. There should be a binding commitment by all nations to eliminate nuclear weapons, in stages, by the year 2010 at the latest.
2. All nuclear weapons States must participate in the process of nuclear disarmament: all other countries must also be part of the process.
3. To demonstrate good faith and build the required confidence, there must be tangible progress at each stage towards the common goal.
4. Changes are required in doctrines, policies, and institutions to sustain a world free of nuclear weapons. Negotiations should be undertaken to establish a comprehensive global security system under the aegis of the United Nations.[87]

Rajiv Gandhi, in his address to the U.N. General Assembly, further said, "The heart of our Action Plan is the elimination of all nuclear weapons in three stages over the next 22 years, beginning now".[88]

Despite Rajiv Gandhi's Action Plan for the time-bound elimination of nuclear weapons, there was little headway, and the results were not as anticipated. However, taking into consideration the slow process of reducing the arms race as agreed in the INF Treaty by the two leaders, the Six-Nation-Five-Continent group again met in Stockholm on July 31, 1988, to continue to build up international pressure for nuclear weapons of mass destruction. Rajiv Gandhi congratulated Ronald Reagan and Gorbachev on the INF Treaty, saying, "This agreement is not, and should not be considered, as more than a beginning, still only a beginning –a historic beginning, a vital beginning, still only a beginning". The survival of humanity depends on the nuclear weapon powers

---

87 J.N.Dixit, Across Borders, Fifty Years of India's Foreign Policy, Picus Books, New Delhi, 1998, pp-203-204.
88 Sumit Chakravarty, Multi-Dimensional Perestroika in Gorbachev's USSR, Mainstream, 37(8) Nov-19, 1988, p-31.

travelling all the way down this road to the complete elimination of nuclear weapons. The world will be really safe only when, as the Delhi Declaration puts it, "the balance of terror gives way to comprehensive international security".[89]

Rajiv Gandhi, who strongly advocated for "a nuclear-weapon-free and non-violent world," left no stone unturned in completing the most challenging task that fell on him. It was also his endeavour to save not only the world from nuclear holocaust but also the lives of millions of people from the jaws of nuclear catastrophe. The majority of peace-loving people in the entire world acknowledged the dynamic role played by Rajiv Gandhi as the leader of the NAM in achieving the same. Remarking on the extraordinary role played by India under the dynamic leadership of Rajiv Gandhi in preserving peace and destroying nuclear weapons, President Gorbachev of the USSR said, "We greatly appreciate India's contribution to the collective effort to preserve peace and remove the nuclear threat. As head of the Non-Aligned Movement, which has become a major factor in international relations, India is doing much to strengthen its unity and beneficial influence in the world... We highly value India's contribution to the strengthening of peace and stability in Asia, her realistic and considered approach to the key problems of the reign".[90]

h) Major Developments in the 1990s:

The year 1990 is said to have been a turning point in Indian history in the context of international and external relations. However, the period also coincided with the end of Rajiv Gandhi's glorious era on the Indian political scene. Besides, it was during the same period that the

89 Rajiv Gandhi, Supra No.24, (Vol-III), p-425.

90 Quoted in Hemen Ray, The Enduring Friendship (Soviet-Indian Relation in Mrs. Indira Gandhi's Days) Abhinav Publications, New Delhi, 1989, p-178.

process to end the Cold War era began and paved the way for political and economic developments in the international sphere. Further, during this time, economic developments took centre stage in the international arena, replacing ideological conflict between communist and non-communist states. This change indirectly influenced India's foreign policy, which was already in the process of economic liberalization introduced by Rajiv Gandhi. The following are some of the significant events in the 1990s that affected India's foreign policy during the post-Rajiv Gandhi period.

End of the Cold War:

The first and most significant event in the 1990s was the end of the Cold War, which marked the beginning of a new era in international relations. The Cold War ended not with détente, mutual understanding, or transcendence of conflicts but because of the collapse of one superpower. But, with the disintegration of the Soviet Union, an era of protracted conflicts and the Cold War between the two superpowers ended. However, "the fall of the Berlin Wall in November 1989 was perhaps the most dramatic event that led to the beginning of ending the Cold War. Besides, the major step was the Malta Summit between President Bush and Gorbachev in December 1989, which can be said to mark the virtual end of the Cold War. During the joint press conference in December, President Gorbachev assured President Bush that;" the Soviet Union would never start a hot war against the USA". He further said that the two leaders agreed that the world was leading "an epoch of the Cold War" and entering "another epoch". The countries were "just at the very beginning of a long road to a long-lasting peaceful period".[91] There were several

---

91　Quoted by Satish Kumar., India and Changing International System, in S.Rasgotra and Others. India's Foreign Policy in the 1990s (Ed) Patriot Publishers, New Delhi, 1990, p-26.

significant events as well, perhaps the most noteworthy being the meeting of the heads of government at the conference on security and cooperation in Europe in Paris in November 1990. Here they signed the Treaty on Conventional Forces in Europe, which for the first time in the history of the world resulted in a multilateral agreement for a significant reduction in conventional military capabilities".[92] In fact, the nuclear-weapons treaties made Rajiv Gandhi's dream of establishing a nuclear-free and non-violent order a reality. Further, the end of the Cold War is undoubtedly a reaffirmation of one of the foremost objectives of India's foreign policy.

Collapse of the Soviet Union:

Following the end of the Cold War and the fall of the Soviet Union, India found itself in an unusual security environment in which local conditions did not correspond to global trends. Further, the sudden dissolution of the Cold War, partly due to Gorbachev's policies and partly because of the collapse of the Soviet Union itself, caused non-aligned countries, particularly those led by India, to reconsider their position due to the vacuum created in the international arena. Besides, India, which has always experienced a bipolar world order system, has to suddenly confront a unipolar (univocal) world order, with the US being the power centre in the absence of the Soviet Union, a strategic partner of India. Naturally, this put India in a dilemma and forced her to look forward to alternatives in the international arena due to the collapse of the Soviet Union. Therefore, without delving into the options, India decided to go ahead with greater self-reliance and self-confidence in a world of insecurity and instability. This significant

---

92   Dipanker Banarjee, The End of Cold War and Its Effects at the Global, Regional and National Level: The Indian Response, in Lalit Mansingh and others, (ed) India's Foreign Policy: Agenda for the 21st Century, Vol-1, Konark Publishers, New Delhi, 1997, p-87-88.

development on the global scene improved relations with both China and the US. Perhaps the downfall of the "evil empire" and the end of the Cold War diluted the American hostility towards India, which had cordial relations with Moscow.

Withdrawal of Troops from Afghanistan:

Another significant development in the early 1990s was the total withdrawal of Soviet forces from Afghanistan under the Geneva Accord. Naturally, this resulted in the end of the Cold War between the USA and the USSR, which were at loggerheads on the issue of Afghanistan. The withdrawal of Soviet forces from Afghanistan and the rapprochement between the United States and Russia opened the door for a more balanced power structure in the South Asian region. In actuality, Pakistan's significance declined in the post-Cold War world order. Once, it was strategically significant for Washington's interests. Given India's emergence as the strongest third-world country in the international arena, the US began to change its position and diminish its hostility towards India. The world leaders praised Rajiv Gandhi for his role in persuading the Soviet Union to withdraw its troops from Afghanistan early, which resulted in the installation of a responsible government in Afghanistan.

Economic Reforms (Development):

The fall of the Soviet Union in the 1990s brought about several changes, not only in the international arena but also in the global economy as a whole and the Indian economy in particular. India's close economic relations with the Soviet Union had to face a peculiar situation soon after its disintegration, wherein its economic interests were in jeopardy in the unipolar world. However, for India, the struggle has become considerably more crucial than ever, and it has begun to seek new routes for its economic and foreign policy. As a result, India decided in the 1990s to turn towards the European Union (EU-15), the world's largest, affluent, and most structured trading bloc. India opened up its economic policies to integrate with the global economy. Due to the economic reforms undergone by India, the Indian economy began to liberalise.

Sudden Eruption of Conflicts:

The end of the Cold War in the 1990s witnessed the sudden eruption of a wide range of regional conflicts. The nature and cause of these conflicts differed from case to case, yet there were some common trends. These conflicts were more intra-state than inter-state. But the most intriguing aspect is that in these cases, there was support either from vested interests or from encouragement from outside powers. These intra-state conflicts owe their origins to ethnic assertions in the local region. Perhaps, even after the end of the Cold War and with the emergence of unipolar world order, there was an era of "intra-state" conflicts in world politics.

India and the Middle East (West Asia):

The history of Indo-Middle East (West Asia) relations reveals that even before independence, India played an important role in maintaining good and friendly relations with nearly all Arab countries. After its independence, India significantly improved its bilateral relations with Arab and Islamic countries by establishing mutually beneficial economic exchanges. The economic ties enabled India to build strong alliances with Iran, Iraq, Egypt, Saudi Arabia, etc., the frontline Arab and Muslim countries of the Middle Eastern region. Firstly, the main objective of improving relations with the Arab countries was to curb Pakistan's growing influence in the Middle East while securing access to Middle Eastern oil resources. Secondly, India also attempted to ease the tension and restore peace and tranquilly in the Middle East through friendly relations with Arab and Jewish countries. However, the Middle East region, which had become entangled with internal conflicts among certain countries, particularly between Arabs and Israelis on the Palestine issue, became a matter of concern in the region. As a result, the Middle East region witnessed a perpetual Cold War between Jews and Arabs over the Palestine issue, which greatly affected Arab-Israeli relations and the NAM's peace process, which India initiated. Indeed, the Arab-Israeli conflict posed a severe threat to the peace and security of the Middle East, and the Palestine issue soured Israel and Arab relations in the region. Naturally, this increased tension in the Middle East region and paved the way for internal strife, namely the Arab-Israel conflict, which lasted several years and proved complicated.

Apart from the dispute over Kashmir and apartheid, which India had taken up in the UN, the Israel-Palestine conflict was one of the first issues that an independent India had to deal with in the UN. International organizations such as the UN and world leaders attempted to defuse tension in the Middle East. However, India's contribution to defusing the conflicts in the Middle East was crucial, particularly among Arab-Israeli countries. In this regard, the roles played by Jawaharlal Nehru and Indira Gandhi are noteworthy. Furthermore, Rajiv Gandhi's role was one of the most significant events in the history of Middle Eastern countries, particularly in resolving the Palestinian question.

A Brief History of the Arab-Israel Conflict: The Palestine Issue:

The conflict between Palestinian Arabs and Jews erupted in the mid-twentieth century. The territorial dispute was said to be the primary cause of the Arab-Israeli conflict. Further, "the Arab-Israel conflict came about from the concept of political Zionism. Zionism is the belief that Jews should establish a state for themselves in Palestine, which was a revolutionary idea of the 19th century".[93] Therefore, the idea of creating a separate Jewish state on the lands of Palestinians created a wide rift between Israelis and Arabs and aggravated an already tense situation. This unjustified ambition of Israel paved the way for hostile relations between Jews and Arabs, ultimately leading to the conflict. As a result, crucial wars fought between Arabs and Israelis over the issue of occupied territories were of great concern. In the 1956 war, Israel captured the Gaza Strip, and subsequently, in 1967, a clash broke out between Arab nations and Israel, which is said to be a watershed in the history of the Middle East. The war lasted six days and "changed the perceived balance of power in the Middle East and created a new reality. Israel had acquired extensive territories- the Sinai desert, the Golan Heights, and the West Bank that were several times larger than the 1948 borders".[94] During the 1967 war, Israel defeated several Arab countries, including Egypt, Syria, and Jordan, resulting in Israel becoming the dominant regional military power. Certain Western and European countries backed Israel in this crucial war against Arabs.

The Arabs were greatly disappointed and questioned themselves following the 1967 war. On both sides, there has been a significant erosion of trust since the outbreak of the war. President Nasser of Egypt openly admitted defeat in the war and lost prestige in the Arab world. Even Palestinians had given up on expecting the Arab countries to save them from their physical plight and uncertain political future. This realization prompted the Palestinians to think in terms of self-reliance and self-help. Because of this, the Palestinians decided to unite themselves and form their movement to fight against the Israelis. As a result, the Palestinian national movement emerged as a most

---

93　http://www.collegetermpapers.com
94　http://www.midestweb.org

significant actor after 1967 in the form of political and military groups that further strengthened the Palestine Liberation Organization (PLO).

To rebuild the lost image, Arabs united to fight against Israel based on the occupied territories, viz., the West Bank, Gaza Strip, etc., aimed at creating an independent Palestine. The Arabs, who constitute the majority in the Middle East region, never tolerated the subjugation of Palestine, an Arab associate. Even the Arabs did not feel equal to the rest of humanity and feared their honour would be jeopardized if Palestine was not liberated. Therefore, the Arabs wholeheartedly supported the Palestinian cause of liberating Palestine from the Israeli occupation. In this regard, India did a commendable job breaking the Arab-Israeli deadlock.

India and Palestine Liberation Organisation: Role of Rajiv Gandhi:

As a colonial country, India suffered greatly under the dominant British rule and experienced humility and subjugation. However, the humility gave India a boost to fight against the world's imperialistic forces and to free itself from the foreign yoke. Perhaps the sufferings under British rule made India lead the freedom movement against colonial rule throughout the globe. India, the NAM's leader and pioneer of developing countries, took up the issue of several countries' independence and supported their movements in achieving it. In fact, extending sympathy and support to other countries in their struggles has always been the hallmark of Indian policy. This unique quality put India on the pedestal of the world. The history of India's struggle for independence reveals that the freedom fighters in India supported the cause of freedom in several countries even before her independence. It can also be in the case of Palestine, where India supported the legitimate right of Palestine's liberation from the Israeli occupation. Indeed, the freedom fighters of India regarded the struggle for the freedom of Palestine as part of their struggle for national independence. Jawaharlal

Nehru, the frontline leader of India's struggle for independence and the architect of India's foreign policy, said in 1963, "The Arab struggle against British Imperialism in Palestine is as much part of the world conflict as India's struggle for freedom".[95] Even, Mahatma Gandhi, who was unwilling to countenance the establishment of a Jewish state, declared that "Palestine belonged to the Palestinians in the same way that England belonged to the English or France belonged to the French. It is wrong and inhuman to impose the Jews on the Arabs...Surely it would be a crime against humanity to reduce the proud Arabs so that Palestine can be restored, to the Jews, partly or wholly as their national home".[96]

Further, the All India Congress Committee resolutions also played a crucial role in supporting the cause of the dependent countries. In 1927, the All India Congress Committee meeting held at Madras extended its moral and material support to many colonial countries during their struggle for independence. Even India's concern for the subject people can be seen in its All India Congress Committee resolution on the foreign policy of 1928, wherein the Congress assured the people of Egypt, Syria, Palestine, and Iraq of its full sympathy with them in their struggle to free themselves from the grip of Western imperialism, which in its view was also a great menace to the Indian struggle".[97]

Therefore, the history of Indian National Congress resolutions on foreign policy and the freedom fighters of the Indian National Movement reveals that India was for the independence of Palestine right from its pre-independence days. As part of its campaign, India raised the

---

95   Prime Minister Rajiv Gandhi Statements on Foreign Policy, April-June 1988, External Publicity Division, Ministry of External Affairs, New Delhi, P-22
96   http://onlinejournal.com
97   N.M.Khilnani, P-85 (Thesis, P-34.)

issue of Palestine's independence in several international forums. Indeed, India took a principled stand on the Palestine issue at the UN even before her independence. Further, India vehemently opposed the partition of Palestine and the creation of a Jewish state until the end. Both Mahatma Gandhi and Jawaharlal Nehru, despite their European education and experiences, were not in favour of the establishment of a Jewish state in Palestine. However, this demonstrates that India was always sympathetic to the Palestine cause. The history of Indo-Palestine relations reveals that India has always pursued a pro-Arab policy in the Arab-Israeli conflict. The main concern behind this move was to free Palestinians from Israeli occupation and achieve enduring peace in the Middle East.

India wanted to see an independent Palestine state in their homeland with an Arab majority called Palestine, which is their inalienable right. India believed that without establishing an independent Palestinian state, there could be no peace in the region. However, the pressure tactics used by some superpowers in the West defeated India's efforts in Palestinian affairs. India, however, continued with its firm and unequivocal support for the Palestinian cause, both bilaterally and in the relevant international forums. In this regard, India went a step ahead under the leadership of Indira Gandhi when it decided to grant diplomatic recognition to the PLO with the intention of raising its status in the international arena without waiting for other countries to follow suit. As part of this ongoing process, then Indian Foreign Minister P.V.Narasimha Rao announced in Parliament on March 26, 1980, that India had decided to accord full diplomatic recognition to the office of the PLO in New Delhi.[98] The announcement came as a boon to the PLO, which naturally strengthened it diplomatically and politically to wean it away from violence and terrorism and to build its image as

---

98   http:// books.google.com.in

a responsible organization. However, this demonstrates India's firm determination to support the Palestinian cause.

The year 1984 is said to have been a turning point in the history of India's foreign policy, which coincided with the entry of Rajiv Gandhi on the Indian political horizon as Prime Minister of India. As a result, things began to change in the domestic and international arenas. During Rajiv Gandhi's tenure, the Palestine issue took a new turn when he started mobilizing the world's opinion in favour of Palestine against Israeli occupation. Even Rajiv Gandhi, the leader of the NAM, left no stone unturned in resolving the Palestine issue. In this direction, Rajiv Gandhi undertook several initiatives to bring about an agreed settlement between Arab and Israeli countries to reduce the heightened tension in the area. Against this backdrop, Rajiv Gandhi played a predominant role in organizing a meeting of the Non-Aligned Committee on Palestine in New Delhi in April 1985. The committee recommended the convening of an international conference under the aegis of the United Nations in order to obtain "a comprehensive, just, and durable peace in West Asia".[99]

During Rajiv Gandhi's tenure, India was the most vocal supporter of the Palestinian cause. As a result, he waged war against imperialistic forces to support colonial countries' independence, adhering to the anti-imperialism and anti-colonialism principles that formed the foundation of India's foreign policy. Rajiv Gandhi, a staunch supporter of the struggle of the dependent countries, made a statement in support of Palestine during the debate in Parliament on April 20, 1988, "In West Asia, our support to the Palestinian cause and the PLO is historic and consistent and dates back to our freedom struggle. We condemn the brutal behaviour of the Israeli forces in the occupied territories... The situation is critical and brooks no piecemeal approach. I believe there

---

99   http://books.google.co.in

is growing support for an international conference on the Middle East. The Palestinians have an inalienable right to self-determination, and we support them in that right".[100]

Further, Rajiv Gandhi was emphatic that Palestine issue needed permanent settlement to establish peace in the region. He put every effort into bringing the Palestine issue to the attention of most international forums, including the United Nations, in order to find a lasting solution. In this regard, he stated at the "Banquet hosted by the Syrian President at Damascus on June 4, 1988, that "To reach such a settlement negotiations must be held at an international conference under the aegis of the United Nations with the participation of all parties to the dispute, including the PLO".[101] Before this, at the forty-second General Assembly of the UN, India reaffirmed its firm support for the Palestinian people in their fight for their right to self-determination and a homeland of their own.

During 1987-88, a significant development with a renewed international focus on the Palestinian question occurred due to the Palestinian mass uprising (*intifada*) in the West Bank and the Gaza Strip against continued Israeli occupation. The uprising, or *intifada* (which means "shaking off" in Arabic), was mainly responsible for the decisive step to establish the state of Palestine. The *intifada* involved hundreds of thousands of people, many with no previous resistance experience, including children, teenagers, and women. Taking note of the uprising of the Palestinians and their genuine struggle for liberation, Rajiv Gandhi, while speaking at Amman on July 11, 1988, said, "The struggle of the brave Palestinian people for their legitimate rights has entered a new and critical phase. Their accumulated anger can no longer be

---

100 http://books.google.co.in

101 Prime Minister Rajiv Gandhi, Statements on Foreign Policy, April-June, 1988, External Publicity Division, Ministry of External Affairs New Delhi, P-24

contained. Not all the brutality and violence unleashed by Israel can crush the Palestinian *intifada*. There can be no peace without justice. The illegal occupation of Arab territories, must be vacated. The Palestinians have an inalienable right to self-determination. They have a right to their homeland. These rights must be recognized".[102]

The *intifada* caught Yasser Arafat by surprise. He never accepted such a mass uprising in the occupied territories. Yasser Arafat, the Chairman of the PLO, seized the opportunity arising out of the rebellion of the Palestinians in the occupied territories and decided to seek a helping hand from India to raise a relentless struggle against Israel for its occupation of the West Bank and Gaza Strip. As a result, in October 1988, Chairman Yasser Arafat visited India to brief the Indian government on various options that were under consideration by the PLO. A warm welcome greeted him and assured him of the country's full support in the cause of liberating Palestine from Israeli occupation. Yasser Arafat and the representatives of the people of Palestine succeeded in getting the help of the international community, particularly from the non-aligned countries under the leadership of India, to make the dream of an independent Palestinian state a reality. The Palestinian revolt and India's support under Rajiv Gandhi, including that of Arab and Islamic (Muslim) countries, put pressure on Israel to restrict its expansion of settlements to establish the state of Palestine on their land.

The declaration of Palestinian independence was possible primarily due to the struggle of the Palestinian activists, coupled with Rajiv Gandhi's unequivocal support for the Palestinians and similar support extended from like-minded countries. At the same time, Palestinian activists in the occupied territories demanded that the PLO adopt a comprehensible political programme to guide the struggle

---

102 Prime Minister Rajiv Gandhi Statements on Foreign Policy, July-September 1988, External Publicity Division, Ministry of External Affairs, New Delhi, P-41

for independence. In response, "the Palestine National Council (a Palestinian Government-in-Exile), convened in Algeria in November 1988, recognized the state of Israel, proclaimed an independent Palestinian state in the West Bank and the Gaza Strip, and renounced terrorism."[103] However, the PLO had no control over any territory during the period. In fact, "India was the first non-Arab country to recognize Palestine as an independent state in 1988,"[104] soon after its proclamation. Yasser Arafat, the Chairman of the PLO, thanked the people of India and Rajiv Gandhi for this gesture during his visit to India in March 1989, when he opened the Embassy of Palestine in New Delhi.

Though Rajiv Gandhi played a predominant role in defusing tension in the Middle East, his dream of an independent state of Palestine with its territories could not become a reality despite his determined efforts. The political strife and violence within the Palestinian community, particularly the Hamas (Islamic Resistance Movement), founded in 1987, complicated the peace process initiated by several countries, both Arab and non-Arab, and also became a barrier to the realization of a united Palestine state. However, this was despite Yasser Arafat leading the Palestinian movement for nearly four decades for an independent homeland with defined boundaries. Above all, the Israeli government did not recognize the PLO's renunciation of terrorism, asserted that nothing had changed, and declared that it would never negotiate with the PLO. Even America failed to convince Israel to change its policies towards Palestine and abandon its adamant stand against Palestine. On account of the indifferent attitude of Israel, peace in the Middle East became an illusion despite the declaration of an independent Palestine state and the recognition of more than 100 countries throughout the

---

103 http://merip.or/palestine
104 Frontline, 21(25) Dec.04-17, 2004.(http://onlinejournal.com. (Asian Recorder, 35 (18) April-30 May-6, 1989, P-20553)

globe. As a result, several factors prevented the Middle East from experiencing lasting peace. The efforts made by Rajiv Gandhi and Yasser Arafat, the towering personalities of the world, to turn the Middle East into a zone of peace remained an unaccomplished mission and an unresolved issue.

CHAPTER – IV

India and Super Powers Under Rajiv Gandhi's Regime

An attempt is made in this chapter to explore India's relations with the super powers under Rajiv Gandhi's dynamic leadership. Historically, the interactions and relations between the two, namely, the US and USSR (Cold War and power politics), have significantly influenced the foreign policy formulation of independent India. The primary objective of the policy of non-alignment was to serve as the guiding principle governing India's relations with the global superpowers. The attitude of the superpowers led to India's foreign policy adopting the concept of non-alignment as its guiding principle. India, along with the newly emerging independent countries of the world, was determined in the 1950s to remain aloof from the politics of the superpowers. When there was competition for supremacy in world politics, these countries, like India, chose non-alignment as their foreign policy principle. Therefore, the influence of the superpowers on India in terms of formulating non-alignment as a strategy of its foreign policy is one of its unique contributions. Thus, understanding the role of the superpowers and their impact on India is critical when analyzing India's foreign policy. Given this, Rajiv Gandhi, during his tenure, gave considerable attention to the normalization of relations with the two superpowers, i.e., the US and the USSR, which had a direct bearing on India's foreign policy. It was also his endeavour to maintain friendly relations with the superpowers.

A Brief History of Indo-American Relations:

India and America, the world's two largest democracies, have undoubtedly been friends since pre-independence days, but their interactions have not been cordial and cooperative. Further, the relations between India and the US have always had ups and downs and have remained complex for quite a long time. Perhaps this is mainly due to India's strategic perceptions. The differences between the two countries have led to abnormal relations on various international issues since the days of Jawaharlal Nehru, followed by Indira Gandhi. Summing up the decades of Indo-US relations, Stanley Hoffmann commented, "Of all the major countries, India is the one whose relations with the United States have been the most baffling. The story since 1947, when India became independent, is one of mutual irritation and missed opportunities".[1]

Despite substantial differences, both India and the US, the world's two largest democracies, shared some perspectives on a variety of issues. Because of British control over India's international affairs, the two countries had friendly ties even before India acquired independence. Hence, there were no significant issues between the two countries. Even America had extended its moral and material support to India in its struggle for independence. Therefore, Jawaharlal Nehru, commenting on the historical relations between India and the US and its support said, "Between the United States and India, there had existed friendly relations even before India gained her independence. No Indian can forget that in the days of our struggle for freedom, we received from your (US) country a full measure of sympathy and support. Our two republics share a common faith in democratic

---

1   Norman D.Palmer., TheUnited States and India, The Dimensions of Influence, Praeger Publishers, USA, 1984, p-1.

institutions and the democratic way of life and are dedicated to the cause of peace and freedom".[2]

During Indira Gandhi's period, particularly in the early 1970s, relations between India and the US were not cordial due to several reasons, such as the continued supply of arms to Pakistan, the uranium supply to Tarapur Atomic Power Plant, the nuclear issue, etc. Further, relations between the two countries deteriorated in the early 1980s with the Soviet Union's intervention in Afghanistan. In fact, the Afghan issue was a crucial cause of concern for India. The US did not like the Soviet invasion of Afghanistan and criticized it as illegal and unethical. As a result, the deterioration of relations between the USSR and the US had a significant bearing on India.

However, 1982 marked an era when India began to turn towards the West with the objective of improving relations with the US. As a result, by 1982, India, under Indira Gandhi's leadership, had begun to move closer to the West to sort out critical issues through bilateral talks, which hampered Indo-US relations. On the contrary, the US also became soft towards India when it approached the International Monetary Fund (IMF) for a loan, as it was functioning under US direction. Taking advantage of this, Indira Gandhi also initiated the dialogue with the US about sending sophisticated technology to India, which resulted in the memorandum of understanding signed between Rajiv Gandhi and Ronald Reagan in early 1985.

Major Issues of Cooperation and Irritants during Rajiv Gandhi's Period:

It is worth noting that India and the US did not agree on some international issues during Rajiv Gandhi's tenure. These include

---

2   P.G.Salvi, India in World Affairs, B.R.Publishing Corporation, New Delhi, 1985, p-127.

the Indian Ocean as a zone of peace, the supply of arms to Pakistan, apartheid in South Africa, the Palestine question, disarmament, the Super 301 trade business, the issue of Afghanistan, and the broader issues of colonialism and neo-imperialism. Such disagreements have hampered Indo-US relations since the beginning. Further, the US was not happy with India's non-alignment policy. Non-alignment, especially in a liberal country like India, was thought to abdicate responsibility for standing with the Soviet threat. More than ever, the US has viewed Indian non-alignment as a mark of tilt towards the Soviet Union.

Despite the increased disagreement between the two countries on several issues, the dynamic leader Rajiv Gandhi made arduous efforts to remove the obstacles that stood in the way of improving Indo-US relations. He was also committed to establishing world peace and left no stone unturned in his efforts. He endeavoured to improve the strained relations between India and the US, if not in all areas, at least in some selected areas of cooperation. Even President Reagan, in his interview with the 'Far Eastern Economic Review, said, "We have our differences with India certainly, but I truly believe that India and the United States have reached a point where we can pursue a mature and constructive relationship based on the values and interests we share rather than points of differences".[3]

However, India's desire to be friendly with the US was voiced by T.N.Kaul the then Ambassador to the US, in the following words, "India would like to be friendly with the USA, but not as a surrogate or client state. If the US administration does not accept equality and reciprocity, mutual respect, and understanding as the basis of friendship, then indeed it would be difficult to improve India-US relations. But such an attitude in the USA cannot endure for long. As India becomes more

---

3   Indo-US Relations, Search for Mature and Constructive Ties, India Quarterly, 42(1), January-March 1985, p-4.

and more self-reliant and strong-economically, politically, and defence wise, America will have to realize her vast potential for peace, security, and development in the region, in Asia, and in the world."[4]

On the contrary, India also expected the US to encourage it to strengthen the bond of friendship without affecting India's policy of non-alignment. Increased economic, technological, and military cooperation with India can help advance this and was considered a step forward in improving Indo-US relations.

a) U.S. Dual-Use Technology Transfer:

Soon after assuming office as Prime Minister, Rajiv Gandhi considered promoting increased technology transfer and foreign investment from the West. At the same time, he was also determined to improve Indo-US relations, which had many difficulties, and were more unfriendly than friendly. Rajiv Gandhi was optimistic about enhancing ties between India and the US relations for a number of reasons. First, compared to his mother, Rajiv Gandhi was regarded as being more Western- friendly. Second, it is expected that he, being Western educated, unorthodox in approach, and with a firm belief in modern technology, engineering, and science, would try to improve India's relations with the US. Thirdly, the growing Indian reliance on Western technology was regarded as a significant factor in fostering better ties.

Therefore, by December 1984, a month after Rajiv Gandhi assumed the office, both India and the US had finalized the memorandum of understanding on technological cooperation, "which was eventually signed in May 1985,"[5] originally initiated during Indira Gandhi's visit

---

4   P.G.Salvi., Supra No.2, p-140.

5   J.N.Dixit., Across Borders, Fifty Years of India's Foreign Policy, Picus Books, New Delhi, 1998, p-173.

in 1982. "The objective of the MOU was to establish a mechanism for the expeditious review of export licence applications for India without jeopardizing US national security and nuclear non-proliferation interests. The agreement permits the use of sophisticated American technology for Indian business and military ventures". [6]

As a result, in June 1985, Rajiv Gandhi, with the avid object of improving friendly relations and getting technological know-how, paid the first-ever official visit to the US within six months of his massive electoral victory, which renewed hopes of a breakthrough in Indo-US relations. Former US diplomat Dennis Kux said of the visit, "Rajiv Gandhi made an excellent impression on his American hosts; the handsome young Prime Minister differed from the preachy, arrogant Indian stereotype. He was quiet, seemed to listen to what American leaders had to say, spoke softly, and had a touch of humour".[7] Even though Rajiv Gandhi made it clear that he was not going to alter the fundamental thrust of his country's foreign policy {he pointedly visited Moscow before Washington}, his change of style from his mother's made India look different". The US Ambassador to India at that time, Harry Barnes, commented, "this was a new start, good for India and good for the USA'. [8]

Rajiv Gandhi, the youngest Prime Minister of the biggest democracy in the world, proved himself an international leader within a short span of time. In recognition of his international stature, he also served as chairperson of the NAM. As a result, during his official visit to the US, "he was accorded the honour of addressing a joint session of the US Congress, a privilege which was not offered even to his mother during

---

6   P.M.Kamath and A.A.Mutalik Desai, Indian Perspective on the US Literature and Foreign Affairs (Ed), Prestige Books, New Delhi, 1993, p-142.

7   Dennis Kux, Estranged Democracies: India and United States 1947-1991, Sage Publications, New Delhi, 1993, p-403.

8   J.N.Dixit, Supra No.5, p-173.

her three official visits to the United States. The Vice President George Bush accompanied Rajiv Gandhi on a trip to the NASA space centre in Houston, Texas, the two developed friendly personal ties."[9], This clearly demonstrated that Rajiv Gandhi had a unique quality of charisma and leadership. This marked a new era in Indo-US relations.

While in America, Rajiv Gandhi decided to visit Houston. The high point of his visit to Houston was his meeting with the representatives of high-tech firms, who informed him about the expertise that America could sell to India. "Rajiv Gandhi evinced keen interest as senior executives of these firms made three sets of presentations. The first pertains to new methods and discoveries in petroleum and metal prospecting, the second to the application of information in the fields of medicine and scientific education, and the third to the development of new materials in space. After the presentations, he said, "India was interested in buying only technology appropriate to its present stage of economic development. "We want to have modern technology relevant to our ambitions. Besides, we should also be able to afford it. Our endeavour is to carry information and education to the countryside."[10]

Rajiv Gandhi successfully developed a connection with the US government during his visit to the US when he met with US President Ronald Reagan and had an in-depth discussion. In addition, his visit also contributed significantly to enriching understanding and cooperation between the two countries. But during this visit, major agreements were not on the agenda of talks. However, during the discussions, both Rajiv Gandhi and Ronald Reagan looked beyond the current problems and moved forward to establishing better relationships on a new basis. From all accounts, Rajiv Gandhi's visit created a new climate

---

9   Dennis Kux Supra No.7, pp-403-404.
10   The Times of India, 17 June 1985.

in the United States relations with India. This did not indicate that all disagreements had settled.

The Indo-US Joint Statement:

After prolonged discussion, the two leaders issued a joint statement on June 15, 1985. The two leaders called on all governments to combat the new danger of organized terrorism as "a threat to peace and democracy". The statement emphasized mutual collaboration in science and technology. They also identified some specific areas of collaboration, like extending the Science and Technology Initiative for another three years, initiating a vaccine action programme, and a long-term research and technology development programme, and a programme for the development of commercial technology."[11]

After Rajiv Gandhi's return from the US, the government of India earmarked four areas where it needed such technology. These are energy, transport, communication, and agriculture. Stressing his commitment to bring high technology to India, Rajiv Gandhi said, "We are looking ahead, removing strife, and removing our petty differences to make India forge ahead as fast as possible to become the equal of any other country."[12] Further, the foremost object of Rajiv Gandhi's visit to the US was to make India one of the strongest nations in the world using the sophisticated technological know-how. And it was also his vision to take India into the 21st century.

Before Rajiv Gandhi's visit, the US sent a fifty-member delegation to the seventh meeting of the Indo-US sub-commission on science and technology in April 1985. William Schneider Jr., Under Secretary of State for Security Assistance, led it. Prof.Yash Pal, Secretary of the

---

11 Rajiv Gandhi, Selected Speeches and Writings 1984-85, Vol-1, Publication Division, Ministry of Information and Broadcasting, New Delhi, 1987, p-344.

12 The Times of India, 17 June 1985.

Department of Science and Technology, led the hundred-member Indian delegation. At the meeting, India and the United States agreed on a new collaborative research programme in material sciences, recommended at the seventh session of the Indo-US science and technology sub-commission. Further, the administrators and scientists of both countries discussed various aspects of Indo-US cooperation in six broad fields, namely "(I) health, medical, and life sciences, (II) physical sciences, (III) earth, atmospheric, and marine sciences, (IV) energy, (V) environment and ecology; and (VI) information sciences."[13] This cooperation between the two countries in science and technology was undoubtedly a step forward in strengthening Indo-US relations. Further, it was considered a milestone in developing collaboration between the two countries after several years.

When Rajiv Gandhi visited the United States in 1985, America agreed to transfer high technology to India in principle. However, the US decision-making process proved slow in its action and began to employ delay tactics concerning technology transfer. In fact, the US was concerned that the transferring technology to India would jeopardize its interests, owing to India's military ties with Moscow. Because of this, the American Pentagon adopted delay tactics, causing significant delays in transferring the technological know-how to India. Therefore, once and for all, the transfer of technology stalled for an indefinite period. Meanwhile, the US also suggested some safeguards to be undertaken by India in the event of the transfer of technology. The main objective behind the US move was to avoid the transfer of sophisticated technology to the USSR via India.

Realizing the same, in October 1985, Rajiv Gandhi again visited the US, renewed his stand and pleaded with the US government to transfer the technological know-how to India at the earliest. As a

---

13   Hindustan Times (New Delhi)9th April 1985.

result, the US administration approved the transfer of sophisticated technology worth 60,000 dollars. In continuation, the US government also declared that the technology would be sent to India at the earliest, without taking into consideration the military linkage with Moscow.

At this point, the US government was said to be on the verge of clearing the sale of the world's most advanced computer to India. This development was followed by the most important meeting of the then scientific advisor to the Defence Ministry, V.S.Arunachalam, with senior US officials. Fred Ikle, the US Under Secretary of Defence, was understood to have assured Arunachalam that the USA would be selling the Supercomputer to India."[14]

The hope generated by Rajiv Gandhi's visit was brightened when the US offered to extend the area of cooperation to defence and, for this purpose, invited India to send senior military officials to important American defence universities and establishments. In October 1986, the US Defence Secretary, Casper Weinberger, paid a visit to India. During this visit, both India and the US reached an understanding regarding the transfer of high technology to India. As per the understanding, the decks were cleared for the transfer of U.S. military related technologies initially in a couple of selected fields and for the likely sale of Supercomputers to India following the U.S. Defence Secretary Casper Weinberger's talks."[15] Further, the US also came forward to supply the critical components for the development and production of a wide range of defence equipment, such as engines and electronics for the light combat aircraft project, radar and telemetry system for testing missiles, anti-tank weaponry, night vision equipment, armour-piercing projectiles and super alloys fire control and transmission

---

14　The Statesman, 20th October 1985.
15　The Times of India, 15th October 1986.

mechanisms for the main battle tank prototypes."[16] In response to Rajiv Gandhi's visit to the US in June 1985, the US Defence Secretary, Casper Weinberger, met Rajiv Gandhi in October 1986 in New Delhi and said, "The US had agreed in principle to sell the supercomputers sought by India, subject to certain safeguards to be worked out by experts of the two governments."[17] The US came forward to help India to modernize its defence. The two countries also reached a wide ranging and substantial agreement on the transfer of high technology equipment, including Supercomputer. The US showed its willingness to sell General Electric's 404 engines for the light combat aircraft being developed by India, technology equipment for missile testing, night vision equipment, etc.

Although a good beginning was made with India, "with the exception of the sale of the 404 engines, the United States remained reluctant to transfer high tech items that may contribute directly to India's weapon capabilities. The United States was not willing to consider India's request for technological assistance for its booster rocket programme since this would contribute to assistance delivery capabilities. Thus, technology for the peaceful programme that involved rocket motors, inertial guidance systems, liquid fuel tanks and components, and propellant technology was excluded."[18]

However, an anti-climax came when Casper Weinberger, during his visit to Pakistan, announced that the US had agreed to supply an airborne warning platform to Pakistan at the earliest, but the system to be provided would be decided later. He further said that the US would assist Pakistan in strengthening its defence capabilities to meet

---

16   The Hindu (Madras) 13th October 1986.
17   The Hindu (Madras) 13th October 1986.
18   Raju C.Thomas, US Transfer of "Dual Use" Technologies of India, Asian Survey, 30(8), 8th August 1990, p-843.

any border threat under a new six-year package. He added that the US felt there was a need to enhance Pakistan's air defence capability in particular."[19] India felt severely upset over the reported statement by Casper Weinberger. India believed that the induction of AWACS to Pakistan's defence would undoubtedly endanger India's security interests. Thus, the US policy towards Pakistan dashed the hope brought out by Casper Weinberger's visit to India.

The Dilemma of the Sale of a Supercomputer:

In spite of all the disagreements and divergent perceptions between the USA and India on certain issues, there were still some agreements and MOUs signed between the two countries. These paved the way for normalizing relations. In fact, the document signed in New Delhi in December 1986 for the sale of a supercomputer was "a landmark in the chequered history of Indo-US relations. Both President Reagan and Prime Minister Rajiv Gandhi played significant roles in getting the deal cleared. Its importance lies in the fact that India is only the third country (after the United Kingdom and West Germany) to such favoured treatment from Washington. Not even Israel, America's closest ally, has been given this facility."[20] This was not successful in improving Indo-US relations due to the delay in transferring the Supercomputers. The US Department of Defence continued to oppose this on the ground that the "misuse" of the machine for purposes other than stipulated. "It was well known that the US Defence Department was initially opposed to the sale of even a single supercomputer to India because it feared that the technology would pass into Soviet hands. By contrast, the State Department and White House were willing to take a "calculated risk"

---

19   Asian Recorder, 33(1), January 1-7, 1987, p-19256.

20   Hindustan Times (New Delhi) 13th December 1986

to wean India away from its dependence on Moscow."[21] Therefore, the deal was thrown into cold storage because of divergent perceptions.

The United States Under Secretary for International Trade, Mr. S Bruce Smart, speaking on the implementation of the memorandum of understanding on the transfer of high technology, said that the fear of diversion was among the major causes of this malaise. Further, he also said, "Within the government, there are differing opinions from time to time on the matter of exporting sensitive technology to third Countries."[22] From the statement, it is clear that the US Congress and the Defence Department were reluctant to transfer technology to India. Despite differing perceptions and the imposition of restrictions and safeguards, at last the US administration agreed to supply a less sophisticated model of the Cray XMP-14 supercomputer instead of the Cray XMP-24 as sought by India. Even, for this, the US administration put a condition that "the officials of Cray Research Inc., manufacturers of supercomputers, will be on-site to ensure that neither the Soviets nor the Japanese gain access to the computer."[23] In fact, India felt greatly perturbed over the carrot-and-stick policy adopted by the US as far as the supercomputer deal was concerned.

In the context of the supercomputer deal, the US demanded to inspect and monitor the end-uses of the facility in order to safeguard it against Indian misuse and accessibility to other countries. "In some quarters in India, this was seen as a compromise on India's sovereignty. The MOU got dubbed as "NPT" in disguise."[24] It should, however, be noted that the Western allies also did not have the freedom to use them according to their requirements or even to transfer the systems

---

21   Hindustan Times (New Delhi) 13th December 1986
22   Hindustan Times (New Delhi) 14th May 1987
23   The Hindustan Times (New Delhi) 4th March 1987.
24   Quoted in P.M.Kamath and A.A.Mutalk Desai, Supra No.6, p-143.

to new sites within their territories. Even India had to deal with the same circumstances as the US and its Western allies concerning to the supercomputer acquisition.

Taking into account the excessive preconditions and restrictions set by the US administration and the Pentagon's callous attitude, made Rajiv Gandhi searched for other avenues to obtain Supercomputers. As a result, he "approached Japan, the only other manufacturer of a similar computer."[25] Sensing Rajiv Gandhi's approach to Japan, the US administration promptly initiated talks with Japan to arrive at an understanding on the terms of the sale of such machines to countries like India that are "neutral but friendly."[26] Therefore, Rajiv Gandhi's approach to Japan to acquire similar computers clearly indicated that his leadership did not compromise India's national interest. Further, it was made clear that there was no shift in India's foreign policy under Rajiv Gandhi's leadership while acquiring sophisticated technology from the US. Even Rajiv Gandhi's leadership proved he was not inclined towards the West, though he was Western- educated and unorthodox while getting the technological know-how.

Taking note of India's disappointment over the sale of supercomputers, the US decided to soothe Rajiv Gandhi's sentiments by offering more computers apart from the one he had already sought. But the US administration's decision to sell Cray XMP-14 Supercomputers to India to keep its promise of transferring high technology just a few days before Rajiv Gandhi visited to the US. However, "the purchase of a supercomputer for weather forecasting and other agricultural related operations from the US was subject to a series of negotiations, particularly because India had initially sought more advanced supercomputers, the Cray XMP-24. The US

---

25   The Times of India, 9th December 1986.
26   The Times of India, 9th December 1986

government finally cleared the sale of lower capacity supercomputers, the Cray XMP-14. Even then, the deal was held up on the question of maintenance fees since it was felt that Cray Company's demand was on the higher side."[27]

Though the decision disappointed Rajiv Gandhi, then Foreign Secretary A.P.Venkteshwaran urged Rajiv Gandhi to "accept the offer in order to gain entry into the US high technology world. Rejecting the offer would freeze India out of high technology cooperation with the United States. This became the rationale for India to accept the sale."[28]

However, during his trip to the US, Rajiv Gandhi confirmed his decision that India would accept the Cray XMP-14 supercomputers. Accordingly, "India had signed the formal contract for the purchase of the Cray-XMP-14 supercomputer from the US. The then financial advisor to the Department of Science and Technology, B.K.Chaturvedi, signed on behalf of the Indian government and Michael Dickey, senior Vice-President of Cray Research Inc., on behalf of his company."[29] Apart from this, the US also promised to provide additional computers in line with "India's need for upgraded capability and the growing mutual confidence that implementation of our agreement will provide."[30] Therefore, the transfer of supercomputers is considered a significant step in the strategic partnership between the two countries.

Rajiv Gandhi's Visit to the US: October 1987

Despite all the irritants, India intended to improve relations with the US to get the sophisticated technological know-how transferred, to develop India into one of the strongest countries in the world by

---

27   The Hindu, 6th May 1988.
28   Quoted in Dennis Kux, Supra No.7, p-108.
29   The Hindu, 6th May 1988.
30   Dennis Kux., Supra No.7, p-414.

making use of the said technology. As a result, in the fall of 1987, Rajiv Gandhi, "after attending the United Nations session, paid his second official visit to Washington – the first time an Indian Prime Minister returned to the US capital after an interval of only two years."[31] Rajiv Gandhi's visit aroused new hopes in Indo-US relations despite certain irritants and disagreements between the two countries. The main idea behind Rajiv Gandhi's visit was to strengthen bilateral ties and expand cooperation in defence and technology. During the meeting, both Rajiv Gandhi and President Ronald Reagan "dealt with various issues, including Islamabad's nuclear ambitions, the US policy towards Pakistan, nuclear proliferation, cooperation in science and technology in several fields, including defence, Afghanistan, the Indo-Sri Lankan Agreement, and East-West relations. During the discussion, Rajiv Gandhi told Reagan that India did not want nuclear weapons and that "we certainly do not want nuclear weapons in our neighbourhood". Conveying his concern over developments in "our immediate vicinity"- an obvious reference to Pakistan-he said, "Yet another country now seems on the threshold of fulfilling a long ambition of acquiring nuclear weapons."[32]

In concrete terms, the outcome of the Rajiv Gandhi and Ronald Reagan talks was the enunciation of new initiatives announced by President Reagan in his farewell speech on October 20, 1987. Briefly stated they were as follows,

    i.   "extension of the three year Indo-US initiative on science and technology;

   ii.   expansion in bilateral trade and reduction in trade barriers, and a check on protectionism;

---

31   Dennis Kux., Estranged Democracies: India and United States 1941-1991, Sage Publications, New Delhi, 1993, p-413

32   The Hindu, 21 October 1987.

iii. cooperation in India's need for upgraded technology dealing with computer science;

iv. pledging cooperation in stemming drug trafficking;

v. expansion in defence cooperation with special reference to LCA;

vi. enhancement in the productivity in arid zone agriculture and water management;

vii. utilization of Indo-US funds for cultural and scientific cooperation;

viii. planning the exchange of visits by dignitaries and parliamentarians of the two countries;

ix. commencing a programme for fellowships in research institutes of science and technology."[33]

Rajiv Gandhi, after his trip to the US, was optimistic about the meetings with Reagan, except on Pakistan's nuclear issue. However, Rajiv Gandhi asserted on the nuclear issue by saying, "If the US really exerts pressure, I have no doubt that Pakistan will change its attitude towards the nuclear weapon programme". On Indo-US defence cooperation, he further stated, "We have seen progress on that confidence building exercise. We have completed everything we had targeted to do. Now we had ups and downs and our differences. But these two years have seen a very substantial improvement in our relations."[34]

b) US Arms Aid to Pakistan:

US arms aid to Pakistan has been a key irritant in Indo-US relations since the beginning. The history of Indo-US relations reveals that

---

33 Quoted in Shri Ram Sharma, Indo-US Relations 1972-91: A Brief Survey Part-II, Discovery Publishing House, New Delhi, 2003, p-76.

34 Quoted in Dennis Kux, Supra No.7, p-414.

Pakistani factors influenced Indo-US relations. The American military aid to Pakistan, which began in 1954, was a cause of great concern to India. Because the supply of US arms to Pakistan always had a significant bearing on the security interests of India. "The United States has been engaged in arms transfers to Pakistan since the mid-1950s, when the Mutual Security Pact was concluded between the two countries in 1954, in utter disregard of Indian interests and susceptibilities. In spite of India's opposition to the US move to aid Pakistan, US President Eisenhower announced on February 25, 1954, that the US had decided to give military assistance to Pakistan for the purpose of strengthening "defence capabilities in the Middle East."[35] During 1954-1965, Pakistan received over $ 630 million in military assistance for weapons; $ 619 million for defence support, and some $55 million worth of equipment purchased on a cash or concessional basis. On September 8, 1965, the US declared an embargo. Pakistan acquired through third countries hardware worth about $ 200 million, including 90 fighters from West Germany, through Iran, and a sizeable number of Patton tanks through Turkey, with the full knowledge of the Pentagon.[36]

Thus, the US arms supply to Pakistan obviously increased the threat perception in the South Asian region. Therefore, Jawaharlal Nehru, the then Prime Minister of India, vehemently criticized American move and said, "It upsets all kinds of balances, the present equilibrium, and all that" and "encourages the Pakistani authorities in their aggressiveness and increases tension and conflict between India and Pakistan."[37]

---

35   Quoted in K.Raman Pillai., Basic Issues and Political Attitudes, Meenakshi Prakashan, Meerut, 1969, pp-42,43.

36   Quoted in Shri Ram Sharma, Lal Bahadur Shastri: An Era of Transition in Indian Foreign Policy, Kanishka Publishers, New Delhi, 2001, p-38.37

37   Quoted by B.S.K.Grover's "India and the United States of America: Problems and Prospects, in Verinder Grover's (Ed) International Relations and Foreign Policy of India, USA and India's Foreign Policy, Deep and Deep Publication, New Delhi, 1992, p-122.

However, in response to Nehru's apprehension and criticism, the US authorities asserted that military assistance to Pakistan "is not directed in any way against India" and that "this is allocated to Pakistan for defence against Russia and China."[38]

Further, during the 1965 Indo-Pak War, America openly supported Pakistan with arms and ammunition despite India's strong protests. It also continued the same in the 1971 Indo-Pak War. In fact, America's open support for Pakistan caused a security imbalance in the South Asian region. Therefore, the supply of US arms to Pakistan has been the single most constant irritant in Indo-US relations. Even during the Soviet Union's intervention in Afghanistan in the1980s, the US again supplied sophisticated weapons to Pakistan to contain the growing Soviet influence in the South Asian region. The Reagan Administration further "announced a $ 3.18 billion arms and economic aid package to Pakistan in 1981. The arms package proposed the sale of forty long-range F-16 fighter bombers to Pakistan, the most modern and sensitive radar, as well as other military personnel carriers". The rationale behind the sale of arms is to give Pakistan the ability to handle "a range of limited cross border threats from Soviet or Soviet backed Afghan forces."[39] However, the arms were meant for the Taliban to fight against the Soviet forces. In fact, the adverse effect was on India. Therefore, the US was the root cause of conflicts, and tensions in South Asia. It also aimed to minimize Soviet influence in South Asia. Inevitably, this led to a security imbalance in South Asia. Therefore, taking into consideration the security threat in the South Asian region, Walter Mondale, former US Vice President, said "It was a mistake to introduce new and more advanced aircraft into the Indian sub-continent. I think the induction of

---

38   D.C.Jha, U.S. Policy Towards India, in Verinder Grovers, Supra No. 37, p-177.

39   Quoted by Moti Lal Govila., Indo-American Relations in the Post War Decade, in Verinder Grover's (ed) International Relations and Foreign Policy of India, USA and India's Foreign Policy, Deep and Deep Publication, New Delhi, 1992, p-251.

F-16 aircraft is a mistake. I would much prefer to encourage attempts by India and Pakistan to resolve their differences, to lay emphasis on peace and diplomatic negotiations and the reduction of tensions, rather than escalate arms, which solves nothing."[40]

The United States Ambassador to the United Nations, Jeane J.Kirk Patrick, categorically stated that the arming of Pakistan "was neither an actual nor an intended threat to India". Further, he said, we call for helping Pakistan to have some confidence as it confronts the problems of refugees and the Soviet presence on its own border."[41] The American view remained dubious as far as the arms aid to Pakistan was concerned. Further, the US Assistant Secretary of State, Richard Murphy, visited India in October 1984 and told the Indian officers that the moment the Afghanistan crisis was over; arms supply to Pakistan would completely be stopped. Meanwhile, efforts were made to see that the sophisticated arms that were in the process of being supplied were immediately stopped."[42]

Taking into consideration the continued US arms supply to Pakistan, Rajiv Gandhi decided to draw the attention of US President Ronald Reagan. As a result, during his visit to the US in October 1985, Rajiv Gandhi conveyed to President Reagan, "India's concern over the continued supply of arms to Pakistan, but it had no effect on the latter, who suggested that the best solution would be for India to improve its relations with Pakistan. He also told Rajiv Gandhi that with American arms aid, Pakistan might abandon its nuclear option."[43] This made it abundantly clear that the US was unwilling to discontinue arms

---

40   P.G Salvi, India in World Affairs, B.R.Publishing Corporation, New Delhi, 1985, p-137.

41   Quoted in Moti Lal Govila., Supra No.39, p-251.

42   Shri Ram Sharma.Supra No.33, p-102.

43   Quoted in Shri Ram Sharma., Indo-US Relations 1972-91 A Brief Survey, Part –II, Discovery Publishing House, New Delhi, 2003, p-91.

supplies to Pakistan due to its strategic interests. Despite this, India was willing to improve relations with Pakistan since it was supporting the terrorists along the Indo-Pak border to disturb the peace process initiated by India.

Therefore, in spite of all the assurances, the US continued to supply sophisticated weapons to Pakistan despite India's protests and serious concerns voiced in numerous international forums. The clear perception of India was that the supply of US arms aid to Pakistan would lead to an arms race in South Asia. Further, the US considered Pakistan a strategic country and used it to serve its vital interests in South Asia. Therefore, Rajiv Gandhi, during his visit to the US in June 1985, said that, "India was worried about US arms supply to Pakistan because "we have to counter it by spending more money by diverting our resources from development". He said, most of the arms Pakistan got were not of the type that could be used against Afghanistan. He referred to the Sea-Skimming missiles, which, he said, could not be used in mountains. "We are keen not to embark on any arms race with Pakistan, and our objective is the reduction of arms in the region."[44]

Further, the decision of the US administration to transfer Airborne Warning and Control System (AWACS) planes to Pakistan became another obstacle in already strained Indo-US relations. India was greatly disturbed and alarmed because she believed that the induction of AWACS in Pakistan's army would pose a grave challenge to its air defence. Further, India also voiced concern that it would threaten India's security and deteriorate relations between the two countries. Therefore, India protested against the US decision and expressed deep concern over the transfer of AWACS to Pakistan. As a mark of protest, then External Affairs Minister, N.D.Tiwari, cancelled his visit to the US against the lease of the AWACS to Pakistan, which were definitely meant

---

44   Asian Recorder, 31(28), July 9-15, 1985, p-18404

to have a substantial offensive against India."[45] However, the American justification for supplying AWACS to Pakistan was to avoid the alleged air intrusion from Afghanistan. Perhaps, "Americans forgot the fact that AWACS were ineffective in the mountainous region of Afghanistan, but they could be of great value in monitoring India's air space as well as a significant portion of the Soviet air space in the Tashkent area."[46] But the "Defence Ministry's Report noted that the US administration's willingness to transfer AWACS planes to Pakistan would only have "minimal impact" on dealing with "alleged" air intrusions from Afghanistan "but a substantial force multiplier effect against India."[47]

Commenting on the reported statement of the US Administration's decision to supply AWACS aircraft to Pakistan, the then Foreign Secretary A.P.Venkateswaran in a threatening version, said, "If the United States decided to sell sophisticated spy planes to Pakistan, there is a possibility of India seeking similar equipment from the Soviet Union. He further said, "So far we have not gone in to ask the Soviet Union for an AWACS (Airborne Warning and Control System), but if some such development (sale by the US of AWACS to Pakistan) takes place, there is a possibility."[48] The ultimate result was that South Asia became a zone of arms race due to the superpower's internal squabbling.

Taking cognizance of India's reports about the sale of AWACS to Pakistan, the American acting Deputy Assistant Secretary of State, Herbert G. Hagerty, said, "The US has not taken any final decision on the sale of Airborne Warning and Control Systems (AWACS) to Pakistan and will take into consideration India's views before taking the

---

45   Quoted in Shri Ram Sharma, Supra No.33, p-105.
46   Quoted in Shri Ram Sharma, Supra No.33, p-92.
47   Asian Recorder, 33 (26), June 25-July 1, 1987, p-19520
48   The Hindu (Madras) 18 January 1987.

decision."[49] In this regard, US foreign policy was inconsistent. On the one hand, the US was displaying interest in moving Indo-US relations forward, while on the other, it was trying to affect the security of India by supplying sophisticated weapons to Pakistan. As far as the issue of Afghanistan and the safety of India are concerned, the US categorically stated, "The United States does not accept the argument occasionally voiced by Indian officials that the Soviet presence in Afghanistan does not constitute a threat to Pakistan and that the United States military sales programme to Pakistan is unnecessary. Here, the choice focuses on the differing Indian and American perceptions of security issues in an area of the world that is important to both."[50] That is why there was a greater than-usual rift in the relationship between India and the US. Because of this, the United States and India have maintained divergent perspectives on security issues.

Despite certain irritants, Rajiv Gandhi strove hard to strengthen friendly relations and technological cooperation with the US. However, it was in October 1987, that is, within two months of Rajiv Gandhi's visit, that shocking news came in when the "US Congress Committee cleared the $ 4.2 billion military and economic aid package for Pakistan on December 4, 1987."[51] Under this package, Pakistan was to get about 60 F-16s, bringing the tally to 100. Besides this, Weinberger in principle agreed to the supply of about 20 F-16s, which were the latest and more sophisticated versions of the already supplied F-16s."[52] Interestingly, the clearing of the aid package was stalled for three and a half months because of new evidence that Pakistani was clandestinely following a nuclear weapon programme. However, this

---

49   Patriot (New Delhi) 1ˢᵗ February 1987.
50   Current History, 85 (509), March 1986, p-100.
51   Asian Recorder, 34(4), January 22-28, 1988, p-19848.
52   Pradyot Pradhan, Nuclear Pakistan and India's Response, India Quarterly, 43(1), January –March 1987, p-4.

was done despite Islamabad's outright refusal to satisfy US law on the "fugitive nuclear weapons programme." This time, before India could object to the military assistance, it was finally stalled in August 1987 because a Pakistani was stealing sensitive materials crucial to the production of nuclear weapons outside the US. With this decision, the US Congress, on the one hand, cleared Pakistan and, on the other hand, branded India's peaceful nuclear programme by equating it with Pakistan's nuclear programme. The US deliberately ignored Pakistan's uranium enrichment capability, a technology that gave rise to a call for halting the nuclear race in South Asia. While making a statement in the Rajya Sabha, Rajiv Gandhi said, "It was made abundantly clear to the United States leaders during his recent visit that there was no comparison between the nuclear programmes of India and Pakistan. The two countries could not be equated in this context. Pakistan was trying to attain nuclear technology clandestinely through stealing and smuggling, and their nuclear programme was targeted at making nuclear weapons. On the other hand, India had developed its nuclear technology on its own, and none of its nuclear programmes was in the military sector."[53] India was agitated due to the biased attitude of the United States.

The US Congress Committee's move to equate India with Pakistan on the nuclear proliferation issue caused a strong reaction in India. "The government of India conveyed to the US Embassy in New Delhi, on December 4, 1987, its adverse reaction to the American Senate panel's amendment on nuclear proliferation, which sought to equate India with Pakistan and permit the US President to continue to give Islamabad military and economic aid despite its nuclear weapons programme.[54] Even Natwar Singh, then External Affairs Minister,

---

53   Asian Recorder, 33 (50) Dec 10-16, 1987, p-19777.

54   Asian Recorder, 34(4) Jan 22-28, 1988, p-19848.

warned in a statement in the Rajya Sabha that Indo-US relations would be "adversely affected unless the clauses seeking to equate India and Pakistan in the US Senate sub-committee recommendations were deleted."[55] Even Rajiv Gandhi conveyed India's concern to the then US Ambassador in India, John Gunther Dean, on the reported remarks by the US on the nuclear issue. He was informed during the meeting that the US Congress Committee's vote would provide an alibi for Pakistan to continue its non- peaceful nuclear programme. The Indian reaction later compelled the US to amend its decision. President Reagan took steps for this purpose, and the US Congress revised the proposal. The crisis was over, but it was a bitter experience for India. The unfriendly friendliness continues to characterize the relations. India's deep and time-tested friendship with the Soviet Union and the American commitment to friendship with Pakistan continue to hinder the growth of Indo-US friendship and cooperation.

Ronald Reagan justified that US arms aid to Pakistan as not aimed at India, and Pakistan's clarification that US aid was not intended to harm any of its neighbours was unconvincing to India and also to the Soviet Union and Afghanistan. Perhaps it was unfair because of the statement made by the then-Bush administration in 1989, wherein he defended the US action in aiding Pakistan, as reported in one of the newspapers.

While "defending the supply of 60 F-16 aircraft to Pakistan, the Bush Administration for the first time admitted at a Congressional hearing that the US military programme for Pakistan was aimed at maintaining the current military balance with India, which is given as 3-to-1. While the previous Reagan Administration had never openly stated this or even hinted that India was a potential aggressor and justified arms sales to Pakistan on the basis of the threat it faced from

---

55   Ibid.

the Soviet Union and the Kabul regime."[56] This clearly indicated and once again proved that the US arms supply to Pakistan appears to be not only directed against India but also indirectly to subdue the Soviet Union.

However, by mid-1986, following the withdrawal of the Soviet troops from Afghanistan, there had been a shift in US policy. In this context, Pakistan has ceased to be a frontline for the US, reducing Washington's attention and importance in the South Asian region. Further, by the end of 1990, the US administration had invoked the Pressler Amendment, which prohibited all forms of economic and military assistance to Pakistan. Thus, for the time being, the United States' support for Pakistan in the form of arms aid ended.

c) "Indian Ocean" Zone of Peace or Military (Zone) Bases:

Not only was the Indian Ocean a problem of concern, but it was also a cause of friction between India and the United States. Along with the north-western and north-east land frontiers, India views the ocean as a crucial frontier for defending its maritime interests. Besides, India regarded the ocean as a significant trade route for its economic development and security. The British, who had sway over the ocean right through the Second World War, found it economically unviable to continue their hold. As a result, "in 1967, Britain announced that "all their military forces outside Europe and the Mediterranean would be withdrawn."[57] The Indian Ocean started gaining importance in the 1970s, when the British withdrew from the east of Suez. This naturally made Indians feel vulnerable and unprotected. Perhaps "they felt even more so when the United States gained a base at Diego Garcia."[58]

---

56   The Hindu, 4 August 1989.
57   Indian Ocean as a Zone of Peace, Lok Sabha Secretariat, New Delhi, 1987, p-6.
58   Kanti Bajapai and Amitabh Mattoo, (Ed) Securing India: Strategic Thought and Practice, Manohar Publishers, New Delhi, 1996, p-65.

Consequent upon the US acquiring Diego Garcia base, "the Soviet Union for the first time sent a small squadron of its navy in March-April 1968, which attracted worldwide attention, and some Western observers considered it as something of a beginning of the Soviet drive to control the Indian Ocean".[59] All these indicate the power politics of the superpowers in establishing their control over the Indian Ocean. When both superpowers began to gain control over the Indian Ocean, the situation in the region started worsening.

Given these developments, India declared the Indian Ocean a zone of peace. The big powers, including the US and Soviet Union, were primarily responsible for converting the Indian Ocean from a peaceful region into a military zone to protect their maritime and security interests and establish supremacy. Perhaps the rivalry between the two superpowers and the establishment of military bases led to an arms race in the region. Obviously, it was a cause of concern for hinterland and littoral states surrounded by the Indian Ocean. This posed a threat not only to the security and integrity of these republics but also trade routes in the Indian Ocean. However, Rajiv Gandhi, commenting on the superpowers rivalry, once said, that "These rivalries are not of our making. We are not parties to them. But they threaten to intrude upon our concern with the progress and development of the littoral and hinterland states of the Indian Ocean."[60]

The politics of the Great Powers became more significant with the British decision to withdraw from the region. The other naval powers believed they could fill the so-called "vacuum" with the British withdrawal. It was this power vacuum theory that tended to militarise the ocean. In the race to fill the vacuum and develop a permanent military base in the Indian Ocean, the US was the first superpower to

---

59   Foreign Affairs Reports, 35 (2) February 1986, p-16.
60   Deccan Herald, 5 July 1986.

do so to counter Soviet naval activity in the region. The competition between the US and the USSR to build a military base in the Indian Ocean disturbed India and other coastal states struggling to keep the Indian Ocean region "a zone of peace". While speaking in New Delhi on April 2, 1985, Rajiv Gandhi said, "The Indian Ocean has become a playground for world navies. It has become infested with nuclear weapons. We are strongly committed to a zone of peace in the Indian Ocean and will work towards this end. The big powers' presence in the Indian Ocean poses a threat to all the littoral states. The continued militarization of Diego Garcia is a matter of deep concern to us. We would like the Indian Ocean to be free from superpower rivalry and tensions."[61]

As a result of the superpower rivalry in the region, Rajiv Gandhi, while speaking at the banquet hosted in his honour by the Prime Minister of Australia at Canberra on October 14, 1986, said, "In 1971, the United Nations declared the Indian Ocean a zone of peace. The declaration has remained a dead letter while the ocean has been transformed into a theatre of tension by the induction of foreign naval presences and their panoply of nuclear war. The United Nations General Assembly is once again considering at its session the question of convening a conference to give effect to that declaration. I hope our discussions here will contribute to a congruence of Indian and Australian positions in New York. The vast riches of the Indian Ocean will be denied to us if the ocean is usurped by the war machines of others.[62]

Rajiv Gandhi had made clear his stand on the complete elimination of superpower rivalry in the Indian Ocean area. He even urged the two

---

61   Rajiv Gandhi, Selected Speeches and Writings, Supra No.11, (Vol-I) , p-300.
62   Rajiv Gandhi, Selected Speeches and Writings, 1986 (Vol-II) Publication Division, Ministry of Information and Broadcasting, Government of India, New Delhi, p-307.

superpowers to make some deal to "freeze" their naval activity in the Indian Ocean in the interests of the littoral states. As a result, there was an opportunity for the two superpowers to discuss the various issues that caused tensions in the international community after the Delhi Declaration.

When Gorbachev became President of the USSR in 1985, a new era of liberalization began. Taking note of the same, Rajiv Gandhi persuaded Gorbachev to stop the arms race in the ocean by converting the Indian Ocean into a zone of peace. Gorbachev, who was also in favour of reducing the naval forces in the Indian Ocean, supported "the United Nations Declaration on the Indian Ocean as a Zone of Peace" and called for the "Demilitarization of the Indian Ocean."[63] thereby joining hands with India to convert the Indian Ocean from a military zone to a zone of peace. However, the US was reluctant to withdraw its naval forces from the Indian Ocean because of the Soviet intervention in Afghanistan and its strategic interests in South Asia. The US insisted that unless the Soviet Union withdrew its military from Afghanistan, it would be difficult to resolve the Afghan issue, and thus no dialogue would occur.

Taking into consideration the adamant attitude of the US and the growing US military activities in the vicinity of the Indian Ocean that were detrimental to the littoral states, the Soviet Union criticized Washington for endeavouring to turn the Indian Ocean into an "American Lake" in order "to train their guns on the independence of other countries". The American naval bases in Kenya, Somalia, Oman, and Diego Garcia "are designed to further American imperial design". These bases should be "dismantled immediately" for the security of

---

63   S.C.Parasher, Gorbachev Visit: A Historical Perspective, India Quarterly 42 (4) October-December 1986, p-457.

the Indian Ocean countries, and offered their aid to India to turn the Indian Ocean into an "Ocean of Peace."[64]

The US linked the Soviet intervention in Afghanistan to the issue of the Indian Ocean and arms aid to Pakistan. Once, "Americans contended that it was the Soviet occupation of Afghanistan that had provoked them to go all out to build up Diego Garcia as a powerful base… One may not agree with them totally, but the Americans went to the extent of saying that all the military bases they might acquire in the Indian Ocean and all their naval bases in the Gulf area could not equal the striking power of the land-based Soviet forces in Afghanistan."[65] Therefore, India pleaded that the US had to delink the Afghan issue from other questions to protect India's security. However, the US continued to supply arms to Pakistan despite India's protests until the withdrawal of Soviet forces from Afghanistan. Therefore, the continued Soviet occupation of Afghanistan was the root cause of strengthening Pakistan's claims for American assistance and heightening tensions in the South Asian region, which provided the US and the Soviet Union with the reason to continue their naval build-up in the Indian Ocean.

It was the Soviet Union that positively responded to Rajiv Gandhi's call for demilitarization of the ocean and accordingly decided to reduce its naval forces in the Indian Ocean. Further, it was also due to the détente that emerged between US and Soviet relations in the latter half of 1985 that India became optimistic about turning the Indian Ocean into an ocean of peace. By this time, the Soviet Union had also withdrawn its military forces, as agreed at the Geneva summit. The result was to reduce US naval forces in the Indian Ocean. In this

---

64   Quoted in Hemen Ray, The Enduring Friendship (Soviet-Indian Relations in Mrs. Gandhi's Days) Abhinav Publishers, New Delhi, 1989, p-183.

65   Quoted in Shri Ram Sharma, Indo-Soviet Relations 1972-1991, A Brief Survey Part-II, Discovery Publishing House, New Delhi, 2003, p-62.

regard, Rajiv Gandhi's leadership proved successful in demilitarizing the Indian Ocean and establishing peace in the region by ending the arms race between the two superpowers.

d) The Super 301 Trade Businesses:

The issue of Super-301, which arose at the beginning of 1989, was another major irritant in Indo-US relations. The US has always maintained a "big brother" attitude towards smaller and developing countries with the object of establishing hegemony and control over their trade relations. As a result, the US introduced new laws "popularly known as Super-301" to bring the countries of the world to its terms. "Super-301 is a provision of the Trade Act of 1974 under which the US Trade Representatives identify, in an annual report, those "priority foreign country practices" that, if eliminated, have the greatest potential for the expansion of US exports. Besides identifying trade liberalization priorities, the United States Trade Representatives (USTR) can initiate Section 301 investigations regarding those practices in countries where the liberalization priorities have not been met."[66]

The Super 301 Trade Law was just one of the draconian laws enacted to punish the countries that had not only adverse business dealings with the US but also those that had not maintained good relations with the US. The rationale behind such a move was to indirectly influence the national and economic interests of the countries that failed to satisfy US business laws. Nonetheless, India was one of those countries that had adverse business dealings with the US. As a result, the US decided to penalise India for several reasons, including its unfavourable business relations with the US. Thus, the US was categorical in punishing India for her stand on the Afghan problem, reluctance to sign the Nuclear Non-proliferation Treaty,

---

66   http://canberra. usembassy.gov./hyper.

violation of human rights in Punjab, etc. Despite the Memorandum of Understanding (MOU) of 1984-85, this marked a significant shift in Indo-US relations in defence cooperation and the sales of military and dual-use technologies. The vital changes in Indo-US relations were short-lived when the US imposed a barrier on Indian trade at the global level. As a result, India decided to take a different approach to its relations with the US.

The differences between India and the US came to the fore when the "United States proposed to include issues related to intellectual property rights (IPR) in the Uruguay Round (UR) negotiations. India vehemently opposed the inclusion of any item dealing with intellectual property rights in the UR negotiations. It could be argued that the US had vested interests in pushing intellectual property rights at the multilateral trade negotiation as she, along with other industrialized countries, held 92% of Patents."[67] India opposed the inclusion of IPR within the GATT framework because It argued that GATT was mainly concerned with trade in goods and was not an appropriate forum to negotiate issues of IPR. India also proposed that the World Intellectual Property Organisation (WIPO), an organization set up for this purpose, host discussion on matters concerning IPR. India expressed its genuine concern about the interests of the developing and least developed countries, believing that the economies of these countries were not ripe enough to concede the demands of the industrialized countries. As a result, the issue of IPR was not on the priority agenda for India, though it was for the US.

Despite strong opposition from India and other countries, the US succeeded in pushing the IPR's item on the eighth Uruguay Round

---

67   Julius Sen., Negotiating the Trade Related Intellectual Property Rights Agreement (Research Report) (CUTS) Center for International Trade, Economic and Environment, Jaipur, 2001, p-22.

negotiation agenda along with three other new areas: agriculture, textiles and clothing, services, and Trade Related Investment Measures (TRIMs) as mandatory issues for negotiation at the GATT Ministerial Conference in Punta Del Este, Uruguay, in 1986. India began negotiating at UR, assuming that no sovereign country could be prevailed upon to negotiate on an issue that was not in its best interest. However, Washington succeeded in bringing the IPR issue to multilateral trade negotiations as a full-fledged item for negotiation.

However, in 1989, India was named under the US Omnibus Trade and Competitiveness Act of 1988 for unfair trade practices. Listing India on the Super and Special 301 (S-301) clause was considered a shrewd strategy to pressurise it to negotiate on trade-related Intellectual Property Rights at the Uruguay Round (UR) multilateral trade negotiations, as she would face retaliatory sanctions unilaterally under the US trade laws. "The national Trade Estimate Report related in early May 1989 by United States Trade Representative (USTR), Carla Hills, named India along with Japan, South Korea, Brazil, Canada, and the European Community as among the offenders."[68] Interestingly, charges against India did not concern restrictions about merchandise trade. Instead, "India was cited for its restrictive policies in respect of foreign investment and an invisible one, namely, insurance. The USTR would like India to revise its policy of requiring government approval of foreign investment and to open its insurance market to foreign companies."[69] The main intention of the US was to take revenge on the countries that refused to be in line with it. However, India, under the dynamic leadership of Rajiv Gandhi, opposed the harsh measures introduced under Super 301 against India. In an oblique reference to the U.S. action of naming India under Super and Special 301, Rajiv

---

68   India Indicated of Putting Unfair Trade Barriers, Indian Express, 5 May 1989.
69   Times of India, 23 June 1989.

Gandhi said, "What is worse, those of us who have dared to raise our voice have been threatened with retribution. We are not going to be cowed by such pressures."[70]

On May 25, 1989, the US put India on the hit list under "Special 301" and Super 301 (alongside Brazil and Japan). The "specific negotiating objectives" Washington expected, among other things, with respect to India were: improved patent protection for all classes of invention; elimination of discrimination against use of foreign trade marks, registration of service marks, effective protection of well known marks, improved access and distribution for US motion pictures, improved enforcement against piracy, conclusion of an intellectual property annex to the bilateral science and technology agreement, and constructive participation in multilateral property negotiations.[71]

America used Super-301 against India less than six months before Rajiv Gandhi faced the General Elections. The US appears to have deliberately chosen this time to put Rajiv Gandhi under pressure over the economy. The US stance naturally upset Rajiv Gandhi, who had all along made sincere efforts to improve Indo-US relations, thereby removing the irritants. As a result, Rajiv Gandhi had to undergo pressure from the US during his last days in office. The US planned to kill two birds with one stone by invoking Super 301, i.e., firstly by affecting the Indian economy and secondly by creating political pressure on Rajiv Gandhi. The US also used Super 301 against India to undermine the increasing influence of Rajiv Gandhi in the international sphere, who withstood all sorts of US pressure tactics and emerged as an able leader in the world. Perhaps the US action in the guise of Super and Special 301 did not deter Rajiv Gandhi, who was working hard to develop India into one of the world's most technologically powerful countries. His

---

70   The Hindu, 5th September 1989.
71   The Hindu, 31 May 1989.

leadership was instrumental in making India self-reliant and putting India on the diplomatic map of the world.

Indo-Soviet Relations:

India and the Soviet Union, the two Asian giants, despite their distinct political systems, are undoubtedly good friends in the eyes of the international community. The two countries were able to establish a high degree of cooperation in almost all spheres of bilateral relations. As a result, the two countries remained role models for peaceful co-existence and cooperation, adhering to principles of equality, mutual respect, and mutual understanding concerns. It is because of the close friendship between the two countries that the Soviet Union has always stood by India in times of crisis. Therefore, warm relations with the Soviet Union were a constant factor in Indian foreign policy. A former Foreign Secretary (and a known Russophile), T.N.Kaul noted "relations between India and the Soviet Union are not a matter of temporary convenience or expediency, but the cornerstone of our foreign policies."[72]

The passage of time has further strengthened the friendship bonds between the two countries and laid the foundations of cooperation and coexistence. Because of this friendship, India and the Soviet Union showed the world community that the history of Indo-Soviet relations is one of ever-increasing cooperation. It is pertinent to note that the study of Indo-Soviet relations reveals that the two countries never had strained relations. This is primarily due to the mutual understanding and principles of cooperation that constitute the Indo-Soviet friendship. An attempt is made here to discuss the beginnings of Indo-Soviet relations under the charismatic leadership of Rajiv Gandhi.

---

72   Ramesh Thakur, India and the Soviet Union, Conjunctions and Disjunctions of Interests, Asian Survey, 31 (9) Sept 1991, p-826.

A Brief History of Indo-Soviet Relations:

The history of India's relations with the Soviet Union dates back to pre-independence days, "when it offered support and sustenance to revolutionaries, like Virendranath Chattopadhyaya, Raja Mahendra Pratap, Mohammed Barakatulla, Pandurang Khankoje, and a host of others. As early as in 1914, a group of freedom fighters, comprising Chamapakraman Pillai, Taraknath Das, Bhagwan Singh, and Lala Har Dayal, arrived from Berlin and were warmly received by officials of the Tsarist Russia. This group was in active contact with the Chadar party and carried on extensive propaganda against British imperialism by smuggling "subversive literature" to India via Kabul."[73]

Taking into consideration the historical relations and bonds of friendship between the two countries Jawaharlal Nehru, during his visit to Moscow in 1927 to attend the 10th anniversary of the October Revolution, said, "India is an Asian country. So is the Soviet Union sprawling over Asia and Europe. Between two such neighbours, there can be amity or enmity; indifference is out of the question."[74] From this, it is apparent that India and the Soviet Union had a long-standing friendship. Since becoming prime minister, Jawaharlal Nehru continued to improve India's friendly relations with the USSR in most areas. Therefore, the role played by Jawaharlal Nehru was one of utmost significance in laying the foundation of Indo-Soviet friendship. Further, the successors of Nehru also faithfully adhered to his policy of coexistence. Because of this, the friendship between

---

73   N.M.Khilnani, Gorbachev and Indo-Soviet Relations PTI Feature Vol-7 (14), November 5, 1986, p- C 271.

74   K.P.S. Menon, The Indo-Soviet Treaty, Setting and Meaning, Vikas Publications, New Delhi, 1971, pp-49-50.

India and the Soviet Union that had existed since pre-independence has persisted unabatedly.

The Soviet Union not only remained by India's side in crisis but also offered its support even at the UN whenever India's territorial integrity was in doubt, as in the case of Kashmir and Goa. Further, it is essential to note that the Western nations were reluctant to criticize India because they feared the Soviet Union's veto power, especially for its invasion of Goa in 1961. Therefore, it is made known to the world's society that "the Indo-Soviet friendship was so deep rooted that none on earth could disturb the friendship, which was based on common interest and cooperation. Commenting on the Indo-Soviet friendship in her message to friends of the Soviet Union meeting in Bombay in May 1981, Mrs. Indira Gandhi said, "Between the people of the Soviet Union and India there is a strong and warm friendship, which has stood the test of time. This friendship is based on shared concern for peace and international brotherhood, common opposition to colonialism and racism, and a deep desire to enlarge economic and cultural relations to mutual benefit.[75]

Therefore, the friendship existed between the two countries stood as a model for the world community. It is because of this that both the Soviet Union and India became a source of inspiration to other countries around the world through their everlasting friendship. Even many countries across the globe appreciated the type of friendship that developed between the two countries. On the whole, the friendship of the Soviet Union with India has remained steady, like, to use a lovely metaphor from the Bhagavad Gita, "a flame in a windless spot which does not flicker." [76]

---

75 P.G. Salvi, India in World Affairs, B.R.Publishing Corporation, New Delhi, 1985, p-143.

76 K.P.S. Menon., Supra No.3, p-5.

The Indo-Soviet Friendship Treaty: 1953

The signing of the Indo-Soviet Friendship Treaty in 1953 marked the beginning of a golden era in Indo-Soviet relations. Despite formidable obstacles, the treaty is thus the most recent fruit of Indo-Soviet friendship. Therefore, the Indo-Soviet Treaty served as a testament to the everlasting friendship between the two countries. Further, relations between India and the USSR steadily developed after the visit of Nehru to the USSR in 1955 and the return visit of Soviet leaders to India in the following year. The Soviet Union also supported India's policies of non-alignment, peace, disarmament, and national independence. In turn, India has also supported the Soviet Union's policy of peace and cooperation. As a result, mutual understanding and collaboration between the two countries significantly helped to build a solid and long-lasting friendship.

In fact, it is no secret, that there was a lot of similarity between India and the Soviet Union on a variety of subjects, "such as ridding the world of the nuclear menace, preventing the spread of militarization to outer space, the need to settle conflict through patient dialogue rather than through military means, and eventually bringing about a climate of peace, harmony, and cooperation, where full respect is given to the aspirations of the different peoples."[77]

Major Issues of Rajiv Gandhi's Period:

Rajiv Gandhi was instrumental in enhancing Indo-Soviet relations and developing cooperation and coexistence to a greater extent. In his broadcast on November 12, 1984, he declared that his government was committed to upholding and fostering India's friendship with the Soviet Union, a trusted ally. Undoubtedly, the Soviet Union had come to India's rescue several times during its critical days and always stood

---

77   Blitz, 29 November 1986, p-31.

behind India to safeguard its security and integrity. Therefore, India attached much significance to the Soviet Union. According to Rajiv Gandhi, "We highly value the wide-ranging and time-tested relationship with the Soviet Union based upon mutual cooperation, friendship, and vital support when most needed."[78] Rajiv Gandhi reiterated his determination to advance India's friendship and cooperation with the Soviet Union in a variety of fields and accorded the utmost importance to the fostering of positive relations.

However, several people in the country became concerned that Rajiv Gandhi would tilt more towards the West than the East because of his Western education, Western culture, new political background, and orthodox personality. Rajiv Gandhi's liberalized policy and his love for modern technology, which he intended to get from the West, were the reasons for his inclination towards the West. Further, the influence of the West on Rajiv Gandhi was another important reason. True to this, Rajiv Gandhi tilted towards the West to acquire modern technology, which includes supercomputers and highly sophisticated military and defence equipment. However, "Rajiv Gandhi had assured the then Soviet Premier Mr.Tikhonov during his visit to India at Mrs. Indira Gandhi's funeral that his government would continue the policies pursued by Indira Gandhi and Jawaharlal Nehru in strengthening friendly ties with the Soviet Union and other countries."[79]

Rajiv Gandhi's views concerning modern technology were inevitable, as he wanted to take India into the 21st century. But Rajiv Gandhi, who extended the hand of friendship and cooperation with the US, had no significant effect on Indo-Soviet relations. It is pertinent to note that he did not compromise in any way India's national interest, her non-aligned policy, or her time-tested friendship with the Soviet

---

78　Rajiv Gandhi, Selected Speeches and Writings, Supra No.11,(Vol-1), p-8.
79　Amrita Bazar Patrika, 1st November 1985.

Union at the cost of Indo-US agreements on the transfer of advanced technology. India, a trusted friend of the Soviet Union, would never forget their friendship, whose relations rested on harmony, reciprocity, and mutual understanding. Therefore, it was unfounded to claim that Rajiv Gandhi was tilting more towards the West than the East, as observed in some corners of the country. Perhaps Rajiv Gandhi made strenuous efforts to strengthen the bond of friendship with the Soviet Union.

a) Towards Greater Cooperation:

Rajiv Gandhi's Visit to Moscow:

As a matter of goodwill and friendship, Rajiv Gandhi undertook a six-day tour of the Soviet Union in May 1985, which was his first official trip since assuming power in October 1984. The main object of his visit was to reaffirm India's stand on friendship and cooperation with the Soviet Union. It was also his endeavour to strengthen the bonds of close friendship and expand the collaboration to a greater extent, involving huge areas between the two countries. During his stay in Moscow, Rajiv Gandhi told the Soviet leaders that "He would continue the splendid record of Indo-Soviet relations built over the last three decades. Friendship and cooperation with the Soviet Union were integral elements of India's foreign policy, and the people of India regarded the Soviet people as friends "who have stood by us in times of need."[80] He assured that India would continue to preserve and promote further relations with the Soviet Union, as it has done in the past. Rajiv Gandhi also got an opportunity to convince the Soviet leaders that India's quest for advanced Western technology would not come in the way of its commitment to promote Indo-Soviet friendship.

80　Amrita Bazar Patrika, 1st November 1985.

Rajiv Gandhi – Gorbachev talk:

During the visit, Rajiv Gandhi met with Gorbachev and discussed bilateral relations apart from international issues covering a wide range of subjects. The worldwide concerns discussed included peace and disarmament and the developments in South-East Asia, South-West Asia, the Iran- Iraq war, South Africa, and Central America. Rajiv Gandhi also briefed Gorbachev on his efforts to foster friendly relations with neighbours and the initiative taken as Chairman of the NAM. The leaders of both countries also signed two significant bilateral agreements on economic cooperation. The first agreement on economic and technological collaboration called for the Soviets to participate in the Seventh Five-Year Plan's vital projects, particularly in the power, coal, and petroleum sectors. There was also provision for Soviet participation in the iron and steel machine- building sectors. This agreement also covered a credit of one billion roubles. The second agreement signed was on the main directions of economic, trade, scientific, and technical cooperation between the two countries up to 2000 AD."[81] The main sectors covered by this agreement are power, coal, the oil and gas industry, science and technology, ferrous and non-ferrous metallurgy, machine building, medicine, and public health.[82] The second agreement was for greater cooperation between the two countries in the diverse spheres of the Indian economy up to the year 2000. With this agreement India became the first non-socialist country to reach a long-term understanding with the USSR. The agreement paved the way for the exploration of hitherto untapped areas. In addition, India received considerable economic assistance from the Soviet Union and increased exports of products from India's heavy engineering and small-scale industries.

---

81   Rajiv Gandhi, Selected Speeches and Writings, (Vol-1), Supra No.11, p-341.

82   Prime Minister Rajiv Gandhi Visits USSR, Allied Publishers, Information Department of USSR Embassy, New Delhi, pp-10, 11.

In terms of international issues, both India and the Soviet Union signed a joint statement in which they expressed grave concern about the ongoing tensions in some areas of Southwest Asia, particularly Afghanistan. They also urged Iran and Iraq to declare a cease-fire in their long-running conflict and to solve their differences through peaceful political means. The joint statement also covered issues including military intervention in Afghanistan, Diego Garcia, Nicaragua, and Palestine. President Gorbachev assured Rajiv Gandhi that his country would not take any initiative to produce nuclear weapons and was ready to end the arms race provided all other countries committed to this endeavour in the interest of the entire world.

Further, the joint statement also expressed "profound satisfaction" on both sides over the results of Rajiv Gandhi's six-day state visit, which "has further strengthened bonds of close friendship between the people of the two countries". The conviction was recorded that it "will be a new and important step on the road to further development of relations.[83] Rajiv Gandhi's visit contributed to increasing bilateral cooperation between the two countries in various fields of human development.

No doubt, Rajiv Gandhi's visit to the Soviet Union aroused new hopes in diverse fields and solidified bilateral relations between the countries. Appreciating the outcome of Rajiv Gandhi's visit to Moscow, the Mainstream rightly observed, "For one thing, the strengthening of mutual trust and cooperation between the two countries of major significance, already bound by more than three decades of tested friendship, is an important event by any international standards. This is precisely the basic achievement of the Prime Minister's trip, the first foreign tour undertaken by him after assumption of office."[84] Rajiv

---

83   Asian Recorder, Supra No.19, p-18373.
84   Mainstream, 23(4), June 1, 1985.

Gandhi's visit provided a good deal of understanding between the two countries and established an excellent personal rapport with Soviet Union leader Gorbachev. The visit significantly helped to maintain friendly relations and further the cause of cooperation with the Soviet Union. Indeed, the visit also strengthened the Indo-Soviet friendship and laid out long-term plans for all-round cooperation. In addition, India and the Soviet Union expressed similar viewpoints during the release of the joint statement on international concerns. However, this demonstrated how these two countries have evolved the concept of mutual understanding and cooperation since pre-independence.

Mikhail Gorbachev's Visit to India: November 1986.

In response to Rajiv Gandhi's visit to Moscow, Mikhail Gorbachev, then General Secretary of the Soviet Communist Party, paid a four-day official visit to India on November 25, 1986, boosting Indo-Soviet relations significantly. The visit also resulted in both countries reaffirming their commitment to the Indo-Soviet Special Friendship Treaty of Peace and Cooperation. Further, Rajiv Gandhi and Gorbachev explored the broad contours of future cooperation from a long-term perspective. The two leaders signed several important bilateral agreements. "The agreement on economic, scientific, and technical cooperation encompasses the Tehri hydroelectric complex, the modernization of the Bokaro steel plant, the setting up of new coking coal mines, and oil exploration in West Bengal. One important element of this agreement was the provision of local cost financing by the Soviet Union."[85]

The economic, commercial, and cultural agreements reflect the growing strength and dynamism of Indo-Soviet relations. The increased cooperation between the two countries under Rajiv

---

85   Rajiv Gandhi, Selected Speeches and Writings, (Vol-II), Supra No.63, p-337.

Gandhi's dynamic leadership was considered a watershed moment in Indo-Soviet ties. On the economic and technical collaboration, Rajiv Gandhi said at the joint conference with Gorbachev, "We have also decided to give a qualitative thrust to our science and technology cooperation. We shall perhaps take a totally new approach in this sphere, doing joint research projects in fresh technology areas together and then moving from that stage to the production stage of these technologies."[86] Further, Rajiv Gandhi described the new arrangement as the "largest economic agreement" ever signed between the two countries. He further said, "There are two new elements in this economic agreement: the local cost financing and the turn-key approach. We have also agreed to increase our trade by about two and a half times by 1992."[87]

After Gorbachev's visit, the two sides issued a joint statement in which they expressed their profound satisfaction with the relations of close friendship and wide-ranging cooperation characterized by mutual respect, warmth, and trust between the peoples and leaders of the two countries". The visit was regarded as a new milestone in the advancement of friendship and successful collaboration between the Soviet Union and India and described the relations as a "model of peaceful coexistence" based on the principles of equality, mutual respect, and non-interference in each other's internal affairs. No doubt, Gorbachev's visit further strengthened the mutual trust between the leaders and the ties of close friendship between the people of the two countries.

Later, Rajiv Gandhi's visit to Moscow in July 1987 to inaugurate the Festival of India further boosted Indo-Soviet relations and the bond of friendship. On July 3, 1987, Gorbachev and Rajiv Gandhi signed

---

86   V.P.Dutt, India and the World, Sanchar Publishing House, New Delhi, 1990, p-89.
87   Quoted in Hemen Ray, Supra No.65, p-196.

a comprehensive long-term scientific and technological cooperation agreement between the Soviet Union and India. "Similarly, in November 1987, the Festival of the USSR opened in India. In a message, Gorbachev said that the festival of the USSR in India and the Indian festival in the Soviet Union were "landmarks in the history of our two countries. They embody the joint response of our two great nations to epoch-making dates: the 40th anniversary of independent India... They graphically prove that our lasting traditional friendly contacts have entered a new stage."[88] During Rajiv Gandhi's tenure, Indo-Soviet relations went far beyond the bounds of official governmental ties," ushering a new era of mutual trust and cooperation. Gorbachev praised Rajiv Gandhi's leadership in strengthening Indo-Soviet relations and stated that India would continue to play a significant role in global politics.

b) The Delhi Declaration:

India, the world's champion of peace, has always advocated for non-violence and peaceful co-existence. Mahatma Gandhi, the founding father of India, led the struggle for disarmament and peace in the world. Jawaharlal Nehru, Indira Gandhi, and Rajiv Gandhi joined the bandwagon of Mahatma Gandhi's peace movement later on. However, Rajiv Gandhi played a predominant role in establishing world peace by persuading the leaders of the two superpowers, resulting in the reduction of nuclear weapons. Furthermore, due to Rajiv Gandhi's efforts, the Soviet Union President also joined hands with India to achieve world peace despite superpower hostility and egoism. Gorbachev's visit to India was undoubtedly a historic event in many aspects, apart from peace and disarmament. His visit introduced new philosophical concepts in the identity of views on

---

88   Hemen Ray, Supra No.65, p-202.

world peace and disarmament. Gorbachev happened to be the first Soviet President who accepted Mahatma Gandhi's philosophy of non-violence as constituting a code of conduct among various nations across the globe. During the meeting, both leaders resolved to work towards establishing global peace. Accordingly, on November 27, 1986, the two leaders signed the historic document for a non-violent and nuclear-free world, popularly known as the "Delhi Declaration." Rajiv Gandhi, in his statement to the Parliament at the end of the Soviet leader's visit and after the joint statement, said, "Moscow had joined India in a common vision of a nuclear-weapon-free and non-violent world" and that "the ideals of Gandhiji and Lenin have found expression in the New Delhi Declaration. The Declaration, he said, "is a vitally important initiative." It sets forth principles that must find universal acceptance if there is to be a peaceful future. The Declaration is being circulated as an official document by the United Nations. We commend the declaration to the world community for acceptance."[89]

As part of the Delhi Declaration, the two leaders agreed that the UN convention should be concluded immediately as an important concrete step towards complete nuclear disarmament. The "Delhi Declaration," aimed at the destruction of nuclear weapons and the establishment of a non-violent world, "called for the barring of all weapons from outer space, which was described as the common heritage of all humankind, the banning of all nuclear tests, prohibition of the development of new types of weapons of mass destruction, banning of chemical weapons, and the destruction of their stockpiles. It also called for the reduction of conventional weapons and armed forces."[90]

---

89   V.P.Dutt, India and the World, Sanchar Publishing House, New Delhi, 1990, p-89.
90   Asian Recorder, 32(52), December 24-31 1986, p-192370

The text of the **"Delhi Declaration"** is as below,

"Today, humanity stands at a crucial turning point in history. Nuclear weapons threaten to annihilate not only all that man has created through the ages, but also man himself and even life on earth. In the nuclear age, humanity must evolve new political thinking, a new concept of the world that would provide credible guarantees for humanity's survival. People want to live in a safer and more just world. Humanity deserves a better fate than being a hostage to nuclear terror and despair. It is necessary to change the existing world situation and to build a nuclear-weapon-free world, free of violence and hatred, fear, and suspicion."[91]

At the final phase of discussion, the two leaders issued a joint statement and supplemented it with a 10 point declaration, which was popularly known as the "New Delhi Declaration".

The two leaders set forth the following principles for building a nuclear-weapon -free and non-violent world.

1. Peaceful coexistence must become the universal norm of international relations.
2. Human life must be recognized as supreme.
3. Non-violence should be the basis of community life.
4. Understanding and trust must replace fear and suspicion.
5. The right of every state to political and economic independence must be recognised and respected.
6. Resources being spent on armaments must be channelled towards social and economic development.
7. Conditions must be guaranteed for the individual's harmonious development.

---

91   Foreign Affairs Reports, 37 (3&4), March-April, 1988, p-91.

8. Mankind's material and intellectual potential must be used to solve global problems.

9. The "Balance of Terror" must give way to comprehensive international security.

10. A nuclear-weapon free and non-violent world requires specific and immediate action for disarmament: it can be achieved through agreements on.

   a. Complete destruction of nuclear arsenals before the end of this century;

   b. Barring of all weapons from outer space, which is the common heritage of Mankind;

   c. Banning of all nuclear weapons tests;

   d. Prohibition of the development of new types of weapons of mass destruction;

   e. Banning of chemical weapons and destruction of their stockpiles;

   f. Reducing the levels of conventional arms and armed forces."[92]

The ten-point "New Delhi Declaration", indeed, constitutes a charter for the transformation of outlook and relations among nations. Gorbachev, taking into consideration the repercussions of the nuclear holocaust, said, "The survival of mankind must be placed above all interests, and the security of any one state is inconceivable without security for all."[93]

The "Delhi Declaration," signed by Rajiv Gandhi and Mikhail Gorbachev, made a significant contribution to the world's largest peace movement, led by India, and was also seen as a turning point in the history of the nuclear era. In this regard, Rajiv Gandhi's leadership

---

92 Rajiv Gandhi Selected Speeches and Writings (Vol-II), Supra No.63, pp-333, 334.

93 S.C.Parasher, Supra No.64, p-457.

that heralded the peace movement succeeded in impressing Gorbachev to join hands with India, which ventured into the riddance of nuclear weapons from the world. Even Ronald Reagan, impressed by the Delhi Declaration's call, responded positively to the cause of establishing a nuclear-free world. As a result, it was in 1987 that both Gorbachev and Ronald Reagan reached an agreement in Geneva that culminated in the signing of the INF Treaty. According to the Treaty, both leaders agreed to eliminate intermediate-range and short-range missiles, not to have systems, and to carry out the other obligations outlined in the Treaty. A considerable part of the credit goes to Rajiv Gandhi for bringing the two superpower leaders together to agree on the INF treaty aimed at the mass destruction of nuclear weapons, thereby saving the world from a nuclear holocaust. Because of Rajiv Gandhi's dynamic leadership, the world can see the era of peace and security today.

c) India's Position on the Politics of Superpowers Regarding the Afghan Crisis:

The Afghan crisis, which became a bone of contention between the US and the Soviet Union in the 1980s, created a schism in Indo-US relations. The Soviet Union's entry into Afghanistan not only created a volatile atmosphere in the South Asian region but also infuriated the United States. Therefore, from 1980, the relations between the superpowers started drifting. In the given context, India had to face a peculiar situation because it was making efforts to normalize its relations with the US while at the same time trying to strengthen its bond of friendship with the Soviet Union, a strategic partner. India was uneasy in the South Asian region because of the US supplied Pakistan with massive arms and ammunition, which posed a threat to India.

India, which maintained good and friendly relations with the Soviet Union since its independence days, had faced an embarrassing situation due to the Soviet Union's intervention in Afghanistan in December 1979. Further, the Soviet Union's intervention in Afghanistan not only changed the whole scenario in the South Asian region but also made the whole world turn its eyes towards India, the leader of the non-aligned countries, for its stance on the Soviet action. Before this, most non-aligned countries, not to mention Washington and Beijing, expressed sharp opposition to the Soviet move. Indira Gandhi, who made a surprise comeback in the midterm elections in January 1980, made India's stand clear that,

1. The Soviets acted on the request of the government existing in Afghanistan prior to the big airlifts;
2. The government of India trusted the Soviet assurance that the troops would be withdrawn as soon as Afghanistan requested it;
3. India perceived more danger to its own security in the concerted Cold War type responses of the United States and china to the Soviet action;
4. Any Sino-American move to arm Pakistan and destabilize the region would compel India to renew its strategic collaboration with the USSR, and
5. By abstaining from voting in the UN General Assembly, India kept some distance from Moscow in order to be able to work patiently – unilaterally or in conjunction with other nations - to ensure at least a sizable and early Soviet withdrawal from Afghanistan."[94]

---

94   Partha S.Ghosh and Rajaram Panda, Domestic Support for Mrs. Indira Gandhi's Afghan Policy: The Soviet Factor in Indian Politics, Asian Survey 33 (3) March, 1983, p-262.

However, the USA did not like India's criticism of the Soviet Union's intervention or its soft corner towards condemning the Soviet Union's action in Afghanistan. Naturally, this put India in a dilemma when the international community was condemning Soviet intervention in Afghanistan, and the US was insisting on the withdrawal of Soviet forces. As a result, the Afghan issue started taking a different shape during the tenure of Indira Gandhi. Therefore, Indira Gandhi adopted a wait-and-watch approach to the Afghan crisis in light of the Soviet Union's friendship.

However, during Rajiv Gandhi's tenure, the situation in Afghanistan became one of the most contentious topics in international forums and organizations. Because of the rivalry between the US and the USSR, the Afghanistan issue became internationalized, and it reached its climax when India was sincerely attempting to normalize its relations with the US. The main objective behind the internal strife between the US and the USSR was that one of the superpowers, America, did not like the USSR's entry into Afghanistan. At this juncture, Rajiv Gandhi also assumed the Chairmanship of the Non-Aligned Movement. Given Rajiv Gandhi's position as Chairman of the NAM, the US started questioning his stance on the Afghanistan crisis. However, Rajiv Gandhi, during his visit to the Soviet Union in May 1985, remarked in response to a question that the subject of Afghanistan did come up in his discussions with Gorbachev, and India had put across its point of view. "Our position on Afghanistan is very clear. We are not for any country interfering or intervening in the internal affairs of another country."[95]

Perhaps it was during the tenure of Rajiv Gandhi that India had to face a similar situation, which existed during Indira Gandhi's period. Due to the ideological rivalry between the US and the USSR, India had to face a peculiar situation. On the one hand, India was seeking the

---

95   Asian Recorder, 31(25) June 18-24, 1985, p-18371.

transfer of Western technology for its development, whilst, on the other, India could not forcefully denounce the Soviet Union's intervention in Afghanistan, as it had been its traditional friend and strategic partner since independence. Therefore, the Afghanistan issue became a cause of concern for India when the US started criticizing the Soviet Union's intervention in Afghanistan and its support for the puppet government in Kabul. Since both superpowers locked horns over the issue, the Afghanistan issue has not only been internationalized but also blown out of proportion. However, Rajiv Gandhi, as the leader of the NAM, decided to ease the Afghanistan crisis, bringing the warring factions to the negotiating table to reach some agreement on the issue.

As a result, Rajiv Gandhi visited the USSR and the US in May and June 1985, respectively, and had the opportunity to discuss the Afghan crisis and nuclear issue with both leaders, urging them to reach an amicable solution at the earliest. Rajiv Gandhi eventually undertook a mediating role in resolving the Afghan crisis by encouraging a negotiated settlement among the warring sections. Against the backdrop of Rajiv Gandhi's visit, Gorbachev and Ronald Reagan first met in Geneva in November 1985 and resolved to end the stalemate in the Afghan issue. Though the meeting between the two leaders eased the tensions somewhat, no substantive progress was accomplished.

However, things began to change in the international arena soon after the signing of the Delhi Declaration in November 1986. Following the declaration, Gorbachev and Ronald Reagan met in Geneva in 1987 and reached an agreement on the Afghan issue, popularly known as the Geneva Agreement. As part of the agreement, "half of the limited Soviet military contingent has been withdrawn from Afghanistan."[96] Further, it was in March 1989 that the Soviet Union completely

---

96   Grigory Bondarevsky, Two Years of the Delhi declaration:Some Reflections, Mainstream, 37 (8), November 19, 1988, p-31

withdrew its remaining military contingent from Afghanistan. Naturally, this contributed to the establishment of permanent peace in South Asia. Indeed, the Geneva agreement was considered a stepping stone in resolving the Afghan crisis. Bringing about a comprehensive settlement between the two superpowers was high on the agenda of Rajiv Gandhi's policy. Therefore, the predominant role played by Rajiv Gandhi in ending the Cold War between the two superpowers over the Afghan crisis was a significant achievement in the history of the international community. Rajiv Gandhi was widely considered a global statesman capable of instilling confidence and trust in the Soviet Union and the United States.

CHAPTER – V

Rajiv Gandhi and Indo–Sri Lankan Relations

As one of the most dominant countries in South Asia, India holds a strategic position in the region. Because of its military power and strategic location, it has been surrounded by big and small countries and has become a helping hand to most of its neighbours. In fact, this has considerably helped India play a significant role in South Asia, apart from China. Above all, India, which imbibed Mahatma Gandhi's ideas of peace, nonviolence, and brotherhood, not only established friendly relations with its neighbours but also developed the concept of peaceful co-existence among countries across the globe. Furthermore, Mahatma Gandhi's views influenced the neighbouring countries to a large extent in developing bilateral ties with India.

But for one reason or another, relations with certain neighbouring countries like China and Pakistan deteriorated, even if India intended to forge amicable and friendly relations with them. As a result, these immediate neighbours threatened the security and integrity of India. Apart from this, there are also countries, like Sri Lanka, Bangladesh, and others, whose relations started souring in the nineties. Since independence, efforts have been made to forge friendly ties between India and its immediate neighbours. However, it was under the dynamic leadership of Rajiv Gandhi that India determined to open a new chapter of peace, harmony, and good neighbourliness in so far as South Asia is concerned. While making a statement on foreign policy matters soon after assuming the office, Rajiv Gandhi aptly said, "Special attention would be given to strengthening ties with our immediate neighbours in South Asia, with whom we have deep historical and cultural links."[1]

A Brief History of Indo-Sri Lankan Relations:

Sri Lanka, a tiny island spread in the Indian Ocean, is India's immediate neighbour, with long-shared cultural and historical relations. The historical ties between the countries can be traced back to the great epic Ramayana. Among the South Asian countries, Sri Lanka has also been one of the members of the SAARC Association since its inception. Though Sri Lanka is our immediate neighbour, it has no land links with India but has had historical relations with India since ancient times. Sri Lanka (formerly Ceylon) is the island that the heroic Rama subdued after his righteous war against Ravana, a king of Lanka. It is the place where Rama liberated Sita from the clutches of Ravana. Further, several missions have also been sent to Sri Lanka from Indian shores. During the reign of the king, great Ashoka of the Mourya Empire sent his daughter Sangmitre and son Mahendra on a mission to spread Buddhism in Sri Lanka. Therefore, for centuries, there have been friendly relations between the two countries.

The relations between India and Sri Lanka since pre-independence were very cordial. But it was the British who, "in order to entrench their designs of commercial exploitation through a plantation economy, introduced a cheap labour force to recruit the Tamils from India into the Kandy area and thereabouts."[2] As a result, a large number of Indian Tamils migrated to Ceylon in the middle of the 19th century, which caused discontentment among the people of Kandyan land. In the meantime, the leaders of the Ceylonese-political and trade union movements began to express concern over

---

1   Asian Recorder, 31 (5), Jan 29-Feb 4, 1985, p-18155.

2   Seminar, No.337, September 1987, p-16.

the effects of free immigration from India. This depression worsened the employment situation on the island, and inescapably, curbs on Tamils free immigration became unavoidable. The Tamil workers, who have been the mainstay of the economy of Sri Lanka for years, were mainly responsible for the country's economic growth. But these workers were subjected to low pay, ill-treatment etc. The Tamils, who constitute nearly one million, have been in Sri Lanka for more than a generation. They have maintained their traditional cultural links with India and have maintained Tamil as their mother tongue without mixing with the local Sinhalese. This separate identity of the Tamils irritated the Sinhalese, who regarded Tamils as people unwilling to join the national mainstream and desirous of securing Sri Lanka's dismemberment. Besides, Sri Lankan Sinhalese did not like the Tamils' tendency to achieve their objectives.

The Tamil plantation labourers who migrated to Sri Lanka dominated the north-eastern part of the Jaffna peninsula. These two provinces of Sri Lanka became highly populated by Tamils. Historically, the conflict between Sinhalese and Tamils was political rather than racial. Firstly, the problem has arisen because the Tamils in Sri Lanka, who had a common heritage, a culture, and a language, have been denied their rights as equal citizens with the rest of the Sinhalese population.

The minorities in Sri Lanka, particularly the Tamils, have been made to feel for too long that they are a part of the country, and this process has been gradually expanded ever since Ceylon was granted independence in February 1948. Taking into consideration the conditions of the Tamils, "the first Prime Minister, D.S.Senanayake, had then appealed to the Tamils to accept the new soul-bury constitution and declared on behalf of the Sinhalese that "I give the minority communities the sincere assurance that no harm need you fear at our hand in Sri Lanka."[3] But the assurance of the Sri Lankan Prime Minister did not last long, and soon things began to change and take a different shape.

To begin with, the Tamil plantation labourers were deprived of citizenship in 1948 and then disenfranchised in 1949 by the Sri Lankan government soon after it assumed power. Apart from this, regulations were enforced wherein proof of citizenship was made mandatory for the issue of travel documents, for obtaining licences, for taking part in business or any other meaningful activity, and for employment in the public and private sectors. These harsh measures imposed by the Sri Lankan government were clearly in violation of the Universal Declaration on Human Rights, which provides that "everyone has a right to a nationality. No one shall be arbitrarily deprived of his nationality, or denied the right to change his nationality.[4]

The Nehru -John Kotelawala Pact: 1953

The citizenship issue became complex during the premiership of Nehru and John Kotelawala later on, which culminated in an ethnic problem. Therefore, to find a lasting solution to the ethnic issue an agreement was signed in 1953 by the two prime ministers. The main features of the agreement were as follows.

1. The Sri Lankan government would register the names of all those people of Indian origin who desired to stay permanently in Sri Lanka.
2. Those who did not wish to become citizens of Sri Lanka would be sent back to India.
3. Illegal migration from India to Sri Lanka was to be effectively checked.

---

3   The Hindu, 2, September 1988.
4   Ibid.

4. Sri Lanka was to quickly dispose of the applications for citizenship that had been pending for two years or more.

5. A separate electoral register was to be maintained for people of Indian origin to enable them to elect their representatives proportionately.

6. Those persons of Indian origin who desired but could not be granted Lankan citizenship, would be allowed to stay on as aliens.[5]

However, the Sri Lankan government did not implement the Nehru-Kotelawala Agreement sincerely. As a result, many people of Indian heritage could not get Sri Lankan citizenship as enshrined in the agreement. Therefore, the people who lost their citizenship became "stateless persons". This naturally aggravated the already tense situation, and then relations between India and Sri Lanka worsened further over the ethnic issue. Annoyed over the non-implementation of the agreement, the stateless persons indulged in large-scale violence and disturbances, for which Sri Lanka blamed India.

The Official Language Act: 1956

During the tenure of then Prime Minister Dudley S. Senanayake, the Tamils were assured justice. However, discrimination against Tamils allegedly began soon after Senanayake's death. The succeeding government abandoned the two-language system used by the United National Party during Senanayake's tenure. The conflict between the majority Sinhalese community and the Tamil minority began in 1956, when the Sri Lankan Freedom Party (SLFP) government headed by S.W.R.D. Bandarnaike passed the Official Language Act in 1956, which declared, "The Sinhala language would be the only official language

---

5   V.N.Khanna., Foreign Policy of India, Vikas Publishing House, New Delhi, 1997, p-168.

of Sri Lanka."[6] In one stroke, it deprived Tamils of their language in official transactions and dealt a severe blow to their employment in government services and public bodies.

Tamils, who constituted a majority in the North-Eastern Provinces, instantly opposed this. Since they were already suffering from a minority complex (despite being the majority in North-eastern Province) with many political and economic disabilities and inequalities, they saw a danger in the language decision, which wanted to keep the Tamils out of the national mainstream and deprive them of the economic benefits of post-colonial economic development. Therefore, the Tamils strongly protested against the move and also took the opportunity to press their demand for autonomy in the Northeastern Province, where they constituted the majority. These events catalyzed the outbreak of ethnic violence in Sri Lanka, which later erupted with varying intensity in 1958, 1961, 1971, 1983, and most recently in 1987.

Subsequently, in 1957, the government led by Bandaranaike signed an agreement with federal party leader S.J.V. Chelvanayakam to reconcile the Tamils. Under this agreement, Tamil was recognized as the official language of the minority. But unfortunately, Bandaranaike backed out of the agreement due to Sinhala nationalist pressure. To soothe the Tamil feeling, the government enacted the Tamil Language (Special Provision) Act in 1958, but in 1960, the government declared that Sinhala would be the only official language as envisaged in the only Act of Sinhala 1956.[7] This indifferent attitude of the Sri Lankan government made the Tamils unhappy and paved the way for further discrimination.

---

6   Foreign Affairs Reports, 36 (7-10) July-October, 1987, p-125.

7   W.Howard Wrigging, Ceylon: Dilemmas of New Nations, Princeton University Press, Princeton, 1960, pp-393-394.

The Shastri-Sirimavo Pact of 1964:

In order to find a lasting solution for the stateless people of Sri Lanka, both Shastri and Sirimavo Bandaranaike signed an agreement on the vexation issue during the latter's visit to New Delhi in October 1964. "According to the agreement, out of 9.75 lakh persons, Ceylon would accept 3 lakh as Ceylonese citizens, and India would accept 5.25 lakh persons. The status and future of the remaining 1.50-lakh people would be the subject matter of a separate agreement between the two governments. It was also agreed that the admission to Ceylonese citizenship should be spread over a period of 15 years and that the two processes should keep pace with each other."[8] This created a permanent barrier between the two ethnic groups, i.e., Tamils and the Sinhalese, towards an amicable relationship.

The Indira Gandhi-Sirimavo Pact of 1974:

The Indira Gandhi–Sirimavo Pact was signed on January 24, 1974, to further the agreement of 1964. In the earlier 1964 Pact, which did not take up the issue of 1,50,000 stateless persons, the matter was taken up by the two, taking the respective quota shares of the two countries to 6,00,000 and 3,75,000."[9] Nevertheless, the notable feature was that the 1974 Pact was not implemented, as the 1964 (Shastri-Sirimavo Pact) was extended up to October 1981. Therefore, the non-starting of the Indira Gandhi-Sirimavo Pact (1974) resulted in the accumulation of a large number of applicants for both Indian and Sri Lankan citizenship. "As per the quota prescribed for India and Sri Lanka under the 1964 and 1974 Agreements, the number of people still to be granted citizenship by the former raised around 2.26 lakh, while the

---

8   Quoted in Shri Ram Sharma "Lal Bahadur Shastri: An Era of Transition in Indian Foreign Policy, Kanishka Publishers, New Delhi, 2001, p-28

9   P.A.Ghosh., Ethnic Conflict in Sri Lanka and Role of Indian Peace Keeping Force, APH Publishers, New Delhi, 1999, pp-65-66.

latter was to absorb a total of 2.12 lakh people. After the inclusion of 75,000 persons in India's quota, it still had a shortfall of around 94,000 persons to fulfil its commitment. In the case of Sri Lanka, the surplus of applications remained substantial."[10]

In 1978, President Jayewardene initiated his efforts to find a solution to the problem of stateless persons. On October 30, 1981, the 1964 agreement was extended until September 1987. By September 1987, all 9,75,000 people who identified as stateless under the 1962 Pact were to be conferred either Indian or Sri Lankan citizenship to solve the problem to some extent.

The Ethnic Crisis during Indira Gandhi's Period:

Indira Gandhi's return to power in 1980 was one of the significant as far as the ethnic conflict in Sri Lanka was concerned. From August 1982-to May 1983, she played a crucial role as mediator in easing ethnic tension through her good offices. However, "it was during July 1983; the worst ever riots broke out between the Sri Lankan security forces and the Tamil militants. It was during this time that attacks were carried out on lives and property, including businesses and industrial establishments. Regarding the 1983 riots, it was suspected that those within the government perpetuated the violence. The large-scale violence was in reply to the government's attempts to accommodate the moderate Tamil leadership by the Tamil Chauvinists.[11]

The most important and immediate provocation for the 1983 riots was the killing of Sri Lankan soldiers by Tamil militants. This resulted in an intense fight between the Tamil militants and the Sri Lankan army, resulting in heavy casualties from both sides and damage to

---

10 P.Sahadevan, *India and Overseas Indians: The Case of Sri Lanka*, Kalinga Publishers, New Delhi, 1995, p-210.

11 M.S Kodandswami, "Sri Lankan Crisis", Authors Press, New Delhi, 2000, pp-92-93.

hundreds of buildings and factories. Some 300-500 prisoners broke out of the high security Wellikada prison and killed nearly 35 Tamils. As a result of these riots, 400 Tamils died and nearly 1,75, 000 were rendered homeless."[12] However, the July 1983 riots badly shaken the political authority of Jayewardene and also exposed the flaws in the administrative system that had been built up under Jayewardene. His image suffered a lot, both locally and internationally. Commenting on the ethnic issue in Sri Lanka Indira Gandhi, then Prime Minister, said, "The loss of property of Tamil speaking people there and of stateless persons and those of Indian origin have sent a wave of anguish not only in Tamil Nadu alone but all over the country."[13] Indira Gandhi reiterated that a political solution would be the only way to resolve ethnic conflict in Sri Lanka. By the 1983 riots, Sri Lanka had also realized that a military solution would be ineffective in suppressing the Tamil militancy.

In the wake of the ethnic violence of July 1983, about 30,000 refugees had entered India from Sri Lanka. Despite grave provocation by the Sri Lankan Prime Minister, New Delhi reaffirmed its desire for peace and its opposition to secession by any group and to all forms of situational violence. In fact, the total mishandling of the ethnic situation by the government of Sri Lanka had taken the island to the brink of a civil war.[14]

After the 1983 riots, the Tamil militants reaffirmed their demand for autonomy and a separate "homeland" comprised of the northern Jaffna peninsula and the eastern district of Batticaloa. However, the Sri Lankan government was reluctant to go beyond the existing

---

12　M.S.Kodandswami, Supra No.9, pp-92-93.

13　P.G.Salvi., India in World Affairs, B.R.Publishing Corporation, New Delhi, 1985, p-57.

14　Quoted in Shipra Mehra, Indo-Sri Lankan Relations 1947 to Present Day, M.G.Publishers, Agra, 1995, p-109.

D.D.C's (District Development Councils), which had little power and meagre funds and were ignored by the local officials. This naturally made the Tamils express resentment at the workings of D.D.Cs. accordingly, in June 1984; President Jayewardene came out with his own formula to solve Tamils' problems. He wanted the TULF to renounce its demand for a separate state. He further assured them that power would be devolved to the Zonal Council, which would be constituted by the merger of the DDC into the Provincial Council. His scheme will be subject to approval by referendum on the entire island. He also wanted Trincomalee to be administered by the central government."[15] However, Jayewardene's new proposals failed to sway the Tamil militants, and the Tamil militants, who refused to discuss anything less than a separate "homeland", rejected them.

Therefore, from 1983 onwards, the Tamils, apart from the issues of citizenship, language, etc., decided to focus more on their demand for a separate "homeland", i.e., Tamil Eelam, comprising the northern and eastern parts of Sri Lanka's Jaffna Peninsula, which were primarily dominated by a significant Tamil population.

Ethnic Crisis during Rajiv Gandhi's Period:

As we have already discussed, Rajiv Gandhi had to deal with several internal as well as external issues while serving as head of the nation. Soon after the assassination of Indira Gandhi, Rajiv Gandhi assumed the office of Prime Minister of India. During his broadcast to the nation after assuming office, he said, "We have inherited a well-tested and consistent foreign policy which serves our national interest. We have always believed in working for peace. Our policy is to be friends with

---

15   Quoted in Ravikant Dubey, Indo-Sri Lankan Relations: With Reference to the Tamil Problem, (second edition), Deep and Deep Publications, New Delhi, 1993, p-95.

all countries on the basis of reciprocity and mutual benefits."[16] Rajiv Gandhi emphasized the need for an immediate solution to the complex Sri Lankan ethnic problem that has become a bone of contention in Indo-Sri Lankan relations. As a result, Rajiv Gandhi appointed Romesh Bhandari as the Prime Minister's special envoy to deal with the crisis and to find a long-term solution.

Therefore, Rajiv Gandhi's first and foremost priority during his tenure was the Tamil stateless issue. In order to find a lasting solution to the issue of stateless persons, India, under the leadership of Rajiv Gandhi, reached an agreement with the Sri Lankan government in January 1985. According to the understanding reached in Colombo, India agreed to go ahead with the process of conferring Indian citizenship on all those who had sought it prior to October 30, 1981.[17]

Following the talks between the then Indian high commissioner to Colombo, J.N.Dixit, Lalith Athulatmudali, and S. Thondaman, and as a continuation of the 1985 understanding, another agreement was reached in January 1986. As per the 1986 settlement, Sri Lanka agreed to confer its citizenship on an additional 94,000 stateless persons. India, on its part, gave an undertaking to grant citizenship to all the 5.06 Lakh persons who had applied until October 30, 1981. The figures were also to take care of the natural increase.[18] Further, 94,000 stateless people were the result of "the breach of the 1964 and 1974 agreements". As part of the settlement India had already granted citizenship to 4, 21,207 persons. It therefore had to absorb the balance of only 84,793 to make a total of 5.06 lakh. As regards Sri Lanka, it agreed to absorb all the 4.69-lakh persons within 18 months. By 1986, only 1,97,535 persons had been conferred Sri Lankan citizenship,

16   India Quarterly, 41 (1), January-March 1985, p-51.
17   Asian Recorder, 32 (9), February-26 March-4, 1986, p-18771.
18   Quoted in P.Saghadevan, Supra No.10, p-219.

and the government was expected to absorb the remaining 2,71,465 persons by September 1987 in order to complete its commitment (i.e., 4.69 lakh)."[19]

However, Sri Lanka, which was supposed to fulfil its obligation of granting citizenship, began to hang around with the remaining stateless persons and took a dilatory approach to granting citizenship. Further, Sri Lanka deliberately linked the issue of residual stateless persons to the ethnic crisis on the island. As a result, Sri Lanka failed to adhere to the period set for granting citizenship to those stateless persons. Naturally, this made the Sri Lankan Tamils unhappy and provoked them to indulge in violence. Perhaps the stateless issue gained prominence during Rajiv Gandhi's tenure, along with the LTTE's demand for a separate, independent homeland, Tamil Eelam.

The denial of fundamental rights and the treatment of Tamil minorities in Sri Lanka as second-class citizens were the main reasons for ethnic strife during Rajiv Gandhi's tenure. The adamant attitude of the Sri Lankan government created an atmosphere of discontent and hostility in the minds of Tamils. It was also due to the ill-treatment meted out to the Tamils by the Singhalese that further widened the gap between the two groups. Therefore, the Tamils in Sri Lanka decided to fight for their rights and wanted to establish their separate homeland, mainly dominated by the Tamils. As a result, the Tamils joined Velupillai Prabhakaran's Liberation Tigers of Tamil Eelam in Sri Lanka to fight against injustice. Further, the LTTE began a campaign for a Tamil homeland in northern and eastern Sri Lanka, where most of the island's Tamils reside. When the LTTE became the saviour and sole representative of the Tamils in Sri Lanka, the Tamils heaved a sigh of relief.

---

19   (Ibid.,) Quoted in P.Sahadevan, Supra No.10, p-219.

The ethnic violence that erupted during the first half of 1987 was one of the bloodiest ever in the history of Sri Lanka. The main reason behind the violence was the minority Tamil's demand for an independent Eelam, which should be an autonomous body as an integral part of the federal state of Sri Lanka. However, the Sri Lankan government was reluctant to concede the Tamil's demand. Sri Lanka was under the impression that accepting the proposal of the Tamils might not only endanger its interests but also go against the interests of the Singhalese. This indifferent attitude of the Sri Lankan government towards the minority Tamils naturally aggravated the already tense situation.

During this critical juncture, the Tamils, who were the minority in Sri Lanka, wholeheartedly supported the LTTE, which was fighting for the cause of autonomy in the north-eastern part of the Jaffna peninsula as the sole representative of Tamils. The LTTE, led by V. Prabhakaran, received material and moral support from the Tamils of Sri Lanka and chose to wage a guerrilla war against the Sri Lankan government to protect their interests. Commenting on the role of the then Chief Minister of Tamil Nadu in the financial assistance received by the LTTE leader, Lalith Athulathmudali, the then National Security Minister of Sri Lanka said, "MGR (M.G.Ramachandran) was giving the money not for relief but directly to the LTTE. In the past, all his donations have been used to buy arms and ammunition. We thought this time the money would be used to buy sophisticated anti-aircraft missiles."[20]

The Thimpu Talks:

The Sri Lankan government refused to concede the LTTE's demand for autonomy in the North Eastern Province. As a result, the LTTE geared up its people with arms and ammunition and unleashed

---

20   Sunday, 14 (30), 14-20, June 1987, p-15.

widespread violence across the island to meet their legitimate demands. Killings and counter-killings continued unabatedly despite several appeals by the Sri Lankan government for a ceasefire. Even the Sri Lankan President, who had ongoing talks with Rajiv Gandhi at various levels to grant a reasonable measure of autonomy to the Tamil areas, failed to convince the Tamil militants. In June 1985, at the initiative of Rajiv Gandhi, "the leaders of the Tamil militant movements, which were engaged in an armed struggle for the establishment of a separate Tamil Eelam state in the north and east of the island of Sri Lanka, agreed to a 'cease-fire' as a preliminary step to creating a 'congenial' atmosphere for peace talks.[21] In response to Rajiv Gandhi's initiative, the Sri Lankan government decided to send a delegation led by H.W.Jayewardene, the younger brother of President J Jayewardene, to Thimpu for talks. "On June 18, 1985, a ceasefire was announced, and talks were held at Thimpu from July 8 to 13 between the Sri Lankan government and the Tamils represented by the TULF and the militants; LTTE, TELO (Tamil Eelam Liberation Organization), EPRLF (Eelam People's Revolutionary Liberation Front), EROS (Eelam Revolutionary Organization of Students), and PLOT (Peoples Liberation Organization of Tamil Eelam). However, the offer of the Sri Lankan government marked no substantial advance on the earlier proposals of 1984. They envisaged only District Councils and Provincial Councils with very modest legislatures and executive powers, and furthermore, they were to be totally dependent on the president."[22] However, these proposals were rejected by the Tamil militants, and talks were discontinued, following the massacre of more than 200 Tamils by the Sri Lankan armed forces.

21　www.tamilnation.org.intframe/india.

22　Quoted by A.M.Vohra, Indian Peace Keeping in Sri Lanka, in Satishkumar (Ed) Year Book on India's Foreign Policy 1989, Sage Publications, New Delhi, 1990, p-85.

The Thimpu talks, which had high hopes, failed to provide provincial autonomy to the Tamil areas of the Sri Lankan government's North-eastern Province. Even the efforts made by Indian diplomacy to bring the Sri Lankan government around to accept the legitimate demand for some form of provincial autonomy failed to yield the desired effects. Commenting on the Thimpu talks on July 16, 1985, Bandaranaike said that she had anticipated the results because, in her view, Jayewardene was not sincere about coming to terms with Tamils. She also emphasized the negative approach of Prime Minister Premadasa and National Security Minister Athulathmudali, which would affect the negotiation process as well as India's mediatory efforts."[23] The subsequent developments proved that she was correct in her assessment. Even India expressed its apprehension about the talks. The continued negative approach of the Sri Lankan government made the Tamil militants choose the path of violence to meet their legitimate demands.

The Second Thimpu Conference:

The talks during the first conference in Thimpu failed to arrive at a consensus on the proposals put forth by the Tamil groups to settle the ethnic issue. As a result, the second Thimpu talks were held on August 12, 1985, and H.Jayewardene led the Sri Lankan delegation. Before the talks, "the Tamil militants and the Tamil United Liberation Front (TULF) leaders forwarded four proposals as a framework for resolving the crisis, namely,

a.   recognition of the separate national identity of the Tamils,
b.   respect for the integrity of the traditional Tamil homeland,
c.   recognition of the right to self-determination of the Tamils,
d.   citizenship rights for all the Tamils living in Sri Lanka.[24]

---

23   J.N.Dixit, Assignment Colombo, Konark Publishers, New Delhi, 1998, p-32.
24   Radhika Coomarswamy, Ethnic Myths, Seminar, No.337, September 1987, p-27.

However, at the second Thimpu conference, Hector Jayewardene rejected the demands put forth by the Tamil militant groups and TULF and bluntly stated that the negotiation had taken place between the two governments and in the APC (All Party Conference) meeting, the government had already announced its intention to grant Sri Lankan citizenship to all stateless persons. "He said that implementation of any agreement reached at these talks requires, as a pre-condition, the pre-renunciation of all forms of militant action. All militant groups must surrender their arms and equipment. All training camps inside Sri Lanka and abroad must be closed. Refugees must be permitted to return unmolested to the area in which they reside. An amnesty for all violations of criminal law, pursuant to agitation and the militant group, will only be granted after the government is satisfied that their pre-conditions have been observed."[25]

The preconditions of H. Jayewardene were not in the interests of the Tamil militant groups and therefore decided not to accept them. While the negotiations were going on, reports came in that hundreds of Tamils had been brutally massacred in Vavuniya, in the north. As a result, the six Tamil militant organizations walked out in protest. The Tamil group also called off the ceasefire, which had been in force since June 18 after the Rajiv–Jayewardene summit talk. Since the beginning, the Tamils believed that the Sri Lankan government was indifferent to their demands, especially after the Thimpu talks.

Therefore, "the collapse of the Thimpu process and the failure of fresh attempts in New Delhi left India and Sri Lanka, as well as the Tamil groups, in a bitter mood. By March 1986, New Delhi began to wonder whether Jayewardene was keen on a political settlement at all. A full-scale civil war threatened the island."[26] Further, the continuing

---

25   Quoted in Ravikant Dubey, Supra No.15, p-105.
26   Quoted in Shipra Mehra, Supra No.14, p-122.

violence after the Thimpu talks was primarily due to the dilatory approach that the Sri Lankan government adopted in responding to the legitimate demands of the Tamils.

Sri Lanka, which wanted to solve the Tamil problem exclusively, depended on a military solution despite several appeals made to the Sri Lankan government by India for a political solution to resolve the ethnic issue that went unheeded. Even Rajiv Gandhi asked the Sri Lankan government to exercise restraint from military action and seek a peaceful settlement for the Tamil problem. However, even his appeal did not influence the Sri Lankan government. As a result, the government of India threatened to withdraw its good offices as a mediator in resolving the ethnic issue if Sri Lanka continued its military force. Accordingly, "then the Indian High Commissioner called on President Jayawardene and stated that India saw no point in continuing its peace efforts in the face of a military offensive."[27] Further, Romesh Bhandari Rajiv Gandhi's Special Envoy, commenting on the ethnic issue, said," The problem in Sri Lanka is not our problem, but we have got sucked into it". He also said, "India had offered her good offices for a political solution to the problem. Military interference would not help to solve the problem. "The Tamil movement cannot be crushed, and neither can the Tamils overthrow the government in Sri Lanka."[28]

The December 1986 Proposals:

After the failure of the Thimpu talks, there was no progress in the ethnic conflict between Sri Lankan Tamils. However, Jayewardene and Rajiv Gandhi discussed the ethnic conflict and reaffirmed their commitment to a political solution to the island's ethnic crisis when

---

27   Quoted in A.M.Vohra, Supra, No-22, p-85

28   Indian Express (New Delhi) 23 May 1986.

both attended the second SAARC Summit in Bangalore in November 1986. As a follow-up to the discussion between the two leaders at Bangalore, the then External Affairs Minister K.Natwar Singh and then Home and Public Grievances Minister P.Chidambaram initiated a new round of talks on the Indian side. These talks were devoted to bridging the differences in positions between the Sri Lankan government and Tamil militant leadership. Accordingly, "both Natwar Singh and Chidambaram visited Sri Lanka in 1986 to discuss a political solution along the lines of the "Eastern Province Trifurcation Proposals" of J.R.Jayewrdene. "India suggested that the predominantly Sinhala Amparai electorate be delinked from Eastern Province and attached to Uva Province. The proposals that emerged as a result of discussions with this Indian delegation (which left Sri Lanka on December 19, 1986) came to be known as the "December 19th Proposals."[29] (Also sometimes, as Chidambaram proposals).

In short, these proposals sought to grant the Tamils a significant part of their demand, namely, the continuation of the Northern and Eastern Provinces in a unified form, excluding the Sinhala-dominated Amparai District of the Eastern Province. Therefore, it was an attempt to create a Tamil homeland under another name. Rajiv Gandhi welcomed the finalization of the "December 19 proposals" in Colombo by Natwar Singh and Chidambaram. He planned to use it as a basis for further talks with TULF, LTTE, and other Tamil groups.

However, the Sri Lankan government did not implement these proposals due to the Singhalese's insistence on a military solution to the ethnic conflict. Therefore, the Sri Lankan government had not only gone back on the formula it agreed with the two Indian Ministers, K.Natwarsing and P.Chidambaram, but had rejected the mediating

---

29   www.tamilnation.org/intframe/india

services of India and moved towards a clear military solution. The initiative failed "largely due to President Jayewardene's failure to use either his forceful personality or his towering parliamentary majority to assert himself at such a critical moment in his country's history. At this point of time, Sri Lanka was ready for and required statesmanship of the highest order."[30]

As a result, India's initiative to reconcile the interests of Sinhalese and Tamil communities by elaborating a political formula to meet the legitimate aspirations of the Tamils for one form of autonomy or another within the framework of a united and territorially integrated Sri Lanka failed. It was due to Sri Lanka's move towards a military solution to the ethnic conflict. Given this, the government of India threatened to withdraw its good offices in resolving ethnic problems if the Sri Lankan government continued with its military offensive. However, the Indian government's threat did not bear fruit, as the Sri Lankan government was firm and unwilling to budge on its stance on the military solution to the Tamil ethnic crisis.

But Jayewardene, commenting on the ethnic issue in January 1987, said, "I shall have a military solution to what I believe is a military problem, and that now I have more weapons and countries like Pakistan are training my men."[31] The tough stand of J.Jayawardene on the military solution to the ethnic problem resulted in large-scale violence in the Jaffna peninsula, where a majority of Tamils under the banner of the LTTE renewed their struggle against the Sri Lankan government. However, the determined Tamil resistance, the continued bloodletting in the fratricidal conflict, and the pressure from India compelled Sri Lanka to enter political negotiations.

---

30   N.N.Jha, India – Sri Lanka Relations, India Quarterly, 50(2), January-June, 1994, p-56.
31   Sunday, 14, (6), 28 December 1986 & 3rd January 1987, p-25.

The Economic Blockade:

The talks between India and Sri Lanka over the ethnic issue stalled and were put on hold. As a result, the Tamil militant groups saw no breakthrough in their legitimate demand for Tamil Eelam and lost faith in the Sri Lankan government. Disgusted by the failure of a series of talks the Tamils had with the Sri Lankan government regarding the autonomy issue, they vowed to continue their violent struggle to meet their legitimate demand. The fight ensued between Tamil militants and Sri Lankan security forces. When the violence erupted and spiralled out of control, the Sri Lankan government, intent on a military solution to the ethnic problem, asked the LTTE to declare a ceasefire. "When there was no sign of ceasefire from the LTTE cadre, the Sri-Lankan government decided to end the violence in the Jaffna peninsula through a military offensive. Sri Lanka, which continued with a policy of crushing the Tamils through military force, made all possible efforts to impose an "economic blockade" on the north-eastern part of Sri Lanka. The Sri Lankan government imposed an economic blockade on the Jaffna peninsula in January 1987."[32]

As the first step of the blockade, the Sri Lankan government cut off all communication with the north-eastern province of the island. Food grains, oil, and other essential commodities were barred from entering the province. The Tamils struggled to procure necessities and suffered greatly from the shortage of food, medicine, oil, etc. As a result, Rajiv Gandhi expressed grave concern about the Sri Lankan government's economic blockade of the northern Jaffna Peninsula, where the Tamil community is in the majority. The Indian government asked J.N.Dixit to convey its concern to the Sri Lankan President in light of the inhuman acts of the Sri Lankan government and after learning about the miserable conditions of the Tamils. "Accordingly, he called on

---

32   A.M.Vohra, Supra No.22, p-86.

President Jayewardene and spelled out these concerns in some detail, also stressed the impact these developments would have on the whole situation on the island and particularly the on-going negotiations for a political settlement of the ethnic problem. Dixit also drew the attention of the President to the "serious and grim situation" prevailing in the peninsula for the last few days following the suspension of distribution of petroleum products."[33]

Sri Lankan President Jayewardene was reported to have taken note of the Indian concern but did not commit himself to what his government planned to do to alleviate the hardship of the civilians on the peninsula. "In the meantime, reports from Jaffna said normal life in the area was coming to a standstill due to the shortage of essential commodities. Thirty to forty trucks loaded with petroleum products and other items were held up at the security camp at Elephant Pass, the gateway to the peninsula.[34] Even after expressing grave concern over the conditions of the Tamils in Jaffna, the Sri Lankan government continued its economic blockade and military offensive against the Tamils. Accordingly, it was during this period that the then Indian High Commissioner J.N.Dixit in a message to Jayewardene, said, "The Sri Lanka government should stop pursuing the military option and stop the violence it was unleashing against the Tamils in the North and East. It should immediately lift the economic blockade of the Jaffna Peninsula; it should affirm its commitment to the December 19, 1986 proposals as a basis and a beginning point for negotiations with the representatives of the Sri Lankan Tamils, and if these steps were not taken but the military option pursued by Colombo, the fighting "will be prolonged" and the situation "will escalate."[35] This political message

---

33   Asian Recorder, 33 (11) March 12-18,1987, p-19365.
34   Asian Recorder, 33 (11) March 12-18,1987, p-19365.
35   Asian Recorder, 33, (20), May14-20, 1987, p-19465.

was conveyed to Jayewardene on behalf of Indian Prime Minister Rajiv Gandhi.

After the strong message from India, the Sri Lankan government began to mend its attitude towards Tamils in Jaffna. Further, it was decided to ease the crisis by lifting the fuel blockade in light of the dire situation facing the Tamils and the severity of the situation prevailing in the peninsula. Accordingly, "the Sri Lankan government officially lifted the fuel embargo on Jaffna on March 27, 1987. A government statement said restrictions on the sale of kerosene, engine oil, and firewood had been removed, and petrol and diesel would be rationed.'[36]

When normalcy was returning to the blockade-affected island, suddenly violence broke out, and the massacre took place in the eastern Trincomalee district. 'At least 107 people, the majority of them believed to be Sinhalese, were killed and 60 others were injured on April 17, 1987, when militants sprayed machine-gun bullets on three passenger buses and two Lorries. Within a few days, a powerful blast took place in Colombo, which killed several people, and some 400 injured.'[37] The Sri Lankan government believed that it was the LTTE and EROs (Eelam Revolutionary Organization) together that were behind the massacre and the Colombo blast, respectively.

Immediately after the blast incident, there were several cases of looting of shops owned by Tamils. Some Tamil passengers were dragged out of their vehicles and assaulted."[38] The situation became tense and began to take a different shape on the island because of continued attacks on Tamils. A curfew was imposed, and the police and army were pressed into service to contain the violence. However, the situation was brought under control, and normalcy was restored

---

36   Asian Recorder, 33 (22) May 22-June 3, 1987, p-19482.
37   J.N.Dixit, Assignment Colombo, Konark Publishers, New Delhi, 1998, p-95.
38   Asian Recorder, 33 (25) June 18-24, 1987, p-19516.

to some extent. But the Sri Lankan government, which had decided to crush the militants, continued its air attack on the Jaffna peninsula. Tilak Ratnakar, the then chairman of the government's media centre, said Air Force planes were stuck at four locations in the rebel-dominated Jaffna peninsula. The government would continue bombing raids against known militant targets to try to get them to end their attacks on civilians.[39]

India felt severely upset and deeply disturbed over these developments. As a result, "in a statement, the government of India strongly condemned the escalation of violence represented by the Ariel attacks and other military measures taken by the Sri Lankan government, which had resulted in large-scale civilian casualties. Further, the government also expressed deep concern over the reported statement of then Prime Minister Premadas foreclosing the political option.[40]

However, India's strong protest did not bear fruit, as pressure was mounting on Sri Lankan President Jayewardene both within and outside the government to take possible stringent action against the Tamil militants to wipe them out of the Jaffna Peninsula. Bowing to the pressure, the Sri Lankan government announced a major military offensive called "Operation Liberation" or "Operation Vadamarachchi" in the first week of May 1987 to regain control of the territory from the LTTE and end violence in the Jaffna Peninsula. Sri Lanka continued its policy of crushing Tamils through military force and made all possible efforts to impose an "economic blockade" effectively on the north-eastern part of Sri Lanka, which had already been in effect since the beginning of January 1987. Accordingly, on May 26, 1987, Jayewardene was forced to launch an operation involving 8000 Sri Lankan ground

---

39   Asian Recorder, 33 (25) June 18-24, 1987, p-19517.

40   Ibid.,

troops to fight to the finish."[41] They cut off all food supplies to the Tamil areas. Jayewardene's action resulted in a large-scale influx of refugees into India, thus adding to the already unbearable burden on Tamil Nadu. However, the presence of refugees in the southern state of India posed a threat to the Indian economic and social system.

Taking note of the military action and the ruthless attitude of the Sri Lankan government towards the Tamils, on May 28, Rajiv Gandhi, addressing a press conference, "gave a clear warning to Sri Lanka that India would intervene to safeguard the welfare of Sri Lankan Tamils against the military onslaught. "The military operation is adding to the carnage. Hundreds have died in the last few days. Horrific losses in innocent lives of this magnitude are totally disproportionate to the avowed aim of exterminating the Tamil militant groups. It is apparent now that the Sri Lankan government was buying time over the last few years for pursuing a military option."[42] When the statement was brought to the notice of Jayewardene, he got enraged and reportedly saying "India can go to hell."[43]

The Sri Lankan government's rigid policy towards Tamils was a natural test for Rajiv Gandhi's leadership. The ethnic conflict altogether took a different turn due to the unleashed violence against the LTTE by the Sri Lankan government. The Tamils within Sri Lanka were hard-pressed in a near-chaotic situation. The situation became a boiling cauldron. India remained concerned about the conditions of the Tamil minority in Sri Lanka as it stirred protests and tensions among its Tamil population in the south. At the same time, public opinion in Tamil Nadu was hardening, and there was a real potential for it adopt independent action to support the Tamils in Jaffna. In addition to this, there were

---

41   The Hindu, 28 May 1987.
42   J.N.Dixit, Supra No.23, p-97.
43   Ibid., (J.N.Dixit, Supra No.23, p-98.)

political and emotional pressures on Rajiv Gandhi, compelling him to take some concrete action to safeguard the interests of Tamils and bring the Sri Lankan government to the negotiating table.

This was the context in which Rajiv Gandhi's leadership decided to break the blockade of Jaffna by sending essential supplies by sea on June 2, 1987. Prior to the dispatch of essential supplies, Rajiv Gandhi sent a message to Jayewardene that "India would be sending 20 fishing boats from Rameshwaram, which would reach Kalmunai Point, five kilometres off the northern coast of the Jaffna Peninsula. Escorted by an India offshore patrol vessel, "Vikram" of the Indian Coast Guard fleet."[44] Accordingly, India sent vessels flying the Indian Red Cross Society flag to Jaffna with food and medicine without military escort. However, the Sri Lankan Navy blocked the Indian vessels carrying essential supplies and refused to allow the flotilla to enter the island's territorial waters. India's efforts to raise the profile of its aid efforts sank in the seas off the coast of Jaffna. This naturally prompted Rajiv Gandhi to search for other avenues to supply humanitarian assistance to the Tamils.

The Air–Dropping:

In view of the situation that has developed in the north-eastern part of Sri Lanka, India decided to render urgent humanitarian aid to the people affected by the bombing and economic blockades. Taking into consideration the plight of the Tamils, "Consequent upon the refusal by Colombo to allow our unarmed relief supplies to get through Jaffna on June 3, 1987, New Delhi, decided to airdrop relief supplies on Jaffna on June 4th with five AN-32 transport aircraft and four Mirage fighter-bombers with full authority to return any ground fire or aerial resistance to destroy its source (Operation Poomalai)."[45] The Indian

---

44   J.N.Dixit, Assignment Colombo, Konark Publishers, New Delhi, 1998, p-102.
45   Quoted in Shipra Mehra., Supra No. 14, p-128.

government, with the help of the Indian army, airdropped food grains, medicines, clothing, etc., over the hard-pressed Tamils of the Jaffna peninsula on June 4, 1987, thereby blatantly intervening at the border and violating the air space of Sri Lanka. This act of airdropping by the Indian army evoked strong opposition and resentment from the leaders of the Sri Lankan government. Condemning the airdropping of relief material, then Prime Minister of Sri Lanka, Premadasa, while addressing a function in Colombo to mark Environmental Day, said, "Coming here and dropping food and running away is an act of cowardice. The Sri Lankan people unitedly condemn this act by India and express our opposition and hatred."[46] At this juncture, the leaders of the Sri Lankan government could not do anything except protest.

Nevertheless, prior to the airdropping, the Indian government informed the Sri Lankan government well in advance about the proposed airdrop. It was the then Minister of State for External Affairs who summoned Sri Lanka's High Commissioner to India, Bernard Tilakratne...and told him that "the government of India would commence airdropping relief materials over Jaffna and also gave him a six–point written message asking him to convey this to his government."[47] Therefore, India's act of airdropping the relief materials over Sri Lankan territory was not an act of cowardice, as Sri Lankan Prime Minister Premadasa claimed, but an act of courage (valour), which occurred after prior intimation to the Sri Lankan government.

After the airdropping of relief materials by the Indian Air Force on June 4, 1987, relations between Sri Lanka and India deteriorated further. Following the violation of its airspace by India, Sri Lanka approached Pakistan for a sophisticated air defence cover, which was likely to heighten tension in the region. It also received assistance from

---

46   Asian Recorder, Supra, No-10, p-19600.
47   J.N.Dixit, Supra No.23, p-105.

Israel and Britain in mercenary training and aerial combat. The visit of President Jayewardene to Lahore in 1985 marked the beginning of this bilateral military agreement against India, and the air defence cover to be provided by Pakistan is an open joining of forces against India. Taking into consideration the arming of Sri Lanka, Rajiv Gandhi, on the eve of the mercy mission to Sri Lanka, while addressing a convention of the Gujarat Pradesh Congress (I) in Surendranagar, said, "Foreign mercenary groups were aiding the Sri Lankan army offensive. Forces from Israel, Pakistan, South Africa, and the UK are present in Sri Lanka."[48]

Some leaders at home and abroad criticized the Indian Air Force's action in airdropping (Operation Poomalai) on the Jaffna Peninsula as a violation of Sri Lankan airspace and an infringement of its sovereignty. The general opinion was that India should not have intervened in Sri Lanka's internal affairs. Bangladesh's Chowdhury, commenting on India's airdrop, said "We are clear on our opposition to the violation of our neighbour's airspace. You have not been able to get a single supporter from any country in the world. Even Subramanian Swamy, a hawk on Sri Lanka viewed it as "either we don't violate the air space of a friendly country or we go in for a full-scale invasion and solve the problem. What we are doing is training the militants, violating Sri Lankan air space, and still claiming the right to mediate. No wonder our neighbours hold us in contempt."[49] Even some people equated Indian action of airdropping to the US invasion on Kampuchea, "the Soviet intervention in Hungary (1956) and Czechoslovakia (1968), the British-French intervention in Egypt leading to the Suez crisis, Turkey's intervention in Cyprus, breaking up that country, the USA's uninhibited interventions in Vietnam,

---

48   Sunday, 14 (31) June 21-27, 1987, p-50.
49   Sunday, Vol-14 (31) June 12-18, 1987, p-24.

Cuba, Granada, Panama, Libya, and Haiti, the Chinese intrusion into Vietnam in 1979 and into the South China Sea, to lay claim to the Spritely Islands, etc.[50] But, India's violation of Sri Lankan air space and its intervention in Sri Lankan affairs cannot be equated with the above interventions. But India's airdrop of civil supplies was on humanitarian ground, which was the "closest parallel to the Berlin airlift of 1961."[51]

Further, some countries also held that India's interference in Sri Lanka was not only against the principle of Panchsheel but also against the SAARC declaration of peaceful settlement of disputes and non-interference in the internal affairs of the member countries. Nevertheless, "these countries were not aware of "the consistent violation of human rights of the Sri Lankan Tamils by their own government and the tension it has generated in India, which might have affected the unity and integrity of India itself."[52] However, the decision to airdrop relief supplies was taken under the leadership of Rajiv Gandhi "after much cogitation and extensive consultations with the Cabinet Committee on Political Affairs, intelligence agencies, service chiefs, and the Foreign office.'[53]

On the other hand, none of the critics explicitly stated what India should do under such dire circumstances. The Indian Air Force's in airdropping on Jaffna was justified on humanitarian grounds; otherwise, thousands of innocent Tamil people would have died of starvation. After the airdrop, relations between India and Sri Lanka deteriorated even further. Rajiv Gandhi had four objectives in mind while ordering the airdrops: "help for the Tamils; a message to Colombo

---

50   J.N.Dixit, India's Foreign Policy, 1947-2003, Picus Books, New Delhi, 1998, p-186.

51   J.N.Dixit, Across the Borders: Fifty Years of India's Foreign Policy, Picus Books, New Delhi, 1998, p-186.

52   J.N.Dixit, Supra No.23, p-111.

53   J.N.Dixit, Assignment Colombo, Konark Publishers, New Delhi, 1998, p-106.

that Delhi could not be a silent spectator to a military onslaught on the civilians of Jaffna; a message to the Tamils that in the final analysis it was not the Tiger or even Tamil Nadu which could be their protector but India; and a warning to foreign powers that India was not going silently to suffer their intrigues in the internal affairs of a non-aligned country that belongs to the Indian realm."[54]

The reaction of the Western countries was ambiguous and mildly critical. They, however, acknowledged that the Indian action was a political necessity and inevitable in the context of India's involvement in the Sri Lankan ethnic crisis."[55] It would be pertinent to mention here that states sometimes deviate from the formal stipulations of international law in the interests of stability, security, and peace. Nevertheless, in the Indian context, the airdrop of relief supplies was purely humanitarian and not aimed at interfering in the internal affairs of Sri Lanka.

However, things began to change in Sri Lanka after the June incidents. The Tamils lost faith in the Sri Lankan government and began to look more towards India to protect their rights and save them from the Sinhalese wrath. During this period, the Indian government also decided to take an active role in the Tamil issue. India feared that persistent instability in its tiny southern neighbour might spread to Tamil Nadu or allow other powers to intervene. When the President of Sri Lanka realized that Sri Lanka would not be able to take on the Tamils on its own; he expressed his desire for a bilateral agreement between the two countries to resolve the ethnic problem. As a result, the representatives of the two countries established a framework to work out the modalities for an agreement between the two countries.

---

54   Quoted in Shipra Mehra, Supra No.14, pp-128, 129.
55   J.N.Dixit, Supra No.23, p-111.

The Indo-Sri Lankan Agreement: 1987

To end their long-running ethnic crisis, India and Sri Lanka, led by Rajiv Gandhi and Jayewardene, signed the historic agreement on July 29, 1987, in Colombo. The Accord allowed for joint action by the two countries to resolve the ethnic conflict. Under this accord, "the government of Sri Lanka permitted the northern and eastern provinces to form one administrative unit with one elected provincial council with one Governor, one Chief Minister, and one board of Ministers. A referendum was provided to enable the people of the eastern province to either decide to remain linked with the Northern Province or to constitute their own provincial council. The devolution of power to the councils was a "residual matter" to be negotiated between the two governments within a period of six weeks on the basis of negotiations conducted between May 4 and December 9 of 1986 (between the TULF and the government of Sri Lanka).[56] The objectives of the Indo-Sri Lankan Agreement were as follows.

1. Desiring to preserve the unity and territorial integrity of Sri Lanka:

2. Acknowledging that Sri-Lanka is a "multi-ethnic" and "multi-lingual society" consisting, inter alia, of Sinhalese, Tamils, Muslims (Moors), and Burghers:

3. Recognizing that each ethnic group has a distinct cultural and linguistic identity, which has to be carefully nurtured:

4. Also recognizing that the Northern and Eastern Provinces have been areas of historical habitation for Sri Lankan Tamil speaking peoples, who have at all times hitherto lived together in this territory with other ethnic groups:

---

56 Quoted in Satishkumar., (Ed) Year Book on India's Foreign Policy, 1989, Sage Publications, New Delhi, 1990, p-86.

5. Conscious of the necessity of strengthening the unity, sovereignty, and territorial integrity of Sri Lanka, and preserving its character as a multiethnic, multilingual, and multi religious plural society in which all citizens can live in equality, safety, and harmony, and prosper and fulfil their aspirations:[57]

Further, it was also resolved that the Indian Government would take all the necessary measures to stop any use of Indian territory for activities that would be prejudicial to Sri Lanka's interests. On the contrary, the Sri Lankan government would ensure that no such activities are carried out on its soil, which is detrimental to India's security concerns.

The Indo-Sri Lankan agreement was a testimony that non-aligned countries, through their sincere efforts, had the political will to resolve the crisis in their mutual interests. Undoubtedly, Rajiv Gandhi played a crucial role in solving the Sri Lankan ethnic problem, and his timely action resulted in peace to a considerable extent on the strife-torn island. His role in solving the ethnic conflict was lauded and widely admired by all segments of the international community. "President Ronald Reagan hailed it in a personal message to Rajiv Gandhi. The USSR, France, Australia, Algeria, Bangladesh, the Netherlands, and the EEC welcomed it. Then Soviet Deputy Prime Minister, Y.Kamentsev, officially declared that the Soviet Union regards the Indo-Sri Lankan Accord as an example of how a regional conflict could be solved. Even the weekly *Beijing Review* acknowledged in an article that the "peace accord is bound to bring about at least a temporary truce between Sri Lanka's Tamil minority and the Buddhist majority Sinhalese."[58]

---

57 http://www.tamilnation.org/intframe/
58 A.M.Vohra Supra No.22, p-87.

Rajiv Gandhi, while addressing a public meeting in Madras on August 2, 1987, said, "This Agreement is a major landmark in these four decades of India's freedom. I am told that no such agreement has been signed by any country in the world, at least in this century. It is an agreement, which does not have a parallel in the world. It is an agreement, which vindicates the principles of good neighbourliness, peaceful co-existence, and non-alignment."[59]

Further, the historic peace pact signed between Rajiv Gandhi and Jayewardene on the ethnic issue of Sri Lanka was undoubtedly a significant achievement in establishing peace on the war-torn island. By signing the Indo-Sri Lankan Accord, Rajiv Gandhi demonstrated to the world that the Third World countries could solve their internal problems without the interference or mediation of the superpowers. As a result, the agreement brought popularity and acclaim not only to Rajiv Gandhi but also to the non-aligned countries of the world at large. The anti-imperialist forces of the world welcomed the accord as it defused tension between two neighbouring countries. It frustrated the aggressive designs of imperialism in this part of the world. Further, the Indo-Sri Lankan Accord was also known as the "Rajiv Gandhi-J Jayawardhane Accord".

For the successful implementation of the Accord, certain prerequisites have been included. "They are maintaining the unity and integrity of Sri Lanka, ensuring conditions of peace and security for the Tamils there; and no foreign intrusion or foreign bases of any kind in Sri Lanka."[60] To implement the Accord, the Indian Peace Keeping Force (IPKF) was sent to Sri Lanka to supervise the ceasefire, the surrender

---

59   Rajiv Gandhi., Selected Speeches and Writings 1987, Vol-III, Publication Division, Ministry of Information and Broadcasting, Government of India, New Delhi, p-381.
60   V.P.Dutt, India and the World, Sanchar Publishing House, New Delhi, 1990, p-92.

of arms, and the protection of the interests of the minority Tamils in the North East Province.

The Indian Peacekeeping Force:

Barring the LTTE, all the Tamil groups in Sri Lanka welcomed the Accord. Although during the last stages of Indo-Sri Lankan efforts for peace, the LTTE also decided to accept the agreement. According to the agreement, the LTTE was supposed to lay down its arms. However, in an interview with the *Hindu* on August 27, 1987, at Jaffna, LTTE Chief V. Prabhakakaran said that he was unhappy because "the problems of the affected people have not been taken care of in the agreement... The LTTE could not give up arms without protection, without security for our people and fighters, without any safeguard for their future."[61] India believed that the apprehensions expressed by the LTTE were without any basis as far as security for the Tamils was concerned. However, the LTTE was not satisfied despite the assurances from both governments regarding the safety and security of minority Tamils. As a result, it started to veer away from the Sri Lankan agreement, despite assurances from both countries that the Tamils interests would be protected.

Despite the continued efforts from the Sri Lankan government to implement the agreement, the opposition from the extremists, especially the LTTE, continued unabatedly, thereby hampering the peace process. The Sri Lankan government sought India's assistance to contain the escalating violence when it became impossible and was not in a position to withstand the LTTE's violence. Thousands of Sinhalese had to take shelter in refugee camps in their own country due to the attack of Tamil guerrillas in the Eastern Province of Sri Lanka. Considering the seriousness of the rapidly worsening situation

---

61   A.M.Vohra in Satish Kumar's Supra No-.22, p-87.

on the island, India decided to send a Peacekeeping force as part of the agreement.

Accordingly, the Indian Peace Keeping Force (IPKF) was sent to Sri Lanka in July 1987 to restore peace and normalcy on the violence-ravaged island. The IPKF was sent to Sri Lanka at the request of the Sri Lankan government to honour the Accord. Therefore, Rajiv Gandhi, in his statement to the Rajya Sabha on July 31, 1987, said, "Our troops have landed in Sri Lanka in response to a specific and formal request of the government of Sri Lanka, who have invoked our obligations and commitments under the Indo-Sri Lankan Agreement. Our troops have gone there to help implement the agreement, to end the ethnic strife in Sri Lanka, and their dispatch underlines our firm commitment to the unity and integrity of Sri Lanka".[62]

The Indian Peace Keeping Force was sent not only to meet the obligation as enshrined in the Indo-Sri Lankan Agreement but also due to the apprehension expressed by the Indian strategic thinkers that, in the event of not supporting the efforts of the Sri Lankan government, there was every possibility that the Sri Lankan leadership would seek foreign military assistance. Nonetheless, several foreign countries were ready to assist Sri Lanka in containing the growing violence. However, India expressed concern that if there were foreign intervention in Sri Lanka, it would endanger the security of South Asia. Prior to this, there was a report that Colombo had sought help from the United States, Britain, and Bangladesh, the then External Affairs Minister P.V.Narasimharao, reportedly warned all powers to keep out of the turmoil in Sri Lanka in 1983."[63] Therefore, the rationale behind sending IPKF to Sri Lanka was

---

62 Rajiv Gandhi, Supra No.59, (Vol-III), p-376.

63 S.D.Muni, Pangs of Proximity: India and Sri Lanka's Ethnic Crisis, Sage Publications, New Delhi, pp-185-186.

not only to protect Tamils, but also to avoid the entry of foreign mercenaries into Sri Lanka.

Initially, the IPKF struggled to deal with the LTTE, had trouble with JVP militants, and failed to contain violence. As a result, the situation in Sri Lanka further worsened with the entry of the IPKF instead of the expected normalization. The situation in Sri Lanka was blown out of proportion when the Peacekeeping Force collaborated with the Sri Lankan government to kill hundreds of innocent Tamils instead of establishing peace. Therefore, accusing the IPKF of its role, the LTTE leader Prabhakaran said, "Having engaged themselves in a war with violence, brutality, and terror, the IPKF has lost its status as an instrument of peace but has assumed the role of a repressive invasion army, typically eliminating both the Tamil freedom fighters and innocent civilians."[64] The IPKF, which was sent to establish peace and harmony in war- ravaged Sri Lanka, failed in its primary objective and had to come back to India without achieving the desired results.

Withdrawal of the IPKF:

India sent the IPKF with the objective of bringing peace and tranquillity to the war-torn island but failed in completing the mission because it had to counter the challenges posed by the militant groups as well as the Sri Lankan government. Therefore, India found it difficult and could not succeed in accomplishing the task with the assistance of the IPKF because of poor strategy and a lack of communication with the various agencies. Though the IPKF landed on the island at the request of the Sri Lankan government, it started sabotaging the IPKF operation by supplying weapons to the LTTE to fight against the

---

64 Avatar Singh Bhasin, India and Sri Lankan Relations and Sri Lanka's Ethnic Conflict Documents, 1947-2000, Vol-1, India Research Press, New Delhi, 2001, p-139.

IPKF."[65] Therefore, the main objective of the Sri Lankan government, especially of some ministers in Jayewardene's cabinet, was to make the IPKF unpopular and send it back halfway. Further, Premadasa, then Sri Lankan Prime Minister, who had opposed the induction of the IPKF since the beginning, put pressure on Jayewardene's government for an immediate pullout of the IPKF from the island.

Even the J.V.P (Janatha Vimukti Perumuna) militants, who stubbornly opposed the entry of the IPKF, were involved in large-scale violence and posed stiff resistance to the IPKF. As a result, the IPKF had a tough time dealing with the JVP. Further, the IPKF's presence in Sri Lanka gave a new lease of life to the JVP, which launched a ruthless campaign of murder and mayhem and demanded the IPKF's withdrawal and the scrapping of the agreement.

The IPKF had become unpopular in Sri Lanka by 1989 when Premadasa was elected President. He reaffirmed his earlier position and sought the immediate withdrawal of the IPKF from the island. The pressure mounted for the withdrawal of troops. Despite Rajiv Gandhi's assurance, Premadasa demanded the withdrawal of the forces by July 29, 1989, and put a unilateral deadline on himself without consulting the Indian government. Before this, Premadasa threatened to boycott the Fourth SAARC Summit, which was set for December 1988 in Pakistan, if India did not withdraw by the deadline he set. Rajiv Gandhi initially turned down the demand on the pretext of fulfilling the terms of the Indo-Sri Lankan Agreement. The demand for Premadasa and Rajiv Gandhi's defiance led to a grave impasse between the two countries. In the meantime, the growing criticism of the IPKF in Sri Lanka prompted Rajiv Gandhi to think in terms of withdrawal in a phased manner. But this incident brought tremendous pressure on Rajiv Gandhi's government, which was gearing up to face the country's

---

65   S.D.Muni, Supra No. 63, pp.276-77.

general elections. Therefore, due to pressure from Preamadasa, Rajiv Gandhi decided to pull out the troops in a phased manner before accomplishing the complete task of bringing normalcy to the war-torn island. Accordingly, a contingent of around 5000 IPKF arrived in India by May 1989.

However, "in a sudden development, the LTTE entered into negotiations with the government, in which one of the demands was the IPKF withdrawal. On June 25, 1989, the LTTE and the Sri Lankan government declared the cessation of hostilities, with the obvious desire to send IPKF from the island."[66] Though the pro-Indian groups insisted on the necessity of the IPKF, the LTTE was adamant that normalcy would only be restored, if the IPKF was withdrawn from Sri Lanka. Apparently, the LTTE which earlier welcomed the induction of the IPKF for the safety and security of the Tamils, subsequently joined hands with the Sri Lankan government in pressing for the withdrawal of the IPKF. Even JVP joined the bandwagon of the groups that sought the withdrawal of the IPKF. Owing to the pressure from all corners," the talks were held, and on September 18, 1989, the then Indian High Commissioner, L.L.Mehrotra and Sri Lankan Foreign Secretary, Bernard Tilakratne, signed a communiqué setting out a framework under which Indian forces would leave the island by December 31, 1989."[67] On September 20, 1989, the IPKF suspended its almost two-year long operations against the LTTE and announced that it would not attack the IPKF unless it was attacked.

In a dramatic turn, in December 1989, V.P.Singh, the leader of the National Front, became the Prime Minister of India, replacing Rajiv Gandhi. Taking advantage of the same, the Sri Lankan government drew the attention of V.P.Singh's government for the immediate withdrawal

---

66 P.A.Ghosh, Supra No. 9, p-133.
67 Quoted in Shipra Mehra, Supra No.14, p-147.

of the IPKF. At the insistence of Premadasa, V.P.Singh, decided to withdraw the remaining troops of the IPKF from Sri Lanka as agreed earlier.

Achievements of the IPKF:

The IPKF made remarkable achievements in establishing peace and tranquilly in war-ravaged Sri Lanka. In general, the following are some of the IPKFs accomplishments.

1. The biggest achievement of the IPKF, as stated by A.S.Kalkat, General Officer Commanding of the IPKF, is that it had maintained and accomplished the objectives of the government of India's policy towards Sri Lanka which is to have a friendly and united Sri Lanka, in which the minority Tamil issue is resolved politically to ensure the Tamils' right."[68]

2. The IPKF entered Sri Lanka under the Indo-Sri Lanka Agreement of 1987 to disarm the LTTE and restore normalcy. The IPKF disarmed the LTTE at a time when the Sri Lankan army was desperately fighting on two fronts against the LTTE and the JVP."[69]

3. The IPKF was dispatched to Sri Lanka to prevent the entry of foreign mercenaries that were eager to interfere in the internal affairs of Sri Lanka to assist the Sri Lankan army in pretending to establish peace on the island.

4. As a consequence of the IPKF's operation, out of all the militant groups, four gave up their demand for Eelam, swore their allegiance to the constitution and integrity of Sri Lanka, and joined the political process in September 1988. The

---

68   Quoted in Ravikant Dubey, Supra No.15, p-135.

69   J.N.Dixit, IPKF in Sri Lanka, in USA Journal 19 (497) July –Sept 1989, p-8.

remaining one, the LTTE too, after further operations by the IPKF, reconciled and accepted the sovereignty of Sri Lanka." [70]

5. The IPKF helped step by step in the execution of the agreement and in the peaceful conduct of successive elections to the democratic institutions despite the threats of terrorist violence in the Northeast.

6. The IPKF was ordered not to inflict casualties on civilians and not to annihilate their adversary. The IPKF General told their men, "This war was not to destroy your adversary but to guide him in the right direction to accept the political settlement."[71]

7. The Indo-Sri Lankan Accord led India to dispatch her troops to the island at a time" when the situation seemed headed inexorably towards the break-up of Sri Lanka."[72]

8. The IPKF was greatly responsible for preventing the continuation of the Sri Lankan policy of seeking a military solution to the Tamil problem, on which it had embarked since 1983.

Causes for the IPKF Failure:

The IPKF, which was sent to Sri Lanka to maintain peace, and disarm the militants, failed in its primary task for the following reasons.

1. Though the Indian military used to counter insurgency operations in the north-eastern states of India, it still "failed to counter revolutionary warfare, particularly in fighting an urban guerilla force that had mastered landmine technology."[73]

---

70   Quoted in Shipra Mehra, Supra No.14, p-152.

71   Rohan Gunaratna, Indian Intervention in Sri Lanka: The Role of Indian Intelligence Agencies, South Asian Network on Conflict Research, Colombo, 1993, p-259.

72   Avatar Sing Bhasin, Supra No.64, p-156.

73   Rohan Gunaratna, Supra No.71, p-259

2. At the beginning, the IPKF troops operating in the jungles had machine guns and SLR weapons, while the LTTE used AK-47s and M-16s, which had the greatest firepower,"[74] apart from the shortage of manpower.

3. The IPKF headed to Sri Lanka to protect the interests of the Tamils. But it forgot its fundamental duty and got involved in killing innocent Tamils in Sri Lanka.

4. After the entry of the IPKF, several Sri Lankan Tamils migrated to countries like Canada and Australia because they found themselves placed between the devil and the deep sea within their own country. On the one hand, they had to deal with the Sri Lankan army and the JVP, while on the other; they feared being massacred by the IPKF.

5. The non-cooperation and hostility of the then Sri Lankan Prime Minister, Premadasa, and the National Security Minister, Athulathmudali, and the persistent demands of the Sri Lankan government and the Tamil militants ultimately demoralized the IPKF. As a result, the IPKF had to face an embarrassing situation in Sri Lanka.

6. The biggest failure of the IPKF was that it allowed Prabhakaran to slip out of its net thrice. According to Gamini Dissanayake, this was confirmed to him by no less a person than General Sundarji, the Chief of the Indian Army."[75]

7. Further, there was no involvement of the chiefs of the defence forces in any of the strategic discussions with Rajiv Gandhi, and there was no attempt to set up a joint task force. Consequently, the army units were to be managed from Pune and Chennai, the air force units from Trivandrum, and the navy from Cochin.

---

74 Ibid.

75 Avatar Singh Bhasin, Supra No.64, p-142.

India's Foreign Policy towards Sri Lankan Affairs:

The formulation of foreign policy towards the Sri Lankan ethnic problem was primarily arduous due to the complex nature of the issue. Therefore, India found it difficult to formulate a clear foreign policy strategy as far as the Sri Lankan ethnic conflict was concerned. India firmly believes in the policy of non-interference in the internal affairs of another country, respect for the sovereignty and integrity of other countries, etc., as laid down in the Panchsheel. While dealing with the Sri Lankan ethnic issue, India appears to have diluted its fundamental foreign policy principles. The LTTE openly condemned India's intervention in Sri Lanka and considered that the ethnic problem was between Tamils and the Sri Lankan government, with no role for the Indian government. Further, the LTTE was the primary actor in dealing with the ethnic crisis in Sri Lanka. However, it was neither made a party to the Accord nor invited to witness the ceremony on July 29, 1987, while signing the Indo-Sri Lankan Accord. Therefore, commenting on the Indo-Sri Lankan Accord, Vellupillai Prabhakaran, the LTTE leader, addressing a rally in Jaffna on August 4, 1987, said, "India was overtly keen on striking an Accord (because it) protected India's interests in the region". It was his view that the accord deals with Indo-Lanka relations and that the Tamil question was not central to it."[76]

Therefore, during the ethnic crisis in Sri Lanka, the foreign policy decision-makers found it challenging to formulate a comprehensible policy on the Sri Lankan issue. Perhaps the ineffectiveness of the Sri Lankan accord is not be entirely attributable to the Indian foreign policy mechanism led by the political leadership. As a result, after assuming the office of Prime Minister, Rajiv Gandhi, discussed relations with neighbouring countries with G.Parthasarathy, the then Chairman of the Policy Planning Committee. He also asked the Ministry of External

---

76   B.G.Verghese, Beyond the Truce, Seminar, No-337, September 1987, p-41.

Affairs to examine various possibilities for improving relations with neighbours, including China, Bhutan, and SAARC nations."[77] Before signing the accord, Rajiv Gandhi consulted all the parties involved. It indicates that Rajiv Gandhi adopted a democratic approach in formulating India's foreign policy in the context of the ethnic crisis in Sri Lanka.

The decision-makers (political leaders) are more significant than the bureaucrats in the formation of democratic foreign policy and strategies to meet problems. On the contrary, as the then Foreign Secretary, A.P.Venkteshwaran, once said, "Today diplomats should not be blamed for not framing an effective foreign policy, since they were "mere file carriers", while decisions were taken by the Parliamentarians."[78] But in actual practice, the decision-makers don't have the required skills and are chiefly dependent on bureaucrats. Therefore, bureaucrats play a more significant role than the policymakers. As a result of the lack of coordination in formulating foreign policy by the various agencies, the Indo-Sri Lankan Accord ended in chaos and confusion without bearing fruit. Therefore, Rajiv Gandhi, who was instrumental in signing the Indo-Sri Lankan Accord and sending the IPKF, had to sacrifice his life at the cost of the so-called Accord, which is ironic. The Sri Lankan political leaders even did not implement the Accord in letter and spirit. Besides, the Tamil groups did not cooperate wholeheartedly with the foreign policy makers of both countries.

The Major Irritants and Shortcomings of the Accord:

The Indo-Sri Lankan Accord went awry for several reasons. Firstly, the most significant factor was the desertion of LTTE leader

---

77   Vandana Asthana, India's Foreign Policy and Sub-Continental Politics, Kanishaka Publishers, New Delhi, 1999, p-170.

78   The Times of India, 28 August 1987.

Prabhakaran, who, after having given consent to surrender arms, reverted to the stand taken at the meeting with Rajiv Gandhi in New Delhi. As a result, the LTTE indulged in large-scale violence and soon was on the warpath against the IPKF, which was summoned at the request of the Sri Lankan government to restore order in the embattled island. Obviously, this brought neither glory nor peace to Sri Lanka.

The revolt of the JVP (Janatha Vimukthi Premuna) activists, who carried out the campaign of murder and terrorism against the bureaucrats, monks, and ordinary people, further fuelled the fire. The JVP ruthlessly killed most of the prominent Sinhalese politicians of both the ruling and opposition parties in Sri Lanka. As a result, the administration on the island became increasingly paralyzed, and the peace process came to a standstill. The JVP inflexibly opposed the Indo-Sri Lankan Accord and stood in the way of its implementation.

Another significant factor was the unremitting hostility of the then Sri Lankan Prime Minister, Ranasinghe Premadasa, who openly expressed his dissatisfaction over the signing of the Accord and carried on a virulent campaign against India, accusing her of imperialism, colonialism, hegemony, and visions of dominance. Even Athulatmudali, the then National Security Minister in Jayewardene's cabinet, opposed the Indo-Sri Lankan Accord tooth and nail. Naturally, this hindered the successful implementation of the Accord.

The foremost important factor was that the main actors in the conflict, especially the LTTE, were not made parties to the Indo-Sri Lankan Accord. It was not taken into confidence while signing the Indo-Sri Lankan Accord, though it dealt with the question of Tamils in Sri Lanka. Undoubtedly, this resulted in discontent among the Tamil guerillas.

The mediators and the government's special envoys, entrusted to bring about a conciliatory process among the warring factions, failed in their task. Romesh Bhandari, the special envoy to Sri Lanka to deal with Sri Lankan issues,"was unpopular among the militant leaders for his pressure tactics and insensitivity to the legitimate aspirations of the Tamils."[79], unlike G.Parthasarathy, who was efficiently trying for rapprochement between the Sinhalese and the Tamils.

Lack of coordination between the various governmental agencies and the bureaucracy involved in the preliminaries of the Indo-Sri Lankan Agreement to be signed by Rajiv Gandhi and J. Jayewardene was one of the significant shortcomings of the Indo-Sri Lankan Accord. The Indo-Sri Lankan Accord was prepared by the Indian Foreign Office without the direct involvement of the Ministry of Defence, resulting in very inadequate preparation for military operations in Sri Lanka.

Frequent changes of emissaries and mediators entrusted with the responsibility of dealing with the Sri Lankan ethnic crisis created instability in their positions and broke consistency in the process of dialogue and negotiations. During the peace process, Indian mediators sidelined moderate Tamil groups and leaders, such as A. Amrithlingam of the TULF, who were fighting for the Tamil cause in Sri Lanka and instead promoted the militants to become the sole representatives of the Sri Lankan Tamils, which was a significant factor in the adversity to the Accord.

Despite all the hostile reactions amongst the Sinhalese, the agreement otherwise had been hailed as the "triumph of statesmanship and courage under the most trying and tragic circumstances.

---

79   P.Sahadevan, India and Sri Lanka in Lalit Mansigh and others, (ed) "Indian Foreign Policy: Agenda for the 21st Century", Vol-2, Konark Publishers, New Delhi, 1998, pp-177-78.

From the Mediatory Role to the Participatory Role:

Since the outbreak of the ethnic problem In Sri Lanka, India has played a limited role as a mediator or facilitator of communication between the two adversaries, i.e., the Sri Lankan government and the minority Tamils. Even during Jawaharlal Nehru's period, India chose to be a facilitator and offer good offices to the ethnic problem of the minority Tamils in Sri Lanka rather than become a party. Perhaps during Jawaharlal Nehru's period, there was no pressure from the Sri Lankan government to assume a participatory role or be the guarantor of the Sri Lankan ethnic issue, unlike during Rajiv Gandhi's period. Like Jawaharlal Nehru, Indira Gandhi played a similar role while dealing with the Sri Lankan Tamil issue. However, it was in mid-1983 that the Indian government, under the leadership of Indira Gandhi, "tried several times to become a mediator."[80] It was clear that India wanted to play the role of mediator to secure its interests, which was unacceptable to the Sri Lankan government. However, Jayewardene's leadership, which was not satisfied with India's mediator role, started pressuring it to assume the role of a guarantor (participator) instead of a mediator or intervener role in solving the ethnic issue. Though there was intense pressure to play the role of guarantor in solving the ethnic conflict, Indira Gandhi chose to assume the responsibility of a mediator for the cause of the Tamils. As a result, during Indira Gandhi's period, India chose a mediatory role between the Tamil guerrillas and the Sri Lankan government rather than being a party to the ethnic problem, unlike Rajiv Gandhi. She did everything without stopping, short of direct intervention in the Sri Lankan ethnic crisis. Therefore, it was clear that India was never a party to the ethnic problem. Instead, it has assumed the role of a mediator since the outbreak of ethnic violence.

---

80   Asian Survey, 29 (4) April 1989, p-406.

So far, India has acted as a mediator between the Tamil groups and the government of Sri Lanka to resolve the vexed ethnic issue. India tried her best to bring the two parties together to resolve the ethnic conflict, narrow the misunderstanding and communication gap, and to make them negotiate a peaceful political settlement. This role of a mediator and offering good offices, India played for the most period since August, 1983".[81]

However, during Rajiv Gandhi's period, the Indian mediatory role between Sri Lanka and the Tamils started losing ground when Sri Lankan President Jayewardene insisted on direct participation on behalf of the Tamils. But it became clear, especially after the failure of two rounds of Thimpu talks in July and August 1985, that this limited intermediary role did not yield any concrete result. With the stalemate persisting on the peace front, India was compelled to change its position from that of a communication facilitator to one of actual participation in the conflict by signing a bilateral peace agreement in July 1987. Thus, it took almost three years for India to change its role, much against its desire and interest and at the initiative of the Sri Lankan government. The Indo-Sri Lankan pact was considered the major political decision by Rajiv Gandhi concerning the Tamil issue.

Rajiv Gandhi was reluctant to accept the direct participant stance on the racial issue. However, the Sri Lankan President Jayewardene pressured him to take up the participatory role proposed in early August 1986. But Rajiv Gandhi, taking into consideration the complex nature of the ethnic issue, did not accept Jayewardene's offer of a participatory role and stuck to playing a mediatory role. Early in 1987, Jayewardene emphasized again that any deal to end the conflict had to be between the two governments, not the Sri Lankan government and the Tamil groups. Naturally this posed a challenge to Rajiv Gandhi,

---

81   Quoted in Shipra Mehra, Supra No. 14, pp.140-41.

who was eager to resolve the ethnic problem. However, Rajiv Gandhi, considering the plight of the Tamils and the seriousness of the ethnic issue, hesitantly agreed to become a direct participant by signing the Indo-Sri Lankan Accord. "In envisaging such a role, the Sri Lankan President's objective was very clear. He wanted to use Indian power to disarm the Tamil militants, especially the LTTE, whose position was quite entrenched in Eelam, and accept Sri Lanka's unity and sovereignty. In other words, by seeking India's direct participation, Jayewardene was ultimately aiming for an intervener role for India. His objective was fulfilled when the Indian government committed its forces to implement the Agreement."[82]

At last, President Jayewardene succeeded in pressurizing Rajiv Gandhi to assume India's role as a party to the Sri Lankan ethnic issue by signing the Indo-Sri Lankan Accord. Though the conflict was between the Sri Lankan government and the Tamils, India had no role to play as a party to the Accord. However, India was compelled to become a party to the Accord, which was not in the best interest of the Sri Lankan Tamil militants. Therefore, the LTTE Chief Prabhakaran expressed discontentment over the Accord and said, "The Accord is between India and the Sri Lankan government, and Tamils were consulted ex-post-facto, hence he was not bound by the Accord."[83] As a result, the Indo-Sri Lankan Accord got the first jolt when the LTTE leader opposed India's participatory role in resolving the vexed ethnic issue.

Nevertheless, Jayewardene achieved his goal of making India a party to the Sri Lankan Accord. Although the LTTE made it clear in 1987 that it would not accept peace without the Tamil Eelam,

---

82   P.Sahadevan, India and Sri Lanka, in Lalith Mansingh and Others, (ed) India's Foreign Policy: Agenda for 21st Century, (Vol-II), Konark Publishers, New Delhi, 1998, p-178.
83   The Hindu, 14 August 1987.

considering that India should have encouraged at least moderate Tamil leaders to sign the Agreement with Jayewardene. Further, India should have been a guarantor to implement the agreement rather than a signatory. Perhaps India's overconfidence in involving the LTTE in the peace process in 1987 caused severe problems for the country. The irony is that, despite Rajiv Gandhi's positive attitude and approach, he eventually had to intervene directly in Sri Lanka with the best intention of resolving the crisis.

CHAPTER – VI

Rajiv Gandhi's Contribution to Sino-Indian Relations

The study of Sino-Indian relations is said to be crucial to the entire gamut of India's foreign policy. Sino-Indian relations have been cordial and friendly since India's pre-independence. The relationship between the two countries deteriorated when China invaded Tibet in the early 1950s. Since then, relations between India and China have been at a crossroads. But in reality, the strained relations between India and China developed in the latter half of the 1950s, when the Tibetan question turned into an issue of disagreement between the two nations. Though Rajiv Gandhi's predecessors' attempted to normalize relations with China, no concrete results were achieved, except during Indira Gandhi's period. Perhaps under the leadership of Rajiv Gandhi, the policy towards China began to change. Soon after assuming power, Rajiv Gandhi affirmed his commitment to normalize India's strained relations with China. Accordingly, he undertook several confidence-building measures to that effect. In this regard, his visit to China in 1988 paved the way for improving Sino-Indian relations.

Sino-Indian Relations: A Peep into History

The history of Sino-Indian relations can be traced back to the ancient days of Buddha and Confucius. The most significant aspect of historical contact was the establishment of Buddhism in China. During ancient times, there was an exchange of spiritual ideas between the two countries. Indian Buddhist monks and scholars played a predominant role in this regard. "The Chinese had responded with great enthusiasm to the arrival of Buddhist missionaries and subsequently initiated a wave to bring Indian Buddhist monks and scholars to help teach, explain, and establish Buddhism firmly in China. During the fourth and fifth centuries A.D., a second wave of Buddhist Indian monks sent as missionaries to China created a counter wave of Chinese Buddhists sent to India for advanced training. Kumarajiva and Bodhidharma, who went from India to China, and Fa Hien and Yuan Chuang, who came from China to India, are four familiar names that greatly enriched the knowledge and understanding of their countries of origin for their hosts."[1] This naturally led the two countries to develop intimate relations between themselves.

Even in ancient times, the Silk Road became a successful conduit for trade, commerce, and cultural exchanges between the two countries. However, this resulted in the establishment of friendly relations between the countries. Therefore, there are many similarities between the two countries as far as traditions, customs, culture, civilization, etc., are concerned. Further, India and China, the two ancient countries of the world, played a significant role in international politics due to their geo-strategic and political status. However, there are some differences between the two countries' political systems and how they attained their independence. In the post-Second World War period, democratic India and Communist China achieved independence in 1947 and 1949 and emerged as two powerful nations in South Asia. India gained freedom through the values of peace and non-violence advocated by Mahatma Gandhi, whilst China gained independence through a violent approach by waging a civil war against the Kuomintang. Though there are inherent differences between the two countries, there are still some similarities regarding some fundamental issues.

------

1   Subramanian Swamy, India's China Perspective, Konark Publishers, New Delhi, 2001, p-1.

The boundary dispute was said to be a contentious issue between the two countries. In fact, the boundary dispute played a predominant role in Sino-Indian relations. Immediately after independence, India's relations with China had no crucial problems or irritants. However, it was in the 1950s that India's relations with China began to get strained, primarily due to the boundary dispute and the Tibetan issue. In fact, this was proven true in the words of K.M.Panikkar, the then Ambassador to China: "With a Communist China, cordial and intimate relations were out of the question". The only area where our interests overlapped was in Tibet."[2] Perhaps, the Tibetan issue appeared to be the major irritant in Sino-Indian relations. As a result, the differences came to the fore when there was disagreement between the two countries over the Tibetan issue and the territorial issue.

India, the champion against colonialism and imperialism and sympathizer of dependent people/countries opposed China's interference in the internal affairs of Tibet. Further, India claimed that the Mc Mohan Line was the lawfully demarcated border between India and China. However, China refuted India's contention and condemned the McMahon Line as an "imperialist line". In this context, the boundary dispute and the Tibetan issues became major irritants in Sino-Indian relations. Therefore, the arguments and counter arguments between the two countries over the boundary dispute culminated in the 1962 war.

The Boundary Dispute:

The thorny boundary dispute became the main obstacle and major irritant in Sino-Indian relations. There was no boundary dispute between the two countries immediately after independence. Perhaps

---

2   K.Raman Pillai, India's Foreign Policy: Basic Issues and Political Attitudes, Meenakshi Prakashan, Meerut, 1969, p-126.

it was in 1954 that the cartographic issue began with the publication of an official Chinese map in a book entitled *"A Brief History of Modern China"*, which showed vast areas of Soviet Central Asia and South East Asia to be within the historical frontiers of China. Also, Nepal, Sikkim, Bhutan, and Assam (in India) were depicted similarly."[3] This incident caused enormous concern in India and heightened tension. Accordingly, the then Prime Minister of India, Jawaharlal Nehru, drew the attention of the Chinese to the issue. To India's concern, Zhou-Enlai, the then premier of China, said, "The map was an "old" reproduction of a publication from "the pro-liberation period," and as his government was busy, it would do the needful soon."[4]

Before this, in November 1950, Prime Minister Jawaharlal Nehru proclaimed to Parliament that the "McMahon Line was indeed India's border with Tibet in the North-West, reiterating that it had been "fixed by the Simla Convention of 1914", even as the Survey of India of the Home Ministry then had published the official map of India showing the border as 'undemarcated' and 'unidentified'. He went on to say, "Map or no map, the McMahon Line was India's boundary, and we will not allow anybody to cross [it]."[5] However, China, which was not happy with the demarcation process, rejected the Simla Convention because the Tibetan government was a local government and therefore did not have treaty-making powers. It does not recognize Lhasa's 1913 declaration of independence, nor does it consider the Mc Mahon line a legal boundary."[6] Even China contended that it was not a signatory to the Simla Convention, which mapped out the McMahon Line. Further, in 1959, Zhou-Enlai, the then Premier of China, questioned for the first

---

3　　Quoted in Bidanda M.Chengappa, India-China Relations: Post Conflict Phase to Post-Cold War Period, A.P.H. Publishing New Delhi, 2004, p-20.

4　　Bidanda M.Chengappa Supra No.3, p.20

5　　Subramanian Swamy, Supra No.1, p-43.

6　　http://en.wikipedia.org/wiki/McMahon_Line

time the established boundary between India and China. He contended that the "Sino-Indian boundary had never been formally delimited' and that the so-called 'McMahon Line was a product of the policy of aggression against the Tibet Region of China and therefore an "illegal line."[7]

Therefore, from the above statement, it is clear that China has never accepted the McMahon Line as the boundary between India and China, even though they "accepted the McMahon Line in *toto* with Burma"[8] as the boundary line. The situation along the Line of Actual Control became tense when the boundary dispute began to take a different shape. The 1959 Tibetan revolt further worsened the situation. In the meantime, the paramilitary clashes between the Indian Army and China's People's Liberation Army continued unabatedly along the Line of Actual Control. This hostility between the two countries took a different shape and increased the tension on the Sino-Indian border.

In the face of the increasing tension on the border, the "Chinese Foreign Minister sent notes in the form of a proposal to the Indian Embassy in Beijing on August 4, September 13, and October 3, 1962, that the two sides should meet immediately without preconditions in order to ease the situation. But all the proposals were rejected by India."[9] As a result, India's refusal to accept the Chinese proposal led the two countries to the brink of war. Accordingly, in October 1962, China attacked India and occupied thousands of kilometres of Indian Territory in the Aksai Chin and Ladakh areas in the Western Sector. The 1962 war resulted in heavy casualties and dropped the curtains once and for all on the Sino-Indian boundary dispute. Indeed, the 1962

---

7   Quoted in, K. Raman Pillai, Supra No.2, p-130.

8   Subramanian Swamy, Supra No.1, p-53.

9   Subramanian Swamy, Supra No.1, pp-87,88.

War shattered the principles of the Panchsheel Agreement and further widened the rift between the two countries.

The Tibetan Issue:

Apart from the boundary dispute, the Tibetan issue was another vital source of friction in Sino-Indian relations. As a result, in the 1950s, India's relations with China strained, not with the boundary dispute but with the emergence of the Tibetan Issue. Indeed, the boundary dispute between India and China reached a climax when India became sympathetic towards the Tibetan issue of autonomy in the early 1950s. Naturally, this irked the Chinese government, which termed India's stance as interference in China's internal affairs. Therefore, the Tibetan issue worsened the already aggravated boundary dispute between the two countries. China considered the Tibetan issue more crucial than the boundary issue while improving relations with India, though it was a central issue between the two countries.

As a result, the boundary dispute and the Tibetan autonomy issue ran parallel in terms of India-China relations. The differences cropped up when there was disagreement between the two countries over the Tibetan issue and the territorial issue. India, the champion of anti-colonialism and anti-imperialism, opposed China's interference in the internal affairs of Tibet. Perhaps the relations between the two countries deteriorated when India protested against the Chinese invasion of Tibet in mid-1950. However, the Chinese government took seriously the way India protested on the Tibetan issue, and did not like its role as a saviour, and asserted that Tibet was an intrinsic part of China. Therefore, the Tibetan issue became yet another source of concern for the strained relations between the two countries. The two countries agreed to reach some kind of agreement, to alleviate the situation and prevent further deterioration of relations. In this regard, it was in 1954 that an agreement was signed concerning trade and related issues between India and China. "Under the agreement, India accepted Chinese sovereignty over Tibet and agreed to relinquish those extra-territorial rights in Tibet that it had inherited from the British when the latter transferred power to India. The agreement was based on the following principles:

a. mutual respect for each other's territorial integrity and sovereignty ;
b. mutual non-aggression;
c. mutual non-interference in each other's internal affairs;
d. equality and mutual benefit; and
e. peaceful co-existence.[10]

During this period, the outbreak of an anti-China revolt in Tibet in March 1959 precipitated a rapid deterioration in relations between the two countries. The Chinese government invaded Tibet and ruthlessly suppressed the rebels (Tibetan liberation activists). The military action against the Tibetan rebels elicited a strong response from the general public in India, which expressed resentment over the attack. "With the flight of the Dalai Lama to India, the situation further deteriorated. China resented the sympathy shown by many in India to the Tibetan insurgents and deemed it interference in the domestic affairs of China."[11] Furthermore, India's decision to provide the Dalai Lama with political asylum infuriated China. As a result, the difference between India and China over the Tibetan issue further sharpened and became a bone of contention between the two countries.

But China suspected India's involvement in it, without whose support, the Tibetans dared not revolt against the Chinese army. As a

---

10   Quoted in T. Karki Hussain, Sino-Indian Conflict and International Politics in the Indian Sub-Continent, Thomson Press (India) Ltd., Faridabad, 1977, p-4.
11   T.Karki Hussain, Supra No.10, p-5.

result, China alleged that India, which sympathized with the Tibetan cause, had not only extended her help but also allegedly supported the Tibetan rebellion. The allegations and counter-allegations between the two countries proved to be a crucial obstacle to the normalcy of Sino-Indian relations.

Therefore, it was not only the boundary dispute but also the Tibetan issue that was a significant led to enormous tension between India and China. Despite several attempts to alleviate the situation, for one reason or another, the boundary dispute continued to haunt Sino-Indian relations. But it was only after Rajiv Gandhi's emergence as the Prime Minister of India that some far- reaching developments began to take place, ultimately leading to improved relations between the two countries.

However, as far as India was concerned, the vexed issue between India and China was mainly the border dispute. It was the border issue that caused a significant schism in Sino-Indian relations. In India's view, a genuine reconciliation would follow a territorial settlement. "However, there has been a substantial change in India's approach to the issue. For several years, India insisted that a solution to the border issue should be accorded priority so that India-China ties could be normalized, while China advanced the view that the two countries should normalize their ties, build confidence, and over the years, gradually, a mutually amicable settlement of the border issue would emerge."[12]

The year 1980 was considered a watershed moment in the history of Sino-Indian relations. During this period Indira Gandhi re-emerged as the Prime Minister of India and paid attention to improving

---

12   V.P.Dutt, India's Foreign Policy in Changing World, Vikas Publishing House, New Delhi, 1999, p-205.

Sino-Indian ties. Therefore, in the 1980s, the boundary dispute shifted from antagonism to dialogue and tension to relaxation. Accordingly, Indira Gandhi took the initiative to start the official–level talks in 1981. She succeeded in holding five rounds of negotiations before her untimely death in October 1984. Another three rounds of talks took place during Rajiv Gandhi's period prior to his visit to Beijing in December 1988. But Indira Gandhi strengthened the relations between India and China to some extent, and later on, Rajiv Gandhi's concrete steps towards normalizing relations with China bore fruit.

Rajiv Gandhi's Period:

Soon after assuming the office of Prime Minister, Rajiv Gandhi paid serious attention to improving India's relations with its immediate neighbours, especially with China. The strained relations between the two countries started improving during Rajiv Gandhi's period. Rajiv Gandhi was determined to open a new chapter in Sino-Indian ties, thereby undertaking several confidence-building measures to strengthen India's relations with China.

Before he visited China in 1988, Rajiv Gandhi continued the efforts of his mother to improve relations with China. When Rajiv Gandhi began talks on Sino-Indian relations, several irritants came his way. The Chinese intervention in the Sumdorong Chu Valley of Arunachal Pradesh in early 1986 was a significant cause of concern for India. The said intervention became a major irritant in Sino-Indian relations when both countries completed almost six rounds of talks. Further, the approval of the Indian Parliament to upgrade Arunachal Pradesh to the level of statehood caused a big problem in Sino-Indian relations. Despite certain irritants, Rajiv Gandhi made concerted efforts to improve India's relations with China. As a result, he continued the border talks with China initiated by his mother, Indira Gandhi, in 1981.

The Sixth Round of Border Talks:

The previous rounds of talks on the Sino-Indian boundary dispute were ineffective and failed to produce any desired results for many reasons. However, the Sixth Round of talks provided a framework to the negotiations when Rajiv Gandhi and Chinese Prime Minister Zhao Ziyang met in New York in October 1985. The sixth round of discussions took place in New Delhi in November 1985. The Chinese side said that India should make "matching concessions" in the eastern sector if it wanted China to vacate some areas in the Ladakh sector. Thus, for the first time in official level talks, the Chinese deviated from the "package" line and asked for territory in the eastern sector."[13] Since China had taken a divergent approach concerning the boundary dispute, India refused to accept the Chinese proposal. As a result, the leader of the Chinese delegation to the border talks stated that no settlement could be arrived unless India made some concessions in the east as proposed. Therefore, this new Chinese stand marked a critical departure from the previously held position on the boundary dispute. The result was that the sixth round of border talks ended without any significant progress.

Sumdorong Chu Valley Intrusion:

Hardly a week before the Seventh Round of talks, a dramatic event took place in July 1986 when the Chinese troops committed a significant incursion into Indian territory to the south of the McMahon line in the Thongdrong area of Arunachal Pradesh's Kameng division. Against this backdrop, the then Minister of State for External Affairs, K.Narayanan made a statement in the Lok Sabha on August 8, 1986, that the government had disturbing information about the Chinese intrusion into the Sumdorong Chu Valley of Arunachal Pradesh". He

---

13   J.K.Baral and others, Millenium, 26 (3), July-September 1989, p-265.

further said, "Chinese personnel have not only improvised a helipad there, "it has also been noticed that they are setting up tents and building huts in the area."[14] These developments have caused India great concern for its security and integrity. As a result, India lodged an immediate protest against the Chinese incursion and decided to raise the issue at the Seventh Round of Sino-Indian border talks in July 1986.

However, "on August 22, 1986, China rejected allegations that Chinese forces had intruded into north-eastern India as "unwarranted and distorted propaganda". On the contrary, it accused Indian aircraft and military personnel of "repeated" crossings of the Line of Actual Control in the eastern sector."[15] The Chinese, however, asserted that the area to the north of the Line of Actual Control was in their territory and re-asserted their position that the whole of Arunachal Pradesh (formerly known as NEFA) was their territory. Despite all these developments, the Chinese proposed "mutual concessions" in the valley of Sumdorong Chu, which was not agreeable to India. Instead, Rajiv Gandhi called for "systematic and scientific mapping" of the area, which could help in settling the dispute."[16] India considered this an attempt by China to revive the conflict over the eastern boundary. The border talks, held under the shadow of this latest Chinese intrusion into India, naturally became an obstacle.

The Sumdorong Chu Valley incident drew the world's attention for its gravity and intensity. Nevertheless, there was no briefing for the press and media agencies on the matter. Even international observers predicted that the intrusion would result in another war between India and China. According to a scholar, the Sumdorong Chu Valley episode

---

14   Asian Recorder, 32 (36) September 3-9 1986, p-19060

15   Asian Recorder, Supra No. 14, p-19060

16   Quoted in Kanti Bajpai and Amitabh Mattoo, (Ed) The Peacock and the Dragon: India- China Relations in the 21st Century, Har Ananad, New Delhi, 2000, p-183.

was "a potentially dangerous situation" which "touched off a border buildup by both sides" but was "controlled by diplomatic action."[17]

However, Rajiv Gandhi's dynamic leadership handled the Sumdurong Chu Valley incident diplomatically, preventing a crucial war similar to the 1962 Indo-China War. Even international observers praised Rajiv Gandhi's timely intervention in defusing the tension between the two countries over the Sumdurong Chu incident. Rajiv Gandhi's attempts significantly reduced the anxiety along the boundary line.

The Seventh Round of Border Talks:

Despite the Sumdorong Chu incident, the seventh round of discussions was held in July 1986 as planned. India accused China of its intrusion into the Sumdorong Chu Valley of Arunachal Pradesh and, as expected, raised the issue apart from the border dispute at the Seventh Round of Sino-Indian border talks. China vehemently denied this accusation, but the resulting tension made the seventh round vulnerable to collapse. However, then Foreign Secretary A.P.Venkateshwaran, the leader of the Indian delegation, claimed that the ongoing talks had resulted in a much better appreciation of each other's positions on the various issues."[18] But the discussions on intrusion and border issues ended in Beijing in July 1986 without making any substantial progress. As such, relations between India and China continued to drift throughout 1986.

Conferring Statehood to Arunachal Pradesh:

When efforts were underway to improve relations between India and China, the issue of Arunachal Pradesh became a major irritant. As

---

17   Bidanda M.Chengappa, Supra No.3, p-81.

18   J.K.Baral and Other's, Rajiv Gandhi's China Diplomacy: Dynamics and problems, Millenium, 26(3) July-September, 1989, p-265.

a result, relations between India and China reached their climax when "the Lok Sabha passed two bills on December 8, 1986, conferring statehood on the Union Territory of Arunachal Pradesh."[19] The main objective of the Indian government's decision to confer statehood on Arunachal Pradesh was to ease the situation in the eastern sector, which was considered a disputed area. The relations between India and China were not so cordial before upgrading Arunachal Pradesh, a Union Territory, to the level of the state.

However, considering the developments that had taken place in Arunachal Pradesh, the Chinese government strongly objected to India's declaration of Arunachal Pradesh as an independent state. The spokesperson of the Chinese government stated that "a bill upgrading Union Territory, Arunachal Pradesh, to the level of state established on a part of Chinese territory illegally occupied by India. This act has once again seriously violated China's territorial integrity and sovereignty and deeply hurt the feelings of the Chinese people. The Chinese solemnly declare that the Bill approved by the Indian Parliament is absolutely illegal and that China will never recognize the so-called Arunachal Pradesh established in the most disputed eastern sector of the Sino-Indian boundary.[20] The main idea behind the protest was that China considered the north-eastern sector of the North Eastern Frontier Area (NEFA) a disputed area.

But India refuted the Chinese allegation over the issue of granting statehood to Arunachal Pradesh and categorically stated that the protest from China was against the principle of the Panchsheel Agreement, which envisages non-interference in the internal affairs of other countries. Since granting statehood to Arunachal Pradesh is an internal affair of India, China has no absolute role to play in the matter.

---

19   Asian Recorder, 33 (3), 15-21 January 1987, p-19269.
20   Asian Recorder, 33 (3), 15-21 January 1987, p-19270.

Therefore, India termed China's protests unwarranted and baseless and described the statement as a "clear interference in the internal affairs of this country.[21] Further, India also made it clear that before making any statement against India, China should have considered its commitment to the Panchsheel Agreement in letter and spirit.

Despite these developments, the process of peaceful negotiations continued. Further, India continued its efforts to normalize relations with China. In this context, the then foreign minister, N.D.Tiwari, visited Beijing in June 1987. In their joint statement, both he and Vice Foreign Minister Liu-Shuqing emphasised that peace and friendship were more important than any differences.[22]

The Eighth Round of Border Talks:

A comparatively relaxed atmosphere preceded the eighth round of talks held in November 1987 in New. Delhi. The tensions of the first half of 1987 gradually decreased. "In fact, China was full of appreciation for India's decision not to give any support, moral, or physical, to the agitation that the Tibetans had launched earlier in the year."[23] It was happy about India's stance concerning the Tibetan issue. It was particularly so because of the American criticism of Chinese action. Obviously, at the eighth round of talks, India decided not to raise the border issue for the time being and confined itself to the areas of cooperation to create a conducive atmosphere during the discussions. However, this was perhaps a change of policy under Rajiv Gandhi's leadership over the boundary dispute. "Indira Gandhi had attached the resolution of the boundary issue to the development of relations in other domains. Rajiv Gandhi's leadership deviated from this position and emphasized that the improvement and strengthening of relations

---

21   Asian Recorder, 33 (3) 15-21 January 1987, p-19269.

22   Patriot, (New Delhi), 16 June 1987.

23   Qouted in J.K.Baral and Others, Supra No.14, p-265.

in other spheres such as trade and commerce, science and technology, and culture should not be held hostage to the border issue.[24]. In addition, the two groups also discussed international issues. Therefore, among the earlier rounds of talks, the talks held at the eighth round succeeded in making some breakthroughs in the dialogues. However, the boundary dispute remained unresolved.

After eight rounds of border dispute negotiations, Rajiv Gandhi revised his strategy, resulting in a minor breakthrough. But the boundary question remained unresolved, despite several rounds of talks. However, this prompted Rajiv Gandhi to visit to China in December 1988, which aroused new hopes in Sino-Indian relations. Another significant factor that undoubtedly led Rajiv Gandhi to improve Sino-Indian relations was the initiative of Gorbachev, the General Secretary of the Communist Party of the Soviet Union. "In 1986, he openly declared in Vladivostok that the Soviet Union was interested in improving its relations with China."[25] Also, the All India Congress Committee passed a resolution on November 5, 1988, that authorized Rajiv Gandhi to seek a settlement based on "mutual interest" and "acceptable to the peoples of both countries" through "peaceful negotiations," even if it took time.[26] This further strengthened the hands of Rajiv Gandhi in taking concrete steps to improve Sino-Indian relations by undertaking a trip to China.

From Confrontation to Normalization:

Rajiv Gandhi's visit to China on December 19, 1988, marked a significant turning point in Sino-Indian relations and a step towards

---

24   B.R Deepak, India and China: 1904-2004. A Century of Peace and Conflict, Manak Publications, New Delhi, 2005, p-324.

25   B.R Deepak, Supra No. 24, p-319.

26   Surjit Mansingh, India-China Relations in the Post-Cold War Era, Asian Survey, 34(3), March 1994, p-289.

improving relations between the two countries after a 34- year hiatus. After the Sino-Indian War of 1962, his visit to China opened a new chapter by shattering the barriers of hostility and mistrust and fostering reciprocal trust between the two countries. As a result, there were high expectations for Rajiv Gandhi's visit, which would result in finding a lasting solution to the Sino-Indian border dispute. During the visit, Rajiv Gandhi made it abundantly clear that issues facing the two countries could not be solved in three or four days. He said, "We have to pave the way for creating an atmosphere which may help in solving mutual problems. This visit to China, the first ever by an Indian Prime Minister since 1954, was an endeavour to rebuild the bridges of friendship through peaceful co existence."[27] The primary objective of the visit was to improve the atmosphere and move from confrontation to normalization of relations, i.e., opening up new areas of cooperation in trade, science and technology, education, mass media, etc.

During the visit, though the border question remained a critical concern, it was emphasized that, in light of changing technological advances, both nations should attempt to strengthen the growing goodwill and enlarge the areas of cooperation in cultural, scientific, and socio-economic spheres. Rajiv Gandhi emphasized the purpose of the visit by saying, "The national sentiments and dignity of both countries have to be understood and respected and added, "We shall conduct our dialogue in this spirit". It was agreed during the visit that a joint working group was to be constituted to look into the border question. China has laid claim to 90,000 sq.km. of Indian territory in the Akshai–Chin area of Ladakh in the Western sector."[28]

---

27   Ranjan Kumar Mishra, India and International Relations, Kanishka Publishers, New Delhi, 1996, p-135.

28   M.R.Biju, India's Foreign Policy, National Publishing House, Jaipur, 2000, p-237.

Though the boundary question figured prominently in Rajiv Gandhi's discussion with the Chinese leaders, bilateral agreements were still given priority during the talks. The Chinese leaders, who always insisted on a give-and-take policy, once again brought the package deal during the discussions. But Rajiv Gandhi was not agreeable to the package deal as far as the border dispute was concerned. Before his visit, even Rajiv Gandhi ruled out any territorial concessions to China and said, "There is no question of giving any piece of land while I am in China. Let me make it very clear."[29] Therefore, Rajiv Gandhi was firm in his stance that, under his leadership, India would not accept the proposal of the Chinese government on the border issue.

Rajiv Gandhi's visit to China was hailed as "historic" since it marked "a new beginning" in relations between the two countries. Rajiv Gandhi's leadership was mainly responsible for improving Sino-Indian relations, which had remained strained for several years. The "Hindi-Chini bhai bhai" sentiment of the 1950s, which receded in history for several years, resurfaced during Rajiv Gandhi's visit to China in 1988. A significant outcome of this visit was the formation of the Joint Working Group (JWG) in early 1989.

During Rajiv Gandhi's visit, both sides agreed to set up a Joint Working Group (JWG) at the level of Vice Ministers for negotiations on the boundary issue. However, this was considered a significant step forward in Sino-Indian relations. It was clear from Sino-Indian relations that the JWG's establishment paved the way for reducing border tensions and the development of confidence-building measures. With the formation of JWG, the border dispute separated from other bilateral concerns. Among other things, the working group was expected to consider a "re-working of the Deng proposal"

---

29   Times of India, (New Delhi) 28 September 1988.

of 1979-80, which was basically a revival of the Zhou-Enlai "give and take" idea of the late fifties and early sixties.[30]

According to the observers, the decision of the two governments to establish the JWG on the boundary question replaced the long-drawn-out process that included eight mainly metaphysical rounds of official-level talks. As a result of the new decision, India and China's relations speculated to free from the bickering that had characterized them in recent years. Further, it was believed that the formation of the JWG would definitely strengthen the process of normalizing relations between the two countries.

The Bilateral Agreements:

India and China signed three separate agreements on intergovernmental cooperation in civil aviation, science and technology, and a bilateral cultural exchange programme. "The agreement on cooperation in science and technology called for interaction between the scientific communities and institutions in the two countries and envisaged the establishment of a joint committee, which would meet at regular intervals to monitor progress. Under the air services accord, the two countries agreed in principle to establish direct air links between New Delhi and Beijing. The cultural agreement covered the exchange of dance and music troupes, artists, writers, and press delegations, art exhibitions, etc."[31] During Rajiv Gandhi's period, a new era ushered in bilateral cooperation between the countries. As a result, bilateral economic and trade cooperation considerably increased, keeping aside the boundary dispute for the time being. Although the boundary issue was a bone of contention between the two countries, it received little attention during the talks.

------

30   Asian Recorder, 35 (7), February 12-18 1989, p-20434.
31   Asian Recorder, 35 (7), February 12-18 1989, p-20434.

A Joint Communiqué:

A joint communiqué was released on December 23, 1988, after the meeting and stated that the discussions had been fruitful, had advanced mutual understanding and benefited the further improvement and development of bilateral relations. "It further emphasized the importance of the Five Principles of Peaceful Co-existence and reiterated that these should be the basis guarding principles for establishing a new political and economic world order. As regards the boundary issue, the joint communiqué stated that both sides agreed to resolve this problem through peaceful means and consultation. It was also agreed that while seeking a solution to the border issue acceptable to both sides, efforts would be made to develop relations in other spheres so as to create an atmosphere and conditions conducive to settling the border issue reasonably and justly."[32]

During Rajiv Gandhi's visit, though the boundary dispute was the main agenda of the bilateral discussions as discussed earlier, it was put aside as the talks between the Indian and Chinese leaders mostly centred on the bilateral agreements and relations between the two countries. Perhaps Rajiv Gandhi believed that the bilateral agreements would undeniably reduce the tensions in the eastern sector along the Line of Actual Control and pave the way for settling the border issue. Therefore, during the talks, bilateral agreements between the two countries preceded over-the-border talks.

The two sides agreed that in the modern world, conflict gave way to dialogue and tension to relaxation concerning the global situation. The long years of unfruitful struggle by the nations and people who value peace against power politics have given rise to this trend. The two sides realised that time is conducive to world peace and resolving

---

32   B.R.Deepak, Supra No. 24, p-332.

regional problems. As a result, both China and India agreed to global peace, promote complete disarmament, and advance of all-round.

The notable feature of the talks was that China expressed concern over the activities against the motherland by some Chinese Tibetans in India. However, whereas the Indian side reiterated the long and consistent policy of the government of India, Rajiv Gandhi said, "Tibet is an autonomous region of China, and India does not allow these Tibetans to engage in political activities against China in India."[33] But Rajiv Gandhi's concern over the Tibetan issue and his statement became a debatable subject.

The success of Rajiv Gandhi's visit to China in 1988 is as follows:

1. Sino-Indian relations were taken out of the past prejudices and put on a forward looking posture to momentum for an all-round development of relations.
2. Pending a solution to the boundary dispute, both sides agreed to maintain peace along the line of actual control, and at the same time, laid emphasis on cooperation in other areas of mutual concern and benefit.
3. The principles of Panchsheel were reemphasized as a guidepost for relations between the two countries.
4. Formation of a working group at the level of Vice-Ministers for negotiations on the boundary question and for strengthening the maintenance of peace and tranquilly along the border.
5. Formation of a working group at the level of Vice-Ministers to promote trade, economic, and investment relations".[34]

---

33   www.mfa.gov.cn/eng/

34   V.P.Dutt, "India-China Promise and Limitation" (Ed) in Lalit Mansingh and Others, Indian Foreign Policy, Agenda for the 21st Century, Vol-2, Konark Publishers, New Delhi, 1998, pp-242, 243.

Even after Rajiv Gandhi's exit, the spirit of his visit remained intact. There were a series of high-level exchanges between the two countries, and the Joint Working Group (JWG) proposed by Rajiv Gandhi and Li Peng was set up in 1988 to work out modalities to resolve all disputes. It was entrusted with the task of maintaining peace and tranquilly on the border.

The two leaders of the JWG, namely, the Indian Foreign Secretary and the Chinese Vice Minister, were given powers to review and initiate proposals for resolving the border issue. Accordingly, the JWG met in July 1989 to discuss all outstanding issues, including the border dispute. Even though the meeting produced no noteworthy results, it provided a conducive environment for sitting across the table and resolving disputes without resorting to hatred or conflict.

Meeting with Deng Xiaoping:

Rajiv Gandhi also happened to meet the oldest person in China, Deng Xiaoping. In his meeting with Rajiv Gandhi on December 21, 1988, Deng Xiaoping, Chairman of the Central Military Commission of the PRC, said, "Let both sides forget the unpleasant period in our past relations, and let us treat everything with an eye on the future."[35]

The discussions between the two leaders laid the groundwork for the growth of Sino-Indian relations. Both sides reached some understanding on border issues and agreed to settle them through peaceful and friendly negotiations. The visit was marked by two significant events: Deng's meeting with India's young Prime Minister, when the ageing leader of China declared that the future belonged to the generation of young leaders of the world, and Rajiv Gandhi's

---

35 Quoted in Wong Hongyu, Sino-Indian Relations: Present and Future, Asian Survey, 35(6), June 1995, p.546.

acceptance of the Chinese position that the 5,000- kilometre border was negotiable.[36]

Although Rajiv Gandhi's China visit was responsible for achieving several objectives, newspaper columnists and opposition figures criticized his trip. Because they zeroed in on his statement that, "Tibet is an internal matter of China."[37] Rajiv Gandhi's statement achieved significance and became a debatable subject in India. Even the leaders of different political parties questioned India's propriety and the genuineness of its policy towards Tibet, which had been in place since Jawaharlal Nehru's period. As a result, India's stand on Tibet came under the scanner, as it claimed to champion against colonialism and imperialism, which had been followed since pre-independence. Even Rajiv Gandhi's statement during his stay in Beijing elicited criticisms, and was termed a violation of the principle of reciprocity by not asking China about the absence of human rights in Tibet and by neglecting to secure China's recognition of Sikkim's merger in India".[38] On the contrary, some critics argued that Rajiv Gandhi's visit to China would considerably contribute to establishing and preserving peace in the region as well as across the globe.

However, it is pertinent to note that the leaders were not aware of Jawaharlal Nehru, who clarified India's stand on Tibet much before Rajiv Gandhi's statement. In 1954, Jawaharlal Nehru said, "Tibet was a part of China, and in 2003, A.B. Vajpayee, the then Prime Minister, said, "The Tibetan Autonomous Region was part of

---

36   Bhabani Sen Gupta, India: The Next Great Power, in Lalit Mansingh and Others, (Ed) Indian Foreign Policy, Agenda for the 21st Century, (Vol-1) Konark Publishers, New Delhi, 1997, pp-134-135.

37   Sumit Ganguly, the Sino-Indian Border Talks: 1981-1989, Asian Survey, 29 (12), December 1989, p-1133.

38   K.Baral and others, Rajiv Gandhi's China Diplomacy: Dynamics and Problems, Millennium, 26 (3), July-September, 1989, p-268

China."[39] Therefore, it clearly indicates that Rajiv Gandhi's statement on Tibet was nothing but a reiteration of what Jawaharlal Nehru and A.B. Vajpayee had said.

Perhaps "the Indian officials closely associated with the visit took a different view and contended that Prime Minister Rajiv Gandhi's statement was a mere reiteration of a long-standing Indian position that dates back to 1954 when India firmly acknowledged Chinese sovereignty on Tibet. "Furthermore, they argued that it would have been foolish to seek a similar endorsement on disputed Indian territories".[40] India deliberately refrained from inciting controversy about Tibet since it was believed that any comments on the Tibetan Autonomous Region (TAR) would inevitably deteriorate relations between the two countries. Therefore, Rajiv Gandhi dealt with the issue diplomatically to strengthen India's relations with China.

India considered Tibet an issue adversely affecting Sino-Indian relations. The history of Sino-Indian relations demonstrates that the Tibetan issue led to deteriorating relations between the two countries. "For China, Tibet has been a highly sensitive issue". As Jawaharlal Nehru once remarked, it was not clear from whom the Chinese wanted to liberate Tibet, as China talked darkly about imperialist forces even as it sent its army to occupy the "roof of the world". India has had long-standing cultural and religious ties with Tibet but no desire to maintain an "imperialistic" presence there, and so it surrendered the British-maintained installations in Lhasa."[41]

The Package Deal:

39　http:// timesofindia.indiatimes.com/articleshow.

40　Sumit Ganguly, Supra No.37, p-1133.

41　V.P.Dutt, India –China: Promise and Limitation, in Lalith Mansingh and Others,(ed) Indian Foreign Policy, Agenda For the 21st Century, Konark Publishers, New Delhi, 1998, p-229.

When the boundary dispute between the two countries became thorny and remained unresolved, China took the initiative and proposed the settlement of the problem through mutual trust and negotiations. In this context, China proposed resolving the unsolved border issues be resolved under the current Line of Actual Control. About this, the then Chinese Vice Premier Teng Hsiao Ping had reportedly said, "While we recognize the present Line of Actual Control in the Eastern Sector, India should recognize the status quo in the West", meaning the Aksai-Chin and the Karakoram areas, which are under Chinese control at present."[42] But in simple terms, the proposal put forth by the Chinese government was nothing but a "give and take formula". In other words, the package deal involved settling the dispute along the lines of actual control with concessions and adjustments in the eastern sectors.

Further, a similar proposal resurfaced during the tenure of Indira Gandhi. China proposed in June 1980 that the present Line of Actual Control be used as the basis to resolve the border issue. As a result, Deng Xiaoping, the then Chinese leader, announced a "package deal" to settle the Sino-Indian border dispute amicably. But the Indian government played it cool. Prior to Deng, during his talks in New Delhi in 1960, then-Premier Zhou-Enlai had proposed practically the same thing during his discussion, but the Indian government finally rejected it. The deal proposed by Deng Xiaoping was that "in the eastern sector, China recognize the McMahon Line as demanded by India; in turn, India could concede Aksai-Chin to China in the western sector."[43] Further, it was also made clear that if a resolution was not possible to the problem, it should be put on ice in order to improve ties between India and China.

---

42   Verinder Grover ,(ed) International Relations and Foreign Policy of India: China, Japan and India's Foreign Policy, Deep and Deep Publications, New Delhi, 1992, p-116.

43   India Quarterly, 41 (1) January-March 1985, p-20.

The Indian public reacted sharply to Deng's proposal, as it was in Indian interest. Reacting coolly to the proposal, then Foreign Minister P.V.Narasimha Rao stated in the Lok Sabha on July 20, 1980, that other ways than the package solution could prove more 'effective'. India, on its part, hoped to settle the border question in a spirit consistent with national honour and the interests of both sides on the basis of equality."[44] However, it considered that the two governments came to grips with the longstanding and complex border problem as a positive step after a significant amount of time had passed.

During Rajiv Gandhi's period, the "package deal' resurfaced, particularly during the sixth, seventh, and eighth rounds of Sino-Indian border talks. The Chinese also asserted their long-standing claim that the traditional boundary line lay east of the McMahon Line, i.e., the Himalayan crest. India perceived that the Chinese had toughened their position. "In December 1985, the External Affairs Minister stated in the Rajya Sabha that the resolution of the border problem was a prerequisite for a complete normalization of relations."[45] Therefore, the package deal did not bear any fruit but was put on the backburner during Rajiv Gandhi's period.

B.R.Deepak, a scholar on Indo-China relations, suggested that to resolve the boundary dispute, "India must not talk of the 1963 Parliament resolution that talks of taking back "every inch of Indian territory". Similarly, China should stop the rhetoric that it does not recognize the "so-called" Arunachal.[46] As far as the latter suggestion is concerned, it is an internal matter of India, and the former is not acceptable to it. Because, in essence, the suggestion is nothing but a reformed proposal

---

44 Verinder Grover ,(ed) International Relations and Foreign Policy of India: China, Japan and India's Foreign Policy, Deep and Deep Publications, New Delhi, 1992, p-75.

45 Sumit Ganguly, Supra No.37, p-1129.

46 B.R.Deepak, Supra No. 24, p-439.

of a "package deal", i.e., a give-and-take policy. The plain reading of the package deal indicates that it discusses the status quo in the Western sector and negotiation in the Eastern sector, which was one-sided. As a result, this proposal was not acceptable to India. Because India wanted to negotiate sector-by-sector, which considered all the sectors disputed, whereas China only wanted negotiation on the eastern sector. This demonstrates the Chinese intention to resolve the boundary dispute.

Therefore, if Jawaharlal Nehru had accepted the package deal or the give-and-take proposal offered by China, as suggested by the scholar, India would have lost thousands of kilometres of its territory to China. Further, the deal would have gone against the wishes and the public opinion of the Indians, who were against parting even an inch of India's territory with China. In fact, the Indian government under the leadership of Jawaharlal Nehru reaffirmed "the 1963 Parliamentary Resolution that India would not hold substantive discussions with China until the Chinese vacated every inch of Indian territory."[47] In this context, the decision taken by Jawaharlal Nehru, the then Prime Minister, to accept the Chinese proposal appears correct in the interests of the people and the sovereignty of India. In fact, the package deal suggested by the then Premier of China, Zhou-Enlai, and subsequently by Deng Xiaoping was not in India's interest but intended to serve the Chinese only.

The "Tiananmen Square Incident" and the Indian Stance:

During the latter part of the 1980s, some dramatic events surfaced in international politics. More particularly, the Communist countries of the world witnessed such events. Firstly, the Soviet Union collapsed in 1990 due to the liberal policies introduced in 1985. Secondly, the consolidation of forces of liberal democracy and freedom clashed with authoritarianism and oppression in some parts of the world. In this

---

47   Quoted in Sumit Ganguly, supra No. 37, p-1126.

context, Beijing the capital of China, also felt the effects of this situation. "The death of Huo Yaobang on April 15, 1989, who was dismissed in 1987 for being lenient with pro-democracy students, provided an opportunity for the students to vent their anger out on the hard-line Communist leaders, including Xiaoping Deng."[48] In early June 1989, the Chinese government started to crush the pro-democracy movements led by students and reformists, resulting in untoward violence across the country. Chinese students who led the protest movement against the authoritarian attitude of then Premier Zhian Zhou were dealt with harshly. The students, however, withstood the oppressive measures initiated by the Chinese leaders to stifle the movement. When the protest turned violent and out of control, the Chinese government ordered its troops to deal with the protestors firmly. As a result, in early June 1989, Chinese troops ruthlessly suppressed the student-led pro-democracy movement in Beijing. The Chinese government used all physical force against the students assembled in Tiananmen Square in Beijing's capital. The horrific incident left thousands of protestors injured and hundreds of them dead.

The Tiananmen Square incident generated much controversy and argument in the Western world, including the Communist countries. However, the incident did not appear to alter Western policies towards the PRC (People's Republic of China). In fact, the incident shook the whole world and paved the way for widespread condemnation across the globe. Even several pro-democratic countries in the world condemned the incident strongly. Gorbachev, the then General Secretary of the Communist Party of the Soviet Union, told a press conference that he regretted some aspects of what had happened in China. He also indicated that during his visit, he had received letters

---

48   B.R.Deepak, Supra No. 24, p-334.

from the demonstrating Chinese students and said he felt that many of their concerns were legitimate."[49]

Rajiv Gandhi, who had just arrived from China's visit, expressed deep concern over the ghastly incident without making any anti-China statement on the massacre. Rajiv Gandhi made it clear in a press conference on June 16, 1989, that though India approves of democracies in all places, it does not intervene in other countries' internal affairs."[50] This naturally made the pro-democracy countries of the world question the propriety of India's stand and its genuineness. However, the Indian Ministry of External Affairs issued a carefully worded statement that avoided direct criticism of the Chinese leadership. Furthermore, India did not postpone the first meeting of the Joint Working Group.[51] Both of these gestures sent a message to Beijing that, despite Beijing's diplomatic isolation following the Tiananmen Square events, Indian leadership was prepared to continue doing business with the Chinese.

In this context, Rajiv Gandhi meticulously followed the principles of Panchsheel, i.e., non-interference in each other's internal affairs, in letter and spirit. Rajiv Gandhi believed that making anti-China remarks would lead to intervention in Chinese affairs and further deteriorate relations between the two countries. Therefore, Rajiv Gandhi carefully avoided the friction between the two countries by refraining from making anti-China comments on the Tiananmen Square issue.

In the meantime, the first meeting of the JWG took place in Beijing from June 30 to July 4, 1989. K.Natwar Singh, the then External Affairs Minister, led the Indian delegation. The friendly attitude of

49   Asian Survey, 29 (12), December 1989, p-1146.

50   B.R.Deepak, India and China: 1904-2004 A Century of Peace and Conflict, Manak Publications, New Delhi, 2005, p-334.

51   Asian Survey, 29 (12), December 1989, p-1146.

Beijing during the talks was the outcome of the "cautious approach" adopted by India on the Tiananmen incident."[52] Therefore, the Indian approach towards the Tiananmen Square incident elicited appreciation from China, and it expressed happiness. Gulam Nabi Azad, then General Secretary of Congress, elaborated further on the Indian position during his visit to China in July 1989 after the Tiananmen Square incident. During his visit, Azad said, "We strictly adhere to the Five Principles of Peaceful Co-existence, one of these being non-interference in other country's internal affairs. Ziang Zemin appreciated India's approach during the Tiananmen incident and emphasized that China attached great importance to developing relations with India.[53]

India's silence over Tiananmen Square should not mean support for such egregious human rights violations in China. Rajiv Gandhi committed to improving the strained relations between the two countries. It took nearly 38 years for successive Indian leaders to normalize its relations with China. Therefore, Rajiv Gandhi's stance of not making any anti-China remarks over the incident appears to have been correct in that hour, which was determined to improve its relations with China. As a sovereign country, India need not follow the actions of others or accept the acts of the Chinese government. Rajiv Gandhi proved his statesmanship and demonstrated that India adhered to the principles of the Panchsheel Agreement signed between India and China.

In so far as Sino-Indian relations were concerned, Rajiv Gandhi played a significant role in improving relations between the two countries. His bold step in visiting China despite hostility from the

---

52   B.R.Deepak, Supra No.24, p-335
53   B.R.Deepak, Supra No. 24, p-335

opposition parties in India evoked strong appreciation not only from the Indian public but also from the international community. Because of his sincere efforts today, the two Asian giants could closely figure in global politics by signing various bilateral agreements in diverse fields. It was also due to Rajiv Gandhi's leadership that India and China could cooperate in most areas, including the strategic one. Indeed, Rajiv Gandhi's leadership in the post-Cold War era paved the way for reducing tensions and improving strained relations between India and China.

The post-Cold War period was more pragmatic in terms of taking concrete steps to introduce cooperation, and in this context, Sino-Indian relations are crucial. Accordingly, both countries held several talks with their leaders to strengthen bilateral cooperation in information technology, biotechnology, and other related fields. Even during the post-Cold War era, the boundary dispute between the two countries ended due to Rajiv Gandhi's imitative and subsequent talks held by P.V.Narasimha Rao, India's then Prime Minister. The base for negotiations began under the leadership of Rajiv Gandhi, who was responsible for the shift in policy towards the boundary dispute. He heralded a new era of cooperation between India and China. Because of his endeavour, several Chinese dignitaries began visiting India. The first was Li Peng, the then-Chinese Premier, followed by P.V.Narasimha Rao's visit to China, which set the agenda for normalizing bilateral relations between India and China. The exchanges of high-level dignitaries that followed suit accelerated the pace of normalizing relations between the two powerful Asian countries. Therefore, Rajiv Gandhi's visit to China in 1988 substantially helped to improve Sino-Indian relations.

Indeed, Rajiv Gandhi's visit to China in 1988 laid the foundation for dialogue and the mutual opening of trade and cultural contacts. His meetings with Chinese leader Deng Xiaoping and Prime Minister Li Peng laid the groundwork for future success, and India is still reaping the benefits of those meetings. On Deng's suggestion, Rajiv agreed to the formula, putting aside the boundary dispute and focusing on strengthening bilateral ties through collaboration in other areas. Even today, the 1988 framework serves as the foundation for India's China policy, which has significantly helped the two countries' cordial relations until the Doklam standoff in 2020.

CHAPTER – VII

Conclusions

In the present world, no country is self-sufficient as far as its needs and desires are concerned. As a result, the countries of the globe have to depend on one another and vice versa to achieve self-sufficiency by fulfilling their wants and needs. As a result, while fulfilling their demands, the countries come into contact with one another, resulting in interdependence. This interdependence among the countries gave rise to their involvement in international relations. These relations were given concrete shape by specific ideas, which came to be known as the "rational guide," i.e., foreign policy. In the modern world, the foreign policy has become an instrument for protecting a country's national interests.

There are numerous factors that influence a country's foreign policy. However, the leadership factor is significant in the foreign policy formulation of a country, regardless of its political system. According to the present world situation, the very survival of the human race is directly dependent upon the pursuit of the right kind of foreign policy and the leaders who determine it. This kind of foreign policy, no doubt, helps to strengthen friendly relations between countries while also reducing conflicts and tensions around the world. As a result, the responsibility of a leader in formulating a sound foreign policy has increased manifold, as he has to keep in mind country's interests, which are of paramount importance. In a democratic country like India, the general public has little role to play in shaping the country's foreign policy. They were unaware of the international happenings due to a lack of interest in foreign affairs and were preoccupied with their day-to-day problems. As a result, this increased the responsibility of the leaders representing the people in shaping the country's foreign policy.

The study demonstrates that Rajiv Gandhi's leadership was crucial in shaping India's foreign policy. In the Indian context, Rajiv Gandhi made a significant contribution to dealing with foreign policy issues. It also reveals that Rajiv Gandhi was instrumental in improving relations with India's immediate neighbours, particularly Sri Lanka and China. Further, his policy towards the global superpowers strengthened friendly ties, especially with the US. Undoubtedly, Rajiv Gandhi was able to demonstrate leadership and succeeded in his mission of acquiring sophisticated technological know-how from the US.

The study of Rajiv Gandhi's foreign policy reveals that Rajiv Gandhi did not dominate the policy planning machinery on foreign policy, as criticized in some quarters. However, Rajiv Gandhi firmly believed in the democratic method of formulating India's foreign policy by allowing all the actors to be involved. Nevertheless, he was the crucial instrument behind the foreign policy mechanism that chalked out the policies and the External Affairs Ministry that implemented them. Indeed, Rajiv Gandhi wielded authority over the foreign policy mechanism to effectively monitor external affairs. Though Rajiv Gandhi had established domination over the External Affairs Ministry, he was very liberal in giving scope to the respective wings of the Policy Planning Committee to formulate an effective foreign policy. Naturally, this resulted in the stability of the foreign policy machinery. He even utilized properly the talent available among the Indian Foreign Service personnel, especially G.Parthasarathy, who was well versed in dealing with Tamil problems since Indira Gandhi's period. Besides, he appointed the then Foreign Secretary, Romesh Bhandari, as the Prime Minister's special envoy to deal with the Sri Lankan crisis. Even

J.N.Dixit, the then High Commissioner to Sri Lanka, was entrusted with the task of preparing an outline of the Indo-Sri Lankan Accord to be signed by Rajiv Gandhi and Jayewardene. However, this indicates that Rajiv Gandhi was democratic in the country's foreign policy-making process.

The tasks given to bureaucrats by the External Affairs Ministry, show Rajiv Gandhi's democratic approach to foreign affairs. However, concerning the Sri Lankan ethnic conflict, the ineffectiveness (mishandling) of the various agencies of the government of India and the emissaries tasked to deal with the ethnic crisis failed in their responsibilities. As a result, during Rajiv Gandhi's tenure, India primarily struggled to formulate an effective policy towards Sri Lanka. As a result, Rajiv Gandhi, who was instrumental in signing the Indo-Sri Lankan Accord, was confronted with the poignant situation in which the LTTE and other Tamil militant groups strongly opposed the Accord and proved hurdles to its implementation. Further, the IPKF, which was dispatched to Sri Lanka to protect Tamil interests, was involved in the massacre of innocent Tamils and thus failed in its mission. Naturally, this infuriated Rajiv Gandhi, who had intended to bring peace and normalcy to the war-ravaged island.

The brief history of India's foreign policy also reveals that it was not rigid but, in fact, flexible. Besides, it was also not clear, especially when dealing with the Sri Lankan ethnic issue and Chinese relations. India's foreign policy also proved that it is not static but adjustable. It was evident in the case of America, where India leaned towards the West during Indira Gandhi's period (1982-84) and Rajiv Gandhi's period (1984-88) to normalize relations. Naturally, this created a sense of mistrust and discontent in India's relations with the Soviet Union. India's shift in policy towards the West, especially during Rajiv Gandhi's period, was widely perceived as a deviation from the actual path laid down by his predecessors. However, it is beyond dispute that there was no shift in India's foreign policy towards the West during Rajiv Gandhi's regime to acquire US technological know-how and advance the country economically. He extended the hand of friendship towards the US in an effort to improve India's relations and get Western technology from that country. Rajiv Gandhi has been pursuing a liberalized policy ever since becoming the Prime Minister of India.

Rajiv Gandhi's visit to China in the second half of 1988 opened a new chapter in Sino-Indian relations. It broke the barrier of hostility and suspicion and established mutual trust between the two countries. Both countries agreed to strengthen their ties and cooperate in all fields. In response to Rajiv Gandhi's visit, Chinese Premier Li-Peng visited India, and both countries decided to have periodic meetings on military and trade issues and high-level exchanges between the two countries. The creation of the Joint Working Group (JWG) gave the two countries a forum to discuss and resolve their issues. The JWG met in July 1989 to discuss all outstanding issues, including the border dispute. Further, in 1990, JWG decided to institutionalize the meeting between the military personnel on the border and agreed to preserve peace and tranquilly along the Line of Actual Control.

Regarding the first hypothesis that Rajiv Gandhi's leadership was primarily responsible for improving relations with the US, it is proved in the study that Rajiv Gandhi made significant attempts to strengthen Indo-US relations despite some disagreements. Rajiv Gandhi's energetic leadership and charismatic qualities enabled India to acquire sophisticated technology. Who had a clear vision to take India into the 21st century using US technological know-how. Rajiv Gandhi's leadership was mainly responsible for India's attainment of self-reliance, which became possible with the development of India's relations with the US. Rajiv Gandhi continued the foreign policy set forth by his predecessors in order to make India strong in the community of nations, thereby getting sophisticated technological know-how from the US.

Regarding the second hypothesis, the responsibility of formulating policy towards Sri Lanka under the leadership of Rajiv Gandhi became more difficult primarily due to the complex nature of ethnic problems in Sri Lanka. The study demonstrated the validity of this hypothesis when Indian foreign policy mechanisms found it challenging to formulate a coherent foreign policy approach towards Sri Lanka's ethnic strife. The irony is that Rajiv Gandhi, who was instrumental in signing the Indo-Sri Lankan Accord and dispatching the IPKF, had to sacrifice his life for the so-called Accord. The pact with Sri Lanka proved very costly to Rajiv Gandhi, who was determined to bring peace on the war-torn island.

The study established and validated the third hypothesis, that Rajiv Gandhi's leadership was primarily responsible for initiating tangible policy measures to normalize India's relations with China. He undertook several confidence-building measures to improve Sino-Indian relations. He mainly concentrated on bilateral agreements to normalize India's relations with China. Rajiv Gandhi's strategy of developing Sino-Indian relations through bilateral agreements proved successful. The best illustration would be the resurfacing of the 1950s sentiment "Hindi Chini bhai bhai", which had faded into history for several years. As a result, Rajiv Gandhi's leadership proved that he was mainly responsible for strengthening India-China relations.

The findings of the present study are as follows:

1. The study reveals that Rajiv Gandhi played a significant role in shaping India's foreign policy. Despite some irritants, Rajiv Gandhi was able to strengthen relations with the US to

some extent. His leadership demonstrated that he did not compromise the national interest while acquiring sophisticated technology for India. During his tenure, there was no shift in India's foreign policy; it was an attempt to normalize relations with the US.

2. This study also reveals that Rajiv Gandhi's leadership was mainly responsible for further cementing the bond of friendship with the Soviet Union. He played a crucial role in signing bilateral agreements with the Soviet Union, which paved the way for strengthening mutual trust and cooperation between the two countries.

3. This study indicates that while dealing with the Sri Lankan ethnic conflict, Rajiv Gandhi's strategy did not work effectively. Naturally, this led to the non-implementation of the Indo-Sri Lankan Accord in letter and spirit.

4. According to this study, under Rajiv Gandhi's leadership, India could improve Sino-Indian relations, which had remained strained for several years. He implemented several confidence-building measures to enhance India's relations with China. During his tenure, Rajiv Gandhi prioritized bilateral agreements, which he regarded as a significant contribution to Sino-Indian relations.

5. This study demonstrated that Rajiv Gandhi's leadership was responsible for establishing world peace and waging a relentless war against the proliferation of nuclear weapons. His efforts prevented the world from erupting into a nuclear conflagration. To achieve this objective, Rajiv Gandhi made use of all the international forums where he could draw the attention of world leaders to the danger of nuclear weapons. Rajiv Gandhi was considerably successful in convincing the leaders of the superpowers to sign the INF (Intermediate

Nuclear Forces Treaty), thereby paving the way for peace disarmament around the globe.

6. The study indicates that Rajiv Gandhi's leadership succeeded to a great extent in accomplishing the laborious task of eradicating the inhuman and obnoxious practice of apartheid from the South African continent. He proved himself a great organizer of funds for the economic development of African frontline countries despite the lack of cooperation from Western and developed countries around the globe.

7. His leadership was successful in further strengthening regional cooperation among the SAARC countries. He was responsible for introducing several new areas of collaboration, along with trade and industry, in the SAARC agenda.

In light of the findings of the present study, consider the following:

This study points to the need for an extensive and intensive study of the political leadership of Rajiv Gandhi and its impact on Indian democratic politics.

Bibliography

Primary Sources:

India: Lok Sabha Debates (Government of India)

India: Selected Speeches and Writings of Rajiv Gandhi, Vol-I, Vol-II and Vol-III(Government of India Publication Division)

Prime Minister Rajiv Gandhi, Statement on Foreign Policy, External Publicity Division, Ministry of External Affairs, New Delhi.

Julius Sen., Negotiating the Trade Related Intellectual Property Rights Agreement (Research Report) (CUTS) Center for International Trade, Economic and Environment, Jaipur, 2001.

Indian Ocean as a Zone of Peace, Lok Sabha Secretariat, New Delhi, 1987.

From Surprise to Reckoning "The Kargil Review Committee Report, Govt. of India, National Security Council Secretariat, Sage Publication, New Delhi, 2000.

National Policy Studies,(Ed) Secretary General, Lok Sabha Secretariat, Tata Mc Graw Hiil Company, New Delhi, 1990.

Secondary Sources:

Books

Adair John, *The Skill of Leadership*, Wildwood House Ltd., West mead, 1994.

Andrew. W.P. "India and Her Neighbours", Inter IndiaPublication, New Delhi, 1981.

Appadorai A and Rajan.M.S., *India's Foreign Policy and Relations*, South Asian Publishers Ltd., New Delhi, 1985.

Appadorai.A., *Domestic Roots of India's Foreign Policy* 1947-1972, Oxford University Press, New Delhi, 1981.

Asthana Vandana., *India's Foreign Policy, and Sub-Continent Politics*, Kanishka Publishers, New Delhi, 1999.

Attar Chand., *Prime Minister Deve Gowda The Gain and Pain*, Gyan Publishing House, New Delhi, 1997.

Bajapai Kanti and Mattoo Amitabh., (Ed) *Securing India: Strategic Thought and Practice*, Manohar Publishers, New Delhi, 1996.

Bajpai Kanti and Mattoo, Amitabh., *The Peacock and the Dragaon: India China Relations in the 21st Century*, (ed) Har Ananad, New Delhi, 2000.

Banarjee Dipanker., *The End of Cold War and Its Effects at the Global, Regional and National Level: The Indian Response*, in Lalit Mansingh and Others (ed) *India's Foreign Policy:Agenda for the 21st Century*, Vol-1, Konark Publishers, New Delhi, 1997.

Bandyopadhayaya J., *The Making of India's Foreign Policy Determinants*, Institutions, Processes and Personalities, Allied Publication, New Delhi, 1980.

Bhabani Sen Gupta, *India: The Next Great Power*, in Lalit Mansingh and Others, (ed) *Indian Foreign Policy, Agenda for the 21st Century*, (Vol-1) Konark Publishers, New Delhi, 1997.

Bhasin Avatar Singh., India and Sri Lankan Relations and Sri Lanka's Ethnic Conflict Documents, 1947-2000, (Vol-I), India Research Press, New Delhi, 2001.

Bidanda Chengappa, M., *India-China Relations: Post Conflict Phase to Post-Cold War Period*, A.P.H. Publishers, New Delhi, 2004.

Biju, M.R., *India's Foreign Policy*, National Publishing House, Jaipur, 2000.

Bimla Prasad., "*The Origins of Indian Foreign Policy.*" Book Land Pvt. Ltd., Calcutta, 1960.

Brecher, Michael., "*Nehru – A Political Biography*, Oxfprd University Press, London, 1959.

Chandra, Prakash., *International Relations (Foreign Policies of Major Powers and Regional Systems)* 2nd edition, Vikas PublishingHouse Pvt Ltd., New Delhi, 1994.

Dawa Norbu, *India and Tibet* in Lalit Mansingh and Others (Eds) Vol-2, Indian Foreign Policy, Konark Publishers, New Delhi, 1998.

Deepak B.R., *India and China: 1904-2004. A Century of Peace and Conflict*, Manak Publications, New Delhi, 2005.

Dessler Garry., *Management Fundamentals: Frame Work Reason*, Reston Publishing Company Inc, Reston, 1977.

Dixit, J.N., *Across Borders, Fifty Years of India's Foreign Policy*, Picus Books, New Delhi, 1998.

Dixit, J.N., *Assignment Colombo*, Konark Publishers, New Delhi, 1998.

Dixit, J.N., *India and Regional Development Through Prism of Indo-Pak Relations*, Gyan Publishing House, New Delhi, 2004.

Dixit, J.N., *India's Foreign Policy*, 1947-2003, Picus Books, New Delhi, 1998.

Dubey Ravikant., *Indo–Sri Lankan Relations: With Reference to the Tamil Problem*, (Second Edition) Deep and Deep Publications, New Delhi, 1993.

Dutt, V.P., "*India-China Promise and Limitation*" in Lalit Mansingh and Others (ed), *Indian Foreign Policy, Agenda for the 21st Century*, Vol-2, Konark Publishers, New Delhi, 1998.

Dutt, V.P., *India and the World*, Sanchar Publishing House, New Delhi, 1990,

Dutt, V.P., *India's Foreign Policy in Changing world*, Vikas Publishing House, New Delhi, 1999.

Dutt, V.P., *India's Foreign Policy*, Vikas Publishing House, New Delhi, 1984.

Frankel Joseph., *The Making of Foreign Policy: An Analysis of Decision Making*, Oxford University Press, London, 1971.

Ghosh P.A., Ehtnic *Conflict in Sri Lanka and Role of Indian Peace Keeping Force*, APH Publishers, New Delhi, 1999.

Grover B.S.K., "*India and the United States of America: Problems and Prospects*, in Grover' Verinder *International Relations and Foreign Policy of India, USA and India's Foreign Policy*, Deep and Deep Publication, New Delhi, 1992.

Grover, Verinder., (ed) International Relations and foreign policy of India: China, Japan and India's foreign Policy, Deep and Deep Publication, New Delhi, 1992.

Gunaratna Rohan., *Indian Intervention in Sri Lanka: TheRole of Indian Intelligence Agencies*, South Asian Network on Conflict Research, Colombo, 1993.

Hartmann Frederick H.., *The Relations of Nations*, Macmillan, 5th edition, New York,1978.

Hatheesing, Krishna., *Dear to Behold: An Intimate Portrait of Indira Gandhi*, IBH Publishing Company, Bombay, 1969.

Hussain, Karki T., *Sino-Indian Conflict and International Politicsin the Indian Sub-Continent*, Thomson Press (India) Ltd., Faridabad, 1977.

Jetly Nancy ., *SAARC: Looking Ahead*, In Lalit Mansingh and others, (Eds) *Indian Foreign Policy: Agenda For the 21st Century*, (vol-1), Konarak, New Delhi, 1998.

Kamath, P.M. and Mutalik Desai, A.A., (ed) *Indian Perspective on the US Literature and Foreign Affairs*, Prestige Books, New Delhi, 1993.

Karunakaran.K.P., *India in World Affairs*, August 1947- January 1950, Oxford University Press (London) Calcutta, 1952.

Khanna Devender., "*Mother And Son*", Affiliated East-West Press Pvt. Ltd., New Delhi, 1986.

Khanna, V.N., *Foreign Policy of India*, Vikas Publishing House, New Delhi, 1997.

Khilanani, N.M., *Panorama of Indian Diplomacy*, S. Chand and Co., New Delhi, 1981.

Kodandswami M.S., *Sri Lankan Crisis*, Authors Press, New Delhi, 2000.

Koontz H and O'Donnell C., *Management: A Systems and Contingency Analysis of Managerial Functions*, (6th Edition) Mc Graw-Hill Kogakusha Ltd., Tokyo, 1976.

Kual, T.N., *Diplomacy in Peace and War*, Vikas publishing House, New Delhi, 1979.

Kux Dennis., *Estranged Democracies: India and United States 1941-1991*, Sage Publications, New Delhi, 1993.

Luthans Fred ., *Organisational Behaviour* (5th Edition), Mc Graw-Hill Company, Singapore 1989.

Luthans Fred ., *Organizational Behaviour*, (8th Edition), Mc Graw-Hill Book Company, Singapore, 1998.

Malhotra Vinay Kumar., *International Relations* (ed), Anmol Publications Ltd., New Delhi, 2001.

Mansingh, Surjit., *India's Search for Power: Indira Gandhi's Foreign Policy 1966-1982*, Sage Publications, New Delhi, 1984.

McGinnie.C.Elliot, *Social Behaviour*, Houghton Mifflin Company, Boston,1970.

Mehra, Shipa., *Indo-Sri Lankan Relations 1947 to Present Day*, M.G.Publishers, Agra, 1995.

Menon, K.P.S., The *Indo-Soviet Treaty, Setting and Meaning*, Vikas Publications, New Delhi, 1971.

Mishra, Ranjan Kumar., *India and International Relations*, Kanishka Publishers, New Delhi, 1996.

Misra, K.P., *Non-aligned Movement India's Chairmanship*, Lancers Books, New Delhi, 1987.

Moti Lal Govila, *Indo-American Relations in the Post War Decade*, in Grover, Verinder's,(Ed) *International Relations and Foreign Policy of India, USA and India's Foreign Policy*, Deep and Deep Publication, New Delhi, 1992.

Muni, S.D., *Pangs of Proximity: India and Sri Lanka's Ethnic Crisis*, Sage Publications, New Delhi, 1993.

Naidu, S.P., *Public Administration, Concepts and Theories, New Age* International Publishers, New Delhi, 1996.

Northedge F.S., and Grieve. M.J., *A Hundred Years of International Relations*, Gerald Duckworth and Co, Ltd., London, 1971.

Ojha G.P., *Mrs. Indira Gandhi's Foreign Policy Choice*, Mrinal Book House, Meerut, 1982.

Paddelford Norman J. and Lincoln George A., *The Dynamics of International Politics*, Macmillan, New York, 1954.

Palmer Norman D., *Foreign Policy of the Indian National Congress Before Independence*, in K.P.Misra.,(Ed) *Studies in Indian Foreign Policy*, Vikas Publications, New Delhi, 1969.

Palmer Norman D., *The United States and India, The Dimensions of Influence*, Praeger Publishers, USA, 1984.

Patagundi S.S., *"Political Parties, Party System And Foreign Policy of India*, Deep and Deep Publications, New Delhi, 1987.

Patagundi S.S., *India's Foreign Policy: An Elitist Perception*, Uppal Publishing House, New Delhi, 1995.

Patel, S.R., *India's Foreign Policy: An Inquiry and Criticism*, N.M.Tripathi Pvt Ltd., Bombay, 1960.

Perkovich, George.,'s, *India's Nuclear Bomb, The Impact on Global Proliferation*, Oxford University Press, New Delhi, 2000.

Prasad Bishweshwar ., *The Foundations of India's Foreign Policy* 1866-1882, Ranjit Printers & Publishers, New Delhi, 1955.

Prime Minister Rajiv Gandhi Visits USSR, Allied Publishers, Information Department of USSR Embassy, New Delhi.

Prime Minister Rajiv Gandhi, Statement on Foreign Policy, April-June1988, Ministry of External Affairs.

Rajasekharaiah, A.M., "International Relations", Kartikeya Publication, Gulbarga, 1976.

Raman Pillai.K., *India's Foreign Policy, Basic Issues and Political Attitudes*, Meenakhsi Prakashan, 1969.

Rana, A.P., *The Imperatives of Non-alignment*, The McMillan Co. of India Ltd., New Delhi, 1976.

Rasgotra M.K., (Ed) *Rajiv Gandhi's World View*, Vikas Publishing House, New Delhi, 1991, p-48.

Ray Hemen., *The Enduring Friendship (Soviet-Indian Relation in Mrs. Indira Gandhi's days)* Abhinav Publications, New Delhi, 1989.

Rosenau, James, N., (ed.) *Linkage Politics, Essays on the convergence of National and international System*, The Free Press, New York, 1969.

Roy C. Macridis, *"Foreign Policy in World Politics"* 5th Edition, Prentice Hall of India (P) Ltd, New Delhi, 1979.

Sahadevan, P., *India and Overseas Indians: The Case of Sri Lanka*, Kalinga Publishers, New Delhi, 1995.

Sahadevan, P., *India and Sri Lanka*, in Lalith Mansingh and Others, (ed) *India's Foreign Policy Agenda for the 21ˢᵗ Century*, (Vol-II), Konark Publishers, New Delhi, 1998.

Salvi, P.G., *India in World Affairs*, B.R. Publishing Corporation, New Delhi, 1985.

SarojKumar Jena, *Political Sociology a Realistic Approach*, Anmol Publications (P)Ltd, New Delhi, 2002.

Satish Kumar, *India and Changing International System*, in S.Rasgotra and Others. India's Foreign Policy in the 1990s (ed) Patriot Publishers, New Delhi, 1990.

Satishkumar. (ed) *Year Book on India's Foreign Policy*, 1989, Sage Publications, New Delhi, 1990.

Shah, A.B., (Ed) India's Defence and Foreign Policies, Manktala, Bombay, 1966.

Sharma Shri Ram., *India-China Relations, 1971-1991, Part-II*, Discovery Publication House, New Delhi, 2003.

Sharma Shri Ram., *Indo-US Relations 1972-91: A BriefSurvey Part-II*, Discovery Publishing House, New Delhi, 2003.

Sharma, Shri Ram., *"Lal Bahadur Shastri: An Era of Transition in Indian Foreign Policy*, Kanishka Publishers, New Delhi, 2001.

Sharma, Shri Ram., *Indo-Soviet Relations 1972-1991, ABrief Survey Part-II*, Discovery Publishing House, New Delhi, 2003.

Sharma, Suman ., *India And SAARC*, Gyan Publishing House, New Delhi, 2001.

Singh, L.P., *India's Foreign Policy: The Shastri Period*, Uppal Publishing House, New Delhi, 1980.

Sultan, Tanveer., Indo-US Relations, Deep and Deep Publication, New Delhi.

Swamy, Subramanian., *India and China Perspective*, Konark Publishers, New delhi, 2001.

Swarankar, R.C., *Political Elite (A Sociological Study of Legislators in Rajastan)* Rawat Publications, Jaipur, 1988.

Terry G.R, *Principles of Management*, (6ᵗʰ edition), Richard.D.Irwin, Inc, Homewood-III, 1972.

Tharoor Shashi., *"Reasons of State, Political Developmentand India's Foreign Policy Under Indira Gandhi*: 1966-1977, Vikas Publishing House New Delhi,1982.

Vidyarthi L.P. (ed) *Leadership in India*, Asia Publishing House, Bombay 1967.

Vohra A.M., *Indian Peace Keeping in Sri Lanka*, in Satishkumar's Year Book on *India's Foreign Policy* 1989, Sage Publications, New Delhi, 1990.

Vohra, A.M., *Indian Peace Keeping in Sri Lanka* in Satish Kumar's (Ed) Yearbook on *India's Foreign Policy* 1989, Sage Publications, New Delhi, 1990.

Worchel S and Cooper J., *Understanding Social Psychology*, The Dorsey Press, Homewood Illinois, 1976.

Wrigging Howard.H., *Ceylon: Dilemmas of New Nations*, Princeton University Press, Princeton, 1960.

Articles:

Arora, V.K., Prospects and Cooperation, *India Quarterly*, 42(1), Jan-Mar,1986.

Baral J.K.and Other's, Rajiv Gandhi's China Diplomacy: Dynamics and Problems, *Millennium*, 26 (3), July-September, 1989.

Baral Lok Raj., SARC, But No "SHARK", South Asian Regional Cooperation in Perspective, *Pacific Affairs*, Vol-58, No.3, fall 1985.

Chakravarty, Sumit., Multi-Dimensional Perestroika in Gorbachev's USSR, *Mainstream*, 37(8) 19 November, 1988.

Coomarswamy Radhika., Ethnic Myths, Seminar, No-337, September, 1987.

Dixit .J.N., IPKF in Sri Lanka, in *USA Journal* 19 (497), July-September 1989.

Foreign Affairs Report, 36 (7-10) July-October, 1987.

Foreign Affairs Report, 37 (3&4), March-April, 1988.

Ganguly, Sumit., The Sino-Indian Border Talks: 1981-1989, *Asian Survey*, 29 (12), December 1989, p-1133.

Grigory Bondarevsky, Two Years of the Delhi Declaration: Some Reflections. *Mainstream*, 37(8) 19November, 1988.

Indian Recorder, Vol-III, September 16-22, 1996.

Jetly Nancy., Sino-Indian Relations: A Quest for Normalization, *IndiaQuarterly*, 42 (1), Jan-March, 1986.

Jha, N.N., India – Sri Lanka Relations, *India Quarterly*, 50(2), January-June, 1994.

Khilnani, N.M. Gorbachev and Indo-Soviet Relations, *PTI Feature,* Vol-7 (14), November 5, 1986.

Mansigh, Surjit., India-China Relations in the Post-Cold War Era, *Asian Survey*, 34 (3), March 1994.

Mathews K., Africa and Non-Alignment, *India Quarterly*, 42(1), Jan-March1987.

Parasher, S.C., Gorbachev Visit: A Historical Perspective, *India Quarterly* 42 (4) October-December 1986.

Partha S.Ghosh and Rajaram Panda, Domestic Support for Mrs. Indira Gandhi's Afghan Policy: The Soviet Factor in Indian Politics, *Asian Survey* 33 (3) March, 1983.

Pradhan, Pradyot., Nuclear Pakistan and India's response, *India Quarterly*, XLIII 43(1) , January –March 1987.

Rajan, M.S., The Goals of India's Foreign Policy, *International Studies*, 35(1), January -March 1998.

Srivastava, B.K., Indo-US Relations, Search for Mature and Constructive Ties, *India Quarterly*, 42(1), Jan-March 1985.

Sunday, 14 (31) June 12-18, 1987.

Sunday, 14 (31) June 21-27, 1987.

Thakur Ramesh., India and the Soviet Union, Conjunctions and Disjunctions of Interests, *Asian Survey*, 31 (9) Sept 1991.

The American Political Science Review, Issue No. 70, 1978.

Thomas, Raju C., US Transfer of "Dual Use" Technologies of India, *Asian Survey*, 30(8), 8th August 1990.

Verghese, B.G., Beyond the Truce, *Seminar*, No-337, September 1987.

Wong Hongyu, Sino-Indian Relations: Present and Future, *AsianSurvey*, 35 (6), June 1995, p-546.

Journals:

Asian Recorder

Asian Survey

Blitz

Commerce

Current History

India Quarterly

Journal of Psychology

Mainstream

Millennium

Pacific Affairs

Seminar

The American Political Science review

Sunday

Foreign Affairs Reports

Newspapers:

Amrita Bazar Patrika,

Deccan Herald.

Economic Times.

Hindustan Times.

Indian Express.

National Herald.

National Herald.

Patriot (New Delhi)

The Hindu

The Hindustan Times.

The Statesman.

The Times of India.

Tribune (Chandigarh)

Encyclopedias/Dictionaries:

International Encyclopedia of the Social Sciences, Vol-6, The Macmillan Co & The Free Press, 1968.

International Relations Dictionary, Holf Rinehart and Winston, New York, 1969.

Websters, New 20th Century Dictionary.

Websites:

http:// www.mofa.gov.bd/

http:// www.nipa-khi-edu.pk.

http://www.changingminds.org/disciplines.

http://www.saarc-sec-org/

http://www.southasianmedia.net.Magzine

http://www.saarc-sec-org/main.

http://www.tamilanation.org/intframe/india

http://timesindia.indiatimes.com/articleshow

http//en.vikipedia.org/wiki/McMahon_Line

http://www.mfa.gov.cn/eng/

http://www.anc.org.zo/ancdocs/historysolidarity.

http://canberra.usembassy.gov/hyper.

Abbreviations

AF	:	Africa Fund
AFRICA	:	Action For Resisting Invasion, Colonialism and Apartheid
AICC	:	All India Congress Committee
ANC	:	African National Congress
APC	:	All Party Conference
ASEAN	:	Association of South East Asian Nation
AWACS	:	Airborne Warning And Control Systems
CBM	:	Confidence Building Measures
CHOGM	:	Commonwealth Heads of Government Meeting
CPC	:	Communist Party of China
CPSU	:	Communist Party of Soviet Union
CTBT	:	Comprehensive Test Ban Treaty
EPG	:	Eminent Persons Group
EPRLF	:	Eelam People's Revolutionary Liberation Front
EROS	:	Eelam Revolutionary Organization of Students
EU	:	European Union
GATT	:	General Agreement on Trade and Tariff
IAEA	:	International Atomic Energy Agency
INC	:	Indian National Congress
INF	:	Intermediate Nuclear Force Treaty

IPKF	:	Indian Peace Keeping Force
IPR	:	Intellectual Property Rights
JVP	:	Janatha Vimukthi Perumuna
JWG	:	Joint Working Group
KPCC	:	Karnataka Pradesh Congress Committee
LAC	:	Line of Actual Control
LCA	:	Light Combat Aircraft
LRM	:	Long Range Missiles
LTTE	:	Liberation Tigers Tamil Eelam
M o U	:	Memorandum of Understanding
NAM	:	Non-Aligned Movement
NASA	:	National Aeronautic and Space Administration
NATO	:	North Atlantic Treaty Organisation
NDA	:	National Democratic Alliance
NEFA	:	North Eastern Frontier Area
NF	:	National Front
NGOs	:	Non Governmental Organisations
NNRC	:	Neutral Repatriation Commission
NPT	:	Nuclear Non-Proliferation Treaty
OAU	:	Organisation of African Union
PLA	:	Peoples Liberation Army
PLO	:	Palestine Liberation Organisation
PLOT	:	Peoples Liberation Organisation of Tamil Eelam
PRC	:	Peoples Republic of China

SAARC	:	South Asian Association of Regional Co-operation
SADCC	:	Southern African Development Co-ordination Conference
SEATO	:	South East Asian Treaty Organisation
SLFP	:	Sri Lankan Freedom Party
SRM	:	Short Range Missiles
SWAPO	:	South West African Peoples Organisation
TAR	:	Tibetan Autonomous Region
TELO	:	Tamil Eelam Liberation Organization
TNLF	:	Tamil National Liberation Front
TRIMs	:	Trade Related Investment Measures
TULF	:	Tamil United Liberation Front
UF	:	United Front
UK	:	United Kingdom
UN	:	United Nation
UNP	:	United National Party
UPA	:	United Progressive Alliance
UR	:	Uruguay Round
US	:	United States
USSR	:	Union of Soviet Socialist Republic
USTR	:	United States Trade Representative
WIPO	:	World Intellectual Property Organisation
WTO	:	World Trade Organisation